PRIVATISATION AND REGULATION
THE UK EXPERIENCE

PRIVATISATION AND REGULATION

THE UK EXPERIENCE

Edited by
JOHN KAY, COLIN MAYER,
and DAVID THOMPSON

CLARENDON PRESS · OXFORD

1986

Oxford University Press, Walton Street, Oxford OX2 6DP

Oxford New York Toronto
Delhi Bombay Calcutta Madras Karachi
Petaling Jaya Singapore Hong Kong Tokyo
Nairobi Dar es Salaam Cape Town
Melbourne Auckland
and associated companies in
Beirut Berlin Ibadan Nicosia

Oxford is a trade mark of Oxford University Press

Published in the United States
by Oxford University Press, New York

British Library Cataloguing in Publication Data
Privatisation and regulation: the UK experience.
1. Privatization—Great Britain
I. Kay, J. A. II. Mayer, Colin
III. Thompson, David
354.4107′2   HD4148
ISBN 0–19–877254–8
ISBN 0–19–877253–X Pbk

Library of Congress Cataloging in Publication Data
Privatisation and regulation.
Bibliography: p.
1. Privatization—Great Britain. I. Kay, J. A.
(John Anderson) II. Mayer, C. P. (Colin P.)
III. Thompson, David.
HD4145.P.72 1986   338.941   86-12704
ISBN 0–19–877254–8
ISBN 0–19–877253–X (pbk.)

Set by Downdell Ltd., Oxford
Printed in Great Britain
at the University Printing House, Oxford
by David Stanford
Printer to the University

PREFACE

This collection of readings has been prepared as part of the programme of research at the Institute for Fiscal Studies on Regulation and Competition Policy which is supported by the Economic and Social Research Council.

The editors are grateful for the co-operation received from the contributing authors in preparing this book. They would especially like to thank Chantal Crevel-Robinson for preparing the manuscript and Judith Payne for assembling the material for publication.

Every effort has been made to trace the copyright-holders. If any have been inadvertently overlooked, the Institute for Fiscal Studies will make due acknowledgement at the earliest opportunity.

John Kay is Director of the Institute for Fiscal Studies and a Fellow of St John's College Oxford.

Colin Mayer is a Research Associate of the Institute for Fiscal Studies and a Fellow of St Anne's College Oxford.

David Thompson is Programme Director of research at the Institute for Fiscal Studies on Regulation and Competition Policy.

CONTENTS

LIST OF TABLES

LIST OF FIGURES

MAP

INTRODUCTION

I. Introduction

Since the election of the Conservative Government in 1979 privatisation has emerged as an important and controversial policy issue. The purpose of these readings is to provide a timely review of the arguments for and against privatisation and to draw together some of the important pieces of research that have been undertaken on the privatisation issue.

In this Introduction we set out an overview of the debate and summarise the results of some of the studies which have been carried out. The discussion in this Introduction broadly follows the six parts of the book:

Part I reviews 'Policies and Issues'. The case for privatisation is presented and some of the difficulties associated with it are considered. The key issue in the debate is undoubtedly efficiency; the case for privatisation points to the claimed inefficiency of public provision and the beneficial impact upon performance of privatisation.

Part II examines evidence on 'The Comparative Performance of the Public and Private Sectors'. Because comparative performance is so central, the readings in this part are selected to provide a wide-ranging survey of the available evidence. We review the results below, and suggest that increasing competition (deregulation) is an important mechanism for stimulating improved performance and one which may be more effective than changing ownership (denationalisation). This points to the importance of deregulation policies.

Part III looks at 'Deregulation and Efficiency' in two sectors where deregulation has been implemented, or is a prospective policy option; the readings show the problems of implementing liberalisation policies and the difficulties in ensuring that fair competition actually takes place.

Part IV looks at 'The Natural Monopolies: Promoting Competition and Regulatory Issues'. Many activities were taken into the public sector in the first place because it was

judged that competition was not appropriate in these particular sectors. It was considered either that competition
would be ineffective (because the industries were natural
monopolies with substantial sunk costs) or that competition
would not promote allocative efficiency (for example because
important external social benefits or costs were significant).
The readings in Part IV look at five sectors which have
typically been regarded as natural monopolies and consider
the scope for introducing competition in the provision of
some of their activities. The requirement for the regulation of
activities which cannot be made competitive and the possible
difficulties associated with regulation are also examined.

Part V looks at the scope for 'Franchising and Competitive
Tendering' as methods of introducing competitive incentives
in sectors where (for the reasons already discussed) direct
competition in the market-place may not be feasible.

Part VI reviews 'Labour and Financial Issues'. Whilst
efficiency is perhaps the central issue in the privatisation
debate other questions have also been important. The
readings in this part look at the financial effects of privatisation and the impact upon labour relations.

II. The course of privatisation since 1979

First, we provide a brief history of the implementation of
privatisation policies since the election of the Conservative
Government in 1979. The term privatisation has been used to
refer to three interrelated strands of policy. A clear delineation
is useful to give a full appreciation of the issues. We review
developments on each in turn:

- denationalisation—the sale of public sector assets
- deregulation—the opening of state activities to private
  sector competition
- tendering—the contracting-out of public provision to
  private firms.

The volume of asset sales by central government has increased
progressively from £377 million in 1979/80 to £1,142 million in
1983/4 (see Table 1 for details); in 1984/5 the sales of British
Telecom (£3,900 million, with payment staged over three fiscal

years) and Enterprise Oil have contributed substantial sums to government receipts. Up to 1983/4 only a few public enterprises had been transferred to the private sector; a substantial part of the receipts from asset sales arose from other sources, such as the sale of small tranches of shares in British Petroleum and of leases of motorway service areas. Many of the enterprises which were transferred to the private sector operated in markets where private sector firms were dominant (e.g. the National Freight Corporation).

The increase in the scale of disposals has also seen a change in their pattern. The largest disposal, the sale of British Telecom, involved a public sector monopoly—a dominant enterprise which enjoys substantial protection from competition by statutory restrictions on market entry (even after the deregulation described below). This is also true of other industries in which the Government is now developing proposals for privatisation—British Airways, the British Airports Authority, the British Gas Corporation, and regional water authorities.

Regulatory restrictions on market entry have been eased in a number of markets. The most substantial deregulation has occurred in the provision of telecommunication services, although even here deregulation has gone considerably less far than would have been feasible technically. A trunk supplier, Mercury, has been permitted to enter the market in competition with British Telecom (BT); BT's statutory monopoly in the supply and installation of subscriber equipment (such as private branch exchanges or telephone sets) has been removed; and the provision of Value Added Network Services has also been liberalised. BT holds a number of advantages (at least in the short term) resulting from its position as dominant incumbent; and it has retained a high market share in the liberalised markets for equipment and services. There is some evidence to suggest, however, that prices have fallen (in some cases substantially) in response to the threat of actual or potential competition. Most conspicuously, BT has instituted major price reductions in call charges between principal cities.

Deregulation in 1980 of express coaching services, where previously particular companies held a monopoly of in-

Table 1. Sales of Public Sector Assets 1979/80 to 1984/5[1]

(£ million)

	1979/80	1980/1	1981/2	1982/3	1983/4	1984/5
SALES OF SHARES						
Amersham International			64			
Associated British Ports				46		51
British Aerospace		43				
British Petroleum	276		8		543	
British Sugar Corporation			44			
British Telecom						1,357
Britoil				334	293	
Cable and Wireless			182		263	
Drake and Scull Holdings	1					
Enterprise Oil						380
National Enterprise Board	37	83	2			142
National Freight Company			5			
Suez Financial Company	22					
Total sale of shares	336	126	305	380	1,099	1,930
SALES OF OTHER ASSETS[2]	41	279	189	108	43	161
TOTAL ASSET SALES	377	405	494	488	1,142	2,091

Source: HM Treasury, 1985, Table 2.14; HM Treasury, 1986, Table 2.23.

1. Figures shown are net receipts; note that in many cases the tranche of shares sold is less than 100 per cent.
2. 'Sales of other assets' includes, for example, the sale of leases on motorway service areas.

dividual routes, has also resulted in price reductions (substantial in some cases) and innovations in the provision of new types of service.

In contrast, the liberalisation of the electricity supply industry, in November 1983, seems to have led to few changes in either market structure or prices. Deregulation enabled private producers to supply power directly to customers by making use of the publicly owned distribution network at pre-specified charges. Private producers can also supply power directly to the public distribution network and again there are pre-specified charges (which in principle are to be based on the avoidable costs of alternative sources of supply) at which the public authorities are required to purchase power offered by private producers. In practice very few private producers have attempted to enter the market. The liberalisation of gas supply (in the Oil and Gas Enterprise Act 1982) has also had little impact; deregulation enabled private suppliers to lease British Gas's transmission network to sell gas directly to large industrial customers. In practice no private suppliers have taken this option up and entered the market.

Various services provided by local government authorities and by health authorities have been put out to competitive tender in some areas of the country: examples are refuse collection services, school cleaning, hospital cleaning, hospital catering. Overall, however, the proportion of such services which have been contracted-out is not substantial. Where tendering has taken place it appears in some cases to have resulted in substantial reductions in costs although there are also cases where the quality of the service provided appears to have fallen. In some cases where tendering has taken place the authority's own 'in-house' service has reduced its costs by a margin sufficient to out-bid other tenderers and the service has continued to be provided by directly employed labour.

III. Part I—Policies and issues

The readings in this part address the basic issues underlying the privatisation debate:

- what are the objectives of privatisation? what are the claimed advantages?

- what are the potential disadvantages?
- what are the problems of effective implementation?

It is not our intention in this Introduction to reach a judgement on the merits of the various arguments for and against privatisation. Rather we want to draw out the main points at issue and thereby provide an agenda for the questions addressed in the analytic studies in the later parts of the book.

In the first article, Michael Beesley and Stephen Littlechild (who have both advised the Government on its privatisation policies) set out the case in favour of privatisation and outline a programme for its implementation. The criterion they adopt to determine whether privatisation in a particular sector is worthwhile is the present value of aggregate net benefits to UK consumers. Their proposed criterion is therefore essentially an economic one; and furthermore, one which excludes the sales proceeds of an asset sale on the grounds that this is simply a part of the transaction between the company's present owners (the taxpayers) and its future owners (the shareholders). The authors believe that privatisation will, on their suggested criterion, often prove worthwhile. They consider that privately owned companies will have a greater incentive to produce goods and services in the quantity and variety which consumers prefer. Essentially, then, their argument is that privatisation will promote greater efficiency. In particular they consider that privatisation will facilitate the promotion of competition, which they regard as the most important mechanism for meeting their criterion of maximising consumer benefits. On this basis the authors conclude that the first priorities in the privatisation programme should be those sectors where multiple ownership (and competing supply) is technically feasible but where little competition exists under public ownership (electricity generation and coal are suggested). In sectors where competing supply is not feasible the authors consider that policy should focus on encouraging competition and that in the case of declining industries (such as British Rail) privatisation should be used to facilitate the movement of resources out of these sectors and into more productive uses.

In the second article, David Heald and David Steel provide a critical review of the advantages claimed for privatisation.

They examine four arguments put forward by government Ministers. First they consider the argument that 'privatisation will enhance economic freedom'. The authors accept that deregulation will generally extend the range of consumer choice by increasing the number of sources of supply. They are sceptical as to whether privatisation of a public sector monopoly will have a positive effect, however. They also believe that deregulation will remove the basis for the cross-subsidisation of loss-making products or services from profitable ones (for example in the case of buses). Whilst accepting that cross-subsidisation is generally undesirable in principle (as Beesley and Littlechild note, cross-subsidies can generally be regarded as an economically inefficient method of support) the authors point to the associated requirement for an increase in explicit public subsidies. On the second argument, that 'privatisation will increase efficiency', the authors are sceptical as to whether the Government's case is supported by the evidence on the comparative efficiency of the public and private sectors; we return to this issue in detail in the next part. The third argument, that 'privatisation will ease the problem of public sector pay', is not seen by the authors as dominant in shaping privatisation policy; they note that denationalisation has not to date been proposed in the sectors where militancy is greatest (coal, electricity, and the railways). The final argument considered is that 'privatisation will reduce public sector borrowing'. The authors note that the short-term gain to the Exchequer from sale proceeds needs to be set against the possible loss of future income streams; they are also sceptical as to whether the sale of assets is less likely to 'crowd out' private sector investment than other methods of financing government expenditure. These are issues which we return to in the final part.

The final readings in this part provide the most comprehensive statements of the Government's case for its privatisation policies in the form of two speeches made by the Financial Secretary to the Treasury (John Moore MP) in November 1983 and in July 1985. The main issues raised have already been touched upon, but three more general points are worth noting. The November 1983 statement places central importance on the objective of improving efficiency: 'Our main objective is to promote competition and improve efficiency'. Objectives such as reducing the size of the public sector or funding the PSBR are regarded as secondary. Furthermore, increasing competition is regarded as the key to improved efficiency: 'The long-term success of the privatisation programme will stand or fall by the extent to which it maximises competition'. The July 1985 statement sets out a development of this position and proposes the privatisation of a number of natural monopolies where competition is considered impractical: 'privatisation policies have now been developed to such an extent that regulated private ownership of natural monopolies is preferable to nationalisation'. This marks a change in the direction of privatisation policy; we discuss the implications further in the conclusions to this Introduction. The speech sets the agenda for the next enterprises to be denationalised, including in particular British Gas, the British Airports Authority, and British Airways.

IV. Part II: The comparative performance of the public and private sectors

What evidence is there to suggest that public enterprises are generally inefficient and why should privatisation improve efficiency? The two readings in this part provide evidence on the first question, although it will be seen that the results are not clear-cut. In this Introduction we will now consider the second question in some detail; this assessment gives some help in understanding the apparent ambiguities and contradictions in the evidence on public and private sector performance.

As we have seen, a belief in the ability of competitive processes to encourage efficient production is central to the argument behind privatisation. These improvements in the production process do not necessarily reflect any changes in the management structures of the companies being privatised. Indeed it could well be the case that the same individuals will one day find themselves in charge of a corporation that on the previous day was under public ownership. In other cases, such as telecommunications and airways, there may be management changes prior to privatisation but these are not seen as the fundamental consequence of the change of ownership. Instead we should focus on the way in which the competitive environment in which the managers operate and the incentive system to which they are subject change as a result of privatisation.

A statutory framework for British nationalised industries was established in the legislation which brought many of today's state enterprises into public ownership immediately after the Second World War. This prescribed objectives only in the most general of terms and saw the role of nationalised industry managers as that of trustees of the public interest. For twenty years thereafter, most of the economic literature on nationalised industries followed the tradition established by Hotelling (1938) and prescribed the pricing and investment criteria which such trustees would wish to follow. It is now apparent that this literature had only a limited influence on what nationalised industries actually did.

An early and perceptive critic of the Hotelling analysis was Little (1950), who was concerned by its neglect of appropriate incentives to productive efficiency. He anticipated the burgeoning literature on business management, which would stress increasingly that efficient organisation required that managers be given specific objectives and their performance be monitored in relation to them (see Drucker, 1974, for an influential popularisation). Little recognised the dangers of an environment in which objectives were ill-defined, and in which it was very difficult to determine *ex post* whether or not they had in fact been achieved. These arguments were to be developed as part of the economic theory of property rights, which was to elaborate a positive rather than a normative view of managerial behaviour (see Furubotn and Pejovich, 1972, for a survey). Public sector managers could be expected to respond to the particular personal incentives with which they were faced. Such incentives might lead to a desire to maximise the scale of operations of the business, subject to any external financial constraint, or to seek a quiet life untroubled by changes in working practices or difficulties in labour relations, rather than to pursue a nebulous public good.

Dissatisfaction with the performance of nationalised industries resulted in repeated attempts to prescribe more specific objectives. These came in White Papers in 1961, 1967, and 1978 (HM Treasury, 1961, 1967, and 1978), and a theme common to all was greater emphasis on commercial rather than public interest considerations and the introduction of more extensive financial controls. Despite the intentions of the authors of these papers, detailed scrutiny by government of day-to-day activities of nationalised industries has tended to increase rather than diminish, and their autonomy in investment and planning decisions, and in industrial relations, has been steadily eroded.

But if neither exhortation to pursue the public interest nor increasing central control has provided an appropriate control structure for nationalised industries, is there reason to believe that privatisation will do better? We are concerned with incentives to both productive and allocative efficiency. Productive efficiency requires that whatever is done should be achieved at minimum cost; allocative efficiency implies that what is done meets consumer needs at prices which reflect the costs of provision.

Competitive forces function in a number of ways in private markets. First, there is competition in the product market which encourages firms to supply the goods desired by consumers at a price which reflects the cost of production. Thus a firm in a competitive product market has incentives to achieve allocative efficiency, provided that the market price reflects the value of its output (implying that external effects and distributional consequences are unimportant, an issue we return to below). Second, there is competition in the market for firms via take-overs. This promotes profit or value maximisation as the objective of managers in line with the goal of shareholders. Third, shareholders may attempt to influence managerial decision-taking directly via their voting power at shareholders' meetings or indirectly in the form of managerial incentive schemes. Finally, there is the threat of bankruptcy.

In the absence of these competitive pressures we might expect that incentives to achieve allocative efficiency (supplying the goods and services that the market desires) and productive efficiency (supplying these goods and services at minimum cost) may be diminished.

These propositions yield the classification of Table 2 (based on Forsyth, 1984). This suggests that it is competitive, privately-owned firms which have incentives to achieve both productive and allocative efficiency. Privatisation tends to promote productive efficiency, competition allocative efficiency.

But this is really to over-simplify the issue; there is a strong presumption that markets do, and will, operate efficiently. Market failure is an issue that has concerned economists for generations and it is important to recognise that it is the belief that private ownership would not achieve allocative efficiency which provided, in many cases, the rationale for nationalisation. Either the industry was inevitably characterised by monopoly or else there were non-commercial objectives, such as external benefits, which implied that some outputs should be produced even if they failed to cover their costs. It is possible, however, that the opportunity to remedy these allocative weaknesses may be outweighed by losses in productive efficiency. And it is clear that some of the early candidates for privatisation—telecommunications, gas, airways—are industries where these non-commercial objectives are comparatively unimportant. But they are all industries in which competition is severely limited, either by the nature of the product or by a history of statutory restriction.

Do private firms which do not face competitive product markets have greater incentives to productive efficiency than their public counterparts? The enterprises that are currently the subject of denationalisation are in many cases well-established firms. They hold substantial competitive advantages, which reflect their expertise, their reputation (for good or ill) and above all the physical assets that they already have in place. They are quite clearly in many cases dominant firms and as such we would expect them to be able to exert substantial control of their product market. Furthermore, from the point of view of any company contemplating a take-over these public companies represent a very large expenditure. For example, the sale of the 50.2 per cent shareholding in British Telecom realised £3.9 billion giving an implicit market capitalisation for BT at the time of sale of £7.8 billion; its current market valuation is considerably higher. It is

Table 2. Ownership, Competition, and Efficiency Incentives

	Publicly owned monopoly	Publicly owned competitor	Large private monopoly	Smaller private monopoly	Competitive private firm
Can the firm go bankrupt?	No	No	Yes	Yes	Yes
Can it be taken over?	No	No	No	Yes	Either
Is the product market competitive?	No	Yes	No	No	Yes
Incentives to—allocative efficiency?	No	Yes	No	No	Yes
—productive efficiency?	No	No	No	Yes	Yes
Kind of firm	Publicly owned monopoly	Publicly owned competitor	Large private monopoly	Smaller private monopoly	Competitive private firm
Example of firm	British Airports Authority	Electricity showrooms	British Telecom	British Aerospace	Many

suggested that British Gas may realise £8 billion. By comparison the largest take-over completed on the UK stock market is the acquisition of Eagle Star Holdings by BAT for £0.97 billion. Enterprises such as British Telecom and British Gas are an order of magnitude larger. Furthermore, any limitations placed on the size of holdings by overseas companies will make the prospect of take-over even less likely. The market for these firms therefore may well be highly imperfect, not least because their managers may be able to employ a variety of devices to prevent any take-over attempt. While the potential for competition must in general be welcomed, its failure to materialise must be treated as a very real possibility and the consequence of creating private sector dominant firms must be considered very carefully.

This discussion shows that the structure of incentives toward the promotion of efficiency (allocative and productive) is substantially more complex than encompassed by a simple distinction between 'public' and 'private'. This complexity is reflected in the findings of empirical studies which have sought to compare the performance of public and private enterprises. In looking at the evidence in the two readings, the difficulties in making meaningful comparisons should be kept in mind. One problem lies in finding a suitable test-bed: particularly in the UK, many of the activities carried out in the public sector are not carried out by the private sector in any significant sense. Moreover, public corporations may have some non-commercial objectives and this may bias comparisons of efficiency. Where outputs are not sold in a competitive market (typically the case for public corporations) appropriate measures of output may need to be devised. Public corporations may sometimes face different input prices as a consequence of being in the public sector; they may have access to cheap capital as a result of explicit or implied government guarantees, but may be requested to purchase more expensive domestically produced inputs.

Even when allowance is made for the problems of comparison, some conclusions emerge clearly from the evidence in the readings. In the first article, Richard Pryke has been able to compare three activities in the UK where services were provided by both the public and private sectors—airlines, ferries and hovercraft, and the sale of electricity and gas appliances. In each of these activities Pryke's analysis shows a picture of a more profitable private enterprise increasing its market share at the expense of the public sector. In cases where comparisons of cost levels and efficiency were feasible, Pryke's analysis generally shows the private enterprises in a favourable light. Pryke concludes that these public enterprises have been badly managed and that the main explanation for this poor performance is a weakening of incentives resulting from public ownership.

It is not difficult to be persuaded that the public enterprises which Pryke has studied have been run inefficiently; the findings on British Airways are supported by a variety of other studies, as Ashworth and Forsyth show in Part III.

However, the whole range of studies reviewed by Robert Millward in the second article show a far less clear-cut picture. A number of studies of the costs and efficiency of electricity generation and distribution in the United States have concluded that, after making appropriate allowance for differences in the mix of outputs provided and for differences in the supply price of inputs, the public sector utilities typically have lower unit costs of supply than their private sector counterparts (Yunker, 1975; Meyer, 1975; Pescatrice and Trapani, 1980). In contrast a comparative study of water utilities in the US (Crain and Zardkoohi, 1978) showed substantially higher costs in the public sector. The authors' analysis suggested that the methods used to regulate private water utilities had resulted in inefficient overcapitalisation (the Averch–Johnson (1962) effect); however, they concluded that any loss of efficiency resulting in this way was substantially outweighed by overmanning in the public sector. In Canada, Caves and Christensen (1978) studied the costs and efficiency of two competing railroads—the privately owned Canadian Pacific and the publicly owned Canadian National. They concluded that Canadian National did not have higher unit costs than Canadian Pacific. A similar study of air services within Australia (Forsyth and Hocking, 1980) compared the public Trans-Australia Airlines and the private Ansett Airlines of Australia. Government policy has imposed a regulatory regime which has sought to maintain a balance between private and public sector operators; the investigation showed very little difference in their performance.

The results of these studies do not suggest that there is anything intrinsically more efficient about private ownership. There are efficient and inefficient public enterprises and efficient and inefficient private enterprises. Some illumination on this apparently perplexing picture can be gained by referring back to Table 2 and looking at the structure of incentives at work in each case. It is interesting to note that each of the public enterprises investigated by Pryke faces competition in its product market. In such circumstances lower efficiency is penalised by falling market shares and/or poor profitability. If capital markets are effective this in turn leads to withdrawal from the industry by unsuccessful private firms or direct penalties in the form of take-over, dismissal or bankruptcy. Managers of public firms do not necessarily suffer corresponding penalties and in the circumstances we would expect product market competition to be more effective in private than public corporations.

It is interesting to note that the industry in Millward's review where public enterprise performance is most strikingly superior to private enterprise performance—electricity supply in the US—is an industry where competition is generally absent and where private enterprises are, for this reason, subject to detailed profit regulation. The higher costs of private firms are partly explained by overcapitalisation induced by the regulatory regime (as suggested by Averch and Johnson, 1962). Analysis of the insurance industry in West Germany shows a similar pattern, where the productive efficiency of private enterprises is generally lower than that of corresponding public enterprises as a consequence of distortions introduced by the form of profit regulation in operation (see Finsinger, Hammond, and Tapp, 1985).

The importance of the interaction of ownership and competition is supported by the cases reported by Millward where competition has been introduced between public and private firms; an analysis of electricity supply in the US has shown that where individual utilities are in competition, costs are generally lower (Primeaux, 1977). In one study of refuse collection costs (Savas, 1977) it was possible to monitor a situation where competition was introduced between private and public suppliers; the difference in costs between the two sectors was largely eliminated in a short time period. The impact of the introduction of competitive tendering for some local authority and health authority services in the UK shows a similar pattern (see the article by Hartley and Huby in Part V). The generally favourable impact of increased competition upon efficiency (both allocative and productive) is further illuminated by experience in sectors which have recently been deregulated (see Bailey, 1985, for a review of US deregulation and also the article by Davis in Part III).

It will be apparent, as was suggested by the analysis of the structure of incentives, that the evidence does not support any simple generalisations about the superiority of private sector performance. But we believe that two very broad conclusions can be drawn out. First, there is support for the view that the economic performance of all firms—public or private—is improved by a competitive environment and that under competition private firms are likely to do better. Second, where competition is absent there can be no presumption in favour of private corporations. Furthermore, the regulation of a private enterprise to prevent abuse of its monopoly power (in an uncompetitive environment) may introduce serious distortions which result in its performance being worse than that of a corresponding public enterprise.

We would conclude from this that denationalising an enterprise into an uncompetitive environment is likely to be positively harmful. Privatisation will tend to improve performance in a company only if supported by liberalisation; and if the two conflict, liberalisation is decidedly to be preferred.

V. Part III: Deregulation and efficiency

Although liberalisation may be (and we have argued should be) a prime policy objective, we have noted already that there are several obstacles to the promotion of competition in the nationalised (or formerly nationalised) industries. Some of these are intrinsic to the industry concerned; several of these industries are 'natural monopolies' and in other cases the significance of external costs or benefits means that an unregulated market solution would not promote maximum allocative efficiency. We consider these problems, and possible solutions, in the next two parts. In this part we consider industries which do not exhibit these features but where, historically, competition has nevertheless been restricted.

It might appear that in these cases matters are straightforward: the response of a government concerned to promote competition should be to repeal the statutes restricting competitive behaviour. The two articles in this section show that matters are not so simple. The case of express coaches (described by Evan Davis) is a telling illustration.

As noted earlier, deregulation of express coaching services in 1980 resulted in substantial price reductions on some routes and innovations in the provision of new types of service. Deregulation appears to have resulted in a significant improvement in allocative efficiency and there are some indications that the productive efficiency of the main incumbent public enterprise (National Express, a subsidiary of the National Bus Company) has improved also. Prior to deregulation National held monopoly rights to the majority of routes and the deregulated market has remained dominated by National. It is possible that National's pre-eminent position in the deregulated market reflects favourably on its efficiency in meeting competition. It seems likely, however, that it has been able to build upon advantages arising from its position as a dominant incumbent to reduce the threat of competitive market entry (in particular by refusing access to some of its city centre coaching terminals to its competitors) and to utilise the financial strength which enables it to outlast competitors when price competition is intense.

These financial and technical advantages are reinforced by the political skills and influence which incumbents have normally acquired. The most striking example comes from aviation. After British Airways (BA)'s success in persuading the Government to reject the Civil Aviation Authority (CAA)'s proposals for restructuring the industry, described in Ashworth and Forsyth, it would clearly be unwise for competitors to assume that the CAA can provide effective protection against predatory activity by BA. The point is reinforced

by reference to the specific allegations of predation made
against BA in the case of Laker Airways. The case was
brought in the US Courts. It was strenuously opposed,
through diplomatic pressures and in other ways, by the
British Government. The case proceeded only because (in
contrast to the position in criminal courts, where charges
were dropped) the US Government has no power to halt a
civil suit. The case concluded with an out-of-court settlement
to the Laker receiver.

In the UK, anti-predation legislation relies on the possibility of complaint to a regulatory agency (the Office of Fair
Trading in the absence of more specific provision) which can,
in some cases of its own volition and in others with the support of the Monopolies Commission, require that the offend-
ing practice cease. The contrast with American legislation,
which permits private action for punitive treble damages,
could hardly be more marked.

The case of aviation illustrates sharply a second problem in
promoting competition. Liberalisation of airline services
prior to privatisation would almost certainly reduce the
revenue received on flotation; to the extent that the proceeds
are regarded as an important benefit of privatisation (an issue
we discuss further in Part V) there is a conflict between the
objective of increasing competition and the maximisation of
sale proceeds.

Competition in the activities which have traditionally been
undertaken by British nationalised industries is thus a tender
plant requiring considerable nurture and shelter if it is to
grow.

VI. Part IV: The natural monopolies:
Promoting competition and regulatory issues

Several of the nationalised industries can be regarded as
natural monopolies. This is most obviously the case in industries which involve distribution networks (for example gas
or electricity distribution). In each of these the costs of providing two competing networks would probably not be a
great deal less than twice what it would cost to provide a
single network. These are not only natural monopolies but

also sustainable monopolies (see Sharkey, 1982, for an exposition of the recent theory of natural monopoly). Not only is it inefficient for competition to emerge but also it is improbable that it will in fact emerge.

Two important issues arise in relation to these industries. The first question is whether it is feasible to introduce competition for at least some of the products or services provided by these industries. Second, where competition is impractical is some form of regulation required and how can this be most effectively implemented? The five readings in this part each examine industries which have been commonly regarded as natural monopolies—railways, electricity supply, airports, telecoms, and gas supply.

A central conclusion emerging from these investigations is that in each case 'natural monopoly' is characteristic of only a part of the industry's activities; and for the remaining activities the scope for introducing competition exists. Thus in the case of railways, David Starkie suggests that the track and signalling system, and the scheduling of trains into particular 'time slots' on this system, can be regarded as a natural monopoly. He argues, however, that the operation of train services does not show characteristics of natural monopoly. It would be feasible, in these circumstances, for individual trains to be operated by different companies. Starkie therefore suggests that the ownership of the railway system should be divided: he proposes that the natural monopoly of the track system should be retained in public ownership but actual train operation could be carried out by a variety of competing companies (both public and private). The train-operating companies would clearly need to purchase track space from the track authority. However, Starkie suggests that this would be little different from the present arrangements in aviation where airlines purchase 'landing slots' (access to the runway at a particular time) from airports.

The feasibility of this proposal is most apparent in the case of rail freight services where 40 per cent of traffic is already carried in privately owned wagons. Passenger services, as Starkie points out, appear a less straightforward case. Many passenger services are at present subsidised, although in a world in which there were several independent train companies there is no reason why subsidised services should not periodically be put out to competitive tender. There are also other issues: for example, is a passenger timetable a natural monopoly and if so who should be responsible for it? are there economies of scale (or scope) between different services in the utilisation of rolling-stock? But these are precisely the types of questions where more detailed study and evaluation might yield solutions for a worthwhile change in the competitive environment in rail operations.

George Yarrow's paper analyses whether electricity supply is a 'natural monopoly'. He argues that the generation of power is not, in particular because of the scope for 'co-generation'—that is, the generation of electricity in conjunction with the production of heat for industrial or commercial purposes. The 1983 Energy Act has removed the statutory barriers to entry into electricity generation. Yarrow argues that this might be ineffective in promoting competition, however. Basically this is because the institutional structure established under the Act involves private suppliers selling power to the (public sector) Area Boards in competition with the established (public sector) Central Electricity Generating Board. Alternatively, private suppliers can, in effect, lease the use of the public distribution network to supply directly to the customer. These arrangements allow scope for the terms and conditions of entry (in particular in relation to prices and charges) to be specified in ways which discourage entry. As in the case of coaching discussed earlier, the removal of statutory entry barriers may not by itself be sufficient to ensure that fair competition takes place.

The paper by David Starkie and David Thompson concludes that airports are only natural monopolies, if at all, to a limited extent. In particular, the authors argue that there are no significant economies of scale (or scope) to be gained by operating London's airports as a system. Competition between these airports should therefore be both feasible and beneficial. The authors conclude that the commercial services (such as shops and cafeterias) provided to passengers at airports could in many cases feasibly be provided on a competitive basis. The authors conclude that the present monopoly provision of these services is a reflection not of the underlying cost structure of those services but of the policies of the British Airports Authority which are directed toward maximising the profits earned on these services by restricting competition.

In the case of telecommunication, John Vickers and George Yarrow argue that it would have been feasible to restructure British Telecom prior to privatisation to promote competition. The authors point to the US where the settlement of an anti-trust suit brought by the Department of Justice resulted in American Telephone & Telegraph (AT&T) divesting itself of its local telephone companies. Vickers and Yarrow identify three ways in which restructuring and dividing an enterprise can promote competition: by facilitating competition between the component parts (although the scope is limited in the case of telecommunications); by providing comparative information on performance for regulators and shareholders; and by reducing both the scope and incentive for predatory activity against market entrants. Instead the Government has chosen to privatise BT as a single entity. More seriously, it failed at the same time to liberalise certain parts of the telecommunications business. The restriction of competition to two firms is a clear recipe for anticompetitive practices. Furthermore, it may be naïve to expect that a regulatory body such as the Office of Telecommunications (OFTEL) will be able to control all forms of abuse. Liberalisation of markets, where possible, was the Government's best weapon against monopolisation and in this respect it is unfortunate that in the important area of resale, particularly in the supply of voice services, the Government acted deliberately to restrict competition (despite the recommendation of a report by Professor Michael Beesley in 1981 endorsing unrestricted resale).

The case of British Gas is in some respects similar to that of British Telecom. In their article Elizabeth Hammond, Dieter Helm, and David Thompson argue that scope exists both to restructure British Gas and to facilitate competitive market entry; we consider the findings of this study in more detail in the conclusions to this Introduction.

The scope for introducing competition in sectors commonly regarded as natural monopolies is thus considerably wider than has hitherto usually been assumed. Nevertheless there remain activities which can be regarded as genuine natural monopolies, in particular, as we noted at the beginning of this section, in sectors with substantial distribution or transmission networks. Gas and electricity distribution, telecoms networks (under present technology), British Rail's track, water systems, and the postal system may all fall into this category. In these cases it is highly unlikely that competing suppliers will emerge. This raises the issue of whether, in the event of privatisation of such a monopoly supplier, there is a requirement for regulation to protect consumers against monopolistic exploitation.

In North America activities such as electricity supply have often been carried out under regulated private ownership rather than (as is typically the case in Europe) under public ownership. Thus whilst experience of the regulation of natural monopolies is limited in the UK, there is a wealth of experience in the US. As has already been indicated, this experience is far from favourable. Two basic problems have been identified.

First, the form of regulatory control adopted can influence industry performance. A common type of regulatory control adopted in the US is rate-of-return (or rate base) regulation. The basic idea is that the level of profits which the regulated enterprise is allowed to make is limited to that required to provide a pre-specified 'fair' rate of return on the enterprise's rate base—a measure of the firm's capital assets. A major limitation of this approach is the well-known overcapitalisation effect identified by Averch and Johnson (1962). The enterprise can increase its total profits by increasing the size of its assets (or rate base) upon which the allowable profit rate is computed (provided, that is, that the allowed rate of return exceeds the cost of capital to the firm). There is therefore an incentive to choose techniques of production which are too capital-intensive. A similar effect has been identified in the regulation of profit levels in the German life insurance industry (Finsinger, Hammond, and Tapp, 1985). Here profits are limited to a specified rate of return on the total value of premium income; this gives an incentive to expand the premium base. This is reflected in overinvestment in marketing and promotional activities to achieve this objective. Rate-of-return regulation also has an effect on price-setting behaviour (Sherman and Visscher, 1982); it encourages the use of multi-part tariffs, price discrimination, and, in some circumstances, the setting of prices below marginal cost for those activities which are comparatively capital-intensive.

The second basic problem identified from North American experience has been characterised as 'regulatory capture' (see Demsetz, 1968, and Bailey, 1973). It is argued that regulatory authorities originally established to protect the interests of consumers against the potential market power exercisable by an industry may come to form a symbiotic relationship with the regulated enterprise in which they effectively promote the interests of the industry (or its more dominant firms) as well as, or instead of, the interests of the industry's customers. Such a situation may arise for a number of reasons but there is a particular danger where the regulatory body is heavily reliant on the regulated enterprise for the information and analysis which it requires to discharge its formal functions. The American airline industry, prior to deregulation, provides an example: the Civil Aeronautics Board, established largely to protect passenger safety, effectively became the co-ordinator of a cartel on behalf of the major carriers (Douglas and Miller, 1974).

The weaknesses identified with regulation in the US have led to a search for more effective measures; before the privatisation of British Telecom, Professor Stephen Littlechild was commissioned to evaluate alternative regulatory schemes (Littlechild, 1983). Vickers and Yarrow discuss the main findings of Littlechild's report in their article. Littlechild's preferred solution was to place a regulatory control on increases in BT's prices. The scheme that has been adopted, the 'RPI minus X' formula as it has come to be known, permits BT to increase the prices of a bundle of its services (a weighted average of line rentals and prices for inland dialled calls by subscribers) by an amount which is X per cent below the increase in the retail price index. Littlechild concluded that the direct regulation of prices, rather than profits, would minimise the incentive to the choice of inefficient (over-capitalised) production techniques which is inherent in rate-of-return regulation. Furthermore, Littlechild believed that the simplicity of the proposed scheme and the absence of significant scope for discretion by the regulatory authorities reduced the dangers of regulatory capture. Vickers and Yarrow take a slightly more cautious view: they have doubts as to whether the level set for the first five years of the regulatory control (RPI minus 3 per cent) places a particularly rigorous constraint upon BT. Separate protection against anti-competitive pricing will also be necessary. Both of these questions indicate that there are disadvantages, as well as advantages, arising from the simplicity of the price regulatory control. A separate issue arises on the respecification of the regulatory control in 1989 at the end of the current phase. Vickers and Yarrow point out that if the specification of X for the next five-year period is, in effect, based upon BT's actual cost performance then the price regulatory control will in practice become very similar to rate-of-return regulation, with all of its associated disadvantages. Furthermore, if in practice the respecification of X involves extensive negotiation with BT on its past and prospective cost performance, then the dangers of regulatory capture become more apparent.

The verdict on the 'RPI minus X' scheme must inevitably remain undecided until evidence becomes available on its performance in practice. Vickers's and Yarrow's discussion shows that the problems of rate-of-return regulation may be hard to avoid in a regulated private monopoly. An alternative mentioned by Vickers and Yarrow is the imposition of an effective incentive scheme on the managers of assets that remain in the public domain. It is not difficult to derive a system of penalties and rewards that encourage managers to implement efficient practices. The problem that is most frequently encountered is one of determining what an efficient cost of production actually is. Since there may be no corresponding assets in the private sector there is no direct measure against which to evaluate the performance of publicly controlled assets. Yarrow suggests in his article that in some cases it may be possible to elicit the required information if the operation of publicly owned assets can be split up. For example, if the prices of electricity produced by CEGB power stations are based on the average unit costs of electricity generated in each of the Area Boards, and if managerial remuneration reflects profits earned, then there will be an appropriate incentive to minimise costs. All that is happening is that, by decentralising operating units, the public sector is replicating the competitive processes of a private industry in which returns reflect the costs of production relative to those of competitors in the industry. It avoids the incumbency problem by allowing several units to operate (albeit in different markets). There may be quite widespread application of this technique for introducing appropriate incentives into the public sector.

The difficulties encountered in the effective regulation of private monopolies led Littlechild to conclude in his report that 'competition is by far the most effective protection against monopoly; regulation is merely a stop-gap until sufficient competition develops'. This conclusion underlines the importance of the positive promotion of competition both by restructuring enterprises to generate effective competition (along the lines suggested by each of the articles in this part) and by taking effective steps (in particular in the implementation of competition policy) to prevent the abuse of the dominant incumbent position enjoyed by many public enterprises.

VII. Part V: Franchising and competitive tendering

The readings in the previous part looked at the scope for introducing competition in activities which are often regarded as natural monopolies. A common theme emerging from these articles is that only a part of the activities carried out by each of the industries investigated could be regarded as a natural monopoly; the introduction of competition for the remaining activities was argued to be both feasible and beneficial.

Nevertheless there remain activities where the introduction of competition either would be ineffective (because the activities are sustainable natural monopolies with substantial sunk costs) or would not necessarily increase social welfare (for example because external costs and benefits are significant or because the activities are unsustainable natural monopolies). The discussion in the previous part showed the problems encountered in regulating private monopolies; this underlined the importance to be attached to the introduction of competition. The two readings in this part show that there may be scope for introducing competitive incentives, and hence easing the regulators' task, even where the direct introduction of competition in the market-place is not feasible.

In the case of natural monopoly, the new theory of contestability (Baumol, Panzar, and Willig, 1982) draws further attention to an old solution to this problem. If it is not possible to have competition *in* the market for the product, why not have competition *for* the monopoly, through franchising? Simon Domberger's article explores a number of possibilities. One variant would simply auction rights to the monopoly, awarding the contract to the bidder who offers to pay most for it. This gives incentives to productive efficiency—the winner of the auction is the producer who minimises costs and will therefore be able to bid a higher sum for the franchise—and it solves the income distribution problems posed by the existence of private monopolies, but it does not deal with the allocative inefficiencies of monopoly. Starkie and Thompson show that this type of franchise is already used extensively by the British Airports Authority for the provision of commercial services (such as cafeterias or car hire) at its airports. In this case the authors note that the allocative inefficiency of monopoly pricing persists.

An alternative type of auction is to award the franchise to the bidder who offers to provide the product or service at the lowest customer prices (Chadwick, 1859; Demsetz, 1968). It is easily shown that this gives appropriate incentives to productive efficiency and to allocative efficiency. The issue is more complex where there are more dimensions to the product than price but, in fact, the products of distribution monopolies are not at all complicated ones. Franchising is the solution which has been pursued in most newly established monopolies—television wavebands, North Sea oil exploration licences, and, most recently, cable television. In principle, it has been applied in telecommunications, where the 1983 Act provides for the licensing of telecommunications suppliers, but it is fanciful to imagine that British Telecom's twenty-five-year licence is likely to be in serious danger of non-renewal. Franchising does, however, raise problems of its own. Domberger identifies two of the most serious of these as how to organise an efficient franchise bidding system and how to ensure a transfer of assets on termination consistent with appropriate incentives to invest, but not to over-invest, in necessary equipment. The existence of substantial sunk costs may weaken the operation of a franchise system which requires repeat bidding. The incumbent may accumulate competitive advantages which diminish the extent of effective competition for the franchise (see, for example, Domberger and Middleton, 1985, on regional ITV franchises).

Where sunk costs are not significant, franchising appears a particularly appropriate policy. In recent years franchising (or competitive tendering) has been introduced for a range of publicly provided services. Examples are subsidised bus services, refuse collection, school cleaning, hospital cleaning, and other services provided by local authorities and health authorities. The article by Keith Hartley and Meg Huby reports experience to date in the case of a number of local authorities and district health authorities which have put services such as refuse collection or hospital cleaning out to tender. Their conclusions are favourable in terms of the feasibility of franchising these services: typically six bids were received for services put out to tender. Their conclusions are also favourable in terms of the impact of tendering: in the cases studied the cost saving from introducing tendering (for a specified level of service) averaged 26 per cent. In a number of the cases where services had been contracted-out, however, there were instances of penalty clauses being invoked because of poor quality work or because of delays in carrying out work. Hartley and Huby point to the importance of ensuring that the tendering process is competitive: they conclude that franchising authorities need to encourage and seek out new entrants to the tendering process and that contracting-out should be subject to the general provisions of competition policy, in particular investigation by the Office of Fair Trading.

VIII. Part VI: Labour and financial issues

Much of the material in this book is concerned with the issue of the efficiency of public enterprises and the related issue of how best to improve performance. We have focused on these issues both because of their importance in the Government's perspective of its privatisation policy (as shown in Moore's speeches in Part I) and because of their importance to academics assessing the Government's policies (see Beesley and Littlechild, Heald and Steel in Part I). Nevertheless it is clear that privatisation, and in particular denationalisation of state enterprises, serves a multiplicity of objectives. The Treasury is greatly interested in the revenue which can be obtained from privatisation. Privatisation may also be seen by the Government as a means of disciplining the power of public sector trade unions (see Heald and Steel in Part I).

In the first reading in this last part David Thomas analyses the unions' response to privatisation. Perhaps his most striking conclusion is that privatisation will not necessarily weaken union power. Thomas argues that privatisation will have a differential impact upon employees in different enterprises. Some will lose but others may gain. Where the privatised enterprise is highly profitable, or where it continues to enjoy substantial market power post-privatisation, then the labour force may gain from privatisation. Thomas also suggests that privatisation may have a differential impact upon different types of labour. He argues that public ownership may have bid up the terms and conditions of less skilled staff (like clerks and some manual workers) with poor bargaining power, and depressed rewards which highly skilled workers (like managers and engineers) would expect in the private sector. Whatever the circumstances, it seems clear that where privatisation does take place it is to the general advantage of the labour force that the newly privatised enterprise retains whatever protection from competition was enjoyed by its predecessor, the nationalised enterprise.

The second reading looks at the financial effects of asset sales. There are two issues that arise here. First, to what extent have the objectives of the Government in achieving a wide share ownership and disposing of assets at minimum costs been met? Secondly, what have been the effects of privatisation on the public and private sectors' financial positions? On the first issue the article by Colin Mayer and Shirley Meadowcroft paints a rather gloomy picture of assets being sold at substantial discounts, with widely dispersed ownership only being sustained for a brief period after privatisation. Apparently straightforward alternatives that significantly diminish discounts are discussed. On the second issue, the authors contend that the financial implications for both public and private sectors have been distorted by accounting conventions. What appears to be a large contribution to government finance is in fact a substantial deficit. The problem arises from the failure of PSBR measures to reflect future as well as current net earnings. This also bears on the effect of privatisation on the corporate sector's cost of capital. Traditional crowding-out arguments are clearly not applicable here and to the extent that there is an effect it is to change the composition, rather than the total, of private sector borrowing.

IX. Conclusions and agenda

The articles in this book raise a wide range of issues and the authors reach many, sometimes conflicting, conclusions. This reflects the complexity of the privatisation debate, the controversial nature of the issues raised and the progressive development of analysis and opinion on the subject. We do not propose an attempt at summarising all the arguments and findings put forward; rather we set out in what follows our own conclusions on the progress and impact of privatisation policies.

Privatisation policy in the UK has increasingly come to emphasise the virtues of denationalisation, as the policy statement by the Financial Secretary to the Treasury in July 1985 shows. (Some of this is reprinted in Part I.) Denationalisation now appears to take precedence over, or even to be carried out at the expense of, the promotion of competition. The conflict between privatisation and liberalisation—noted by Kay and Silberston (1984)—is no longer a conflict but a rout. We do not believe that the change of policy direction is supported by the empirical evidence on the relative performance of public and private enterprise (see Part II). This stresses the role of competition and supports scepticism about the value of denationalisation outside a competitive environment.

The promotion of competition in the areas covered by public enterprises is rarely a straightforward task, however, as the articles in Parts III and IV indicate. Indeed it is often the problems which would arise from unregulated private supply—a belief that some type of significant market failure was likely to be the result—that provided the rationale for public provision in the first instance.

We believe, however, that the range of possibilities for promoting competition is far wider than has hitherto usually been assumed, and the readings in Parts IV and V show the possible opportunities in a number of sectors. Scope exists for introducing competition (in particular through franchising) in industries traditionally regarded as natural monopolies or where significant external benefits and costs require recognition. We have discussed elsewhere why a policy of promoting competition may not have been pursued (Kay and Thompson, 1985). Denationalisation of public enterprises in their existing (usually monopolistic) form can be implemented more speedily than if measures of restructuring (breaking up) or liberalisation are to be implemented in parallel. This is both because the flotation process is more straightforward for an established enterprise and because privatisation options which preserve an enterprise's market power are likely to gain the most support (or generate the least resistance) from the management and workforce of the enterprise. More rapid implementation of denationalisation policies enables the perceived financial and other benefits (whatever their actual substance) to be reaped more quickly. But if this is achieved at the expense of the promotion of competition then we consider that the most significant benefit which might be gained—that is, improving economic efficiency—will be sacrificed. And this may not just be a short-term loss. The denationalisation of monopoly enterprises may make the future task of introducing competition more, not less, difficult.

The topical case of gas—the largest transfer of assets to the private sector proposed by the Government—illustrates both the possibilities and the problems in promoting competition (see the article by Hammond, Helm, and Thompson in Part IV). Gas supply is typically regarded as a natural monopoly and in practice the British Gas Corporation (BGC) is the sole supplier (although, in principle, gas supply was deregulated in 1982). The Government's proposals for privatisation involve the sale of BGC as a single entity.

The authors suggest that an alternative approach is feasible and would also prove more effective in improving the efficiency of the gas industry. The approach aims to create a market for gas by separating activities which have natural monopoly characteristics from activities where competition is possible. The most important source of natural monopoly lies in the distribution network. The authors conclude that the ownership of BGC's National Transmission System (which carries gas from the beach-head to different parts of the country) and of each of the local distribution networks in each region of the country should be separated from the business of buying and selling gas. The transmission system would act as a common-carrier facility charging rental rates to companies selling gas to customers. This would establish a market for the purchase and sale of gas between the owners of the local distribution networks and the producers of gas (the oil and gas companies). Direct market entry by the producers into the supply of gas directly to consumers would be permitted, although in practice this would only be likely to prove attractive for supply to larger industrial customers (because there are some economies of scale in revenue collection from smaller customers). However, such market entry would not be forestalled, as it is at present, by BGC's ownership of both the National Transmission System and contracts for the supply of gas at advantageous prices.

The natural monopoly associated with the transmission system and local gas distribution would still lead to a requirement for regulation. But regulation is focused only on activities where competition is not feasible. And dividing the ownership of the local distribution networks provides competing sources of information to the regulatory authority. The creation of several regional gas companies would also increase capital market incentives both by providing sectoral bench-marks for company performance and by making the threat of take-over more realistic.

The possibility therefore exists of restructuring the gas industry in order to promote competitive incentives. But an intrinsic part of such restructuring is a reduction in the advantages and market power at present enjoyed by BGC. As such it is likely to be opposed by the industry; indeed the Chairman had stated well before gas privatisation came onto the policy agenda that, if privatised, BGC should be sold as a single entity. Even with management support, restructuring is also likely to prolong the timetable for flotation.

The case of gas suggests a conclusion which we have seen applies more generally to other sectors. Options which provide a larger role for competition are feasible in many cases, but their implementation requires a willingness to take a longer-term view of the benefits of increased competition, and a determination to persuade, and engage the support of, those groups (in particular the incumbent management) whose interests are not well served, in the short term, by increased competition.

Part I
POLICIES AND ISSUES

1

PRIVATISATION: PRINCIPLES, PROBLEMS AND PRIORITIES*

Michael Beesley and Stephen Littlechild

I. Introduction

What principles should guide a further programme of privatisation? What kinds of problems will be encountered, and where should the priorities lie? Economists have not written much on these issues. We hope to provide an explicit structure in which relevant questions can be identified and answered.

'Privatisation' is generally used to mean the formation of a Companies Act company and the subsequent sale of at least 50 per cent of the shares to private shareholders. However, the underlying idea is to improve industry performance by increasing the role of market forces. Many other measures can contribute to this, notably freeing of entry to an industry, encouraging competition, and permitting joint ventures. Market forces can also be increased by restructuring the nationalised industry, to create several successor companies which may be publicly owned. To secure maximum benefits, a whole set of measures must be designed for each industry, including privatisation as a key element.

In this paper we seek criteria to decide:

- whether a particular nationalised industry is a serious candidate for privatisation
- how the industry should be structured and the regulatory environment designed
- what the priorities should be for privatisation among the industries.

* This article was first published in the *Lloyds Bank Review*, July 1983; it was written before the 9 June 1983 General Election was announced. Reprinted by permission of the authors.

Michael Beesley is Professor of Economics at the London Graduate School of Business Studies.

Stephen Littlechild is Professor of Commerce in the Department of Industrial Economics and Business Studies at the University of Birmingham.

II. Criteria for privatisation

It is helpful to structure the problem as a cost–benefit analysis. In principle, one might examine the effects of each alternative privatisation proposal on different interest groups such as existing and potential customers, taxpayers, suppliers of labour and capital, etc. Trade-offs between these interest groups could be established and decisions made accordingly.

We propose to short-circuit this procedure somewhat by specifying a single criterion, namely the present value of aggregate net benefits to UK consumers. This is measured primarily by lower prices of currently available goods and services (offset by any price increases). Effects on the level of output, the quality and variety of goods and services available, and the rate of innovation will also be important. Typically, there will be release of resources, benefiting the consumer in other ways. Changes in the distribution of benefits (e.g. by geographical area) and effects on employees, suppliers, exports, and taxpayers must also be considered. Nonetheless, the criterion of aggregate net benefit to consumers seems a simple and appropriate starting point. Unless this promises to be considerable, the political costs of change will scarcely be worth incurring. (Public opinion on privatisation is probably changing. Political 'costs' may prove significantly less than they once appeared.)

We do not assume that privatisation is desirable in itself. Respectable arguments support such a view—for example, that political freedom depends on private property, or that government intervention should be minimised, because the larger the government sector, the larger the threat to liberty. Here, privatisation is strictly an economic instrument. Privatisation in certain industries (or parts thereof) could be ruled out as simply not beneficial to consumers.

Our criterion excludes the stockmarket value of the successor company or companies. This value could clearly be artificially increased (e.g. by granting a monopoly or announcing lesser restrictions on entry), but this would be counterproductive to consumers. Similarly, the (alleged) poor proceeds of sale, realised or in prospect, should not in themselves deter privatisation. The right sale price is simply that which investors are prepared to pay, once conditions and timing of sale have been determined by the criterion of consumer benefit.

Though it should not influence the decision to privatise, the sale value is not unimportant. The proceeds are the price at which the present owners of the company's assets (viz. the taxpayers) transfer these assets to the future owners (viz. the shareholders). The method of flotation should aim to minimise over- or under-subscription. There is no merit in making a gift to 'stags' or imposing losses on underwriters. The difficulties of estimating future stockmarket prices are great, as witness Amersham, Britoil, and Associated British Ports. There is therefore a strong case for supplementing professional advice by the organisation of some form of futures market, e.g. by distributing to customers limited quantities of shares to be traded in advance of the main flotation.[a]

The criterion of benefit to consumers should be used to design the privatisation scheme as a whole. Consider some of the things to be decided in order to write prospectuses for floating one or more successor companies:

- the number of companies, the assets and liabilities of each, and their intended aims and scope of business
- the structure of the industry in which the company (or companies) will operate, especially the conditions of new entry
- the regulatory environment, including competition policy, efficiency audits, controls (if any) on prices or profits
- non-commercial obligations (e.g. with respect to employment, prices or provision of services) and sources of funding for these obligations (e.g. direct subsidies from government or local authorities)
- the timing of the privatisation scheme, including the flotation date and the times at which new competition is allowed and/or regulation instituted
- future levels of government shareholding, and ways in which the associated voting power will be used.

Potential investors will translate this package, which is designed to maximise benefits to consumers, into a stockmarket price. Successful flotation requires an accurate forecast of this price, and a limited futures market in the shares can help.

III. Benefits and costs

Our criterion involves benefits for two sets of consumers: actual or potential consumers of the industry; and other consumers, who benefit from savings in resources which may accompany privatisation. Thus, if lower subsidies are paid, other consumers will benefit via lower taxation. Subsidies represent real resources which could be consumed elsewhere.

Privatisation will generate benefits for consumers because privately owned companies have a greater incentive to produce goods and services in the quantity and variety which consumers prefer. Companies which succeed in discovering and meeting consumer needs make profits and grow; the less successful wither and die. The discipline of the capital market accentuates this process: access to additional resources for growth depends on previously demonstrated ability. Selling a nationalised industry substitutes market discipline for public influence. Resources tend to be used as consumers dictate, rather than according to the wishes of government, which must necessarily reflect short-term political pressures and problems of managing the public sector's overall demands for capital.[1]

But gains are not all one way. Privatisation is intended to change motivations of management towards profit-making. A privately owned company will have greater incentive to exploit monopoly power commercially. To the extent that this is not limited, consumer benefits from privatisation will be less than they might be. Second, a privatised company will be less willing to provide uneconomic services. The resources so released will be used more productively, but particular sets of consumers will lose by the change. This raises the question of how such losses, often thought of as social obligations, should be handled. Third, eliminating inefficient production and restrictive

[1] To support this argument, there is growing empirical evidence, mainly from the USA, that privately owned companies make more efficient use of labour, capital, and other resources, and are also more innovative. See, for example, De Alessi (1974b and 1980).[b]

labour practices means the release of resources. This will benefit taxpayers and consumers outside the industry, but some employees and suppliers will suffer. The short-cut criterion does not explicitly recognise these losers. Ways of coping with these three problems are discussed below.

Some have argued that ownership is largely irrelevant. But could the benefits of privatisation be obtained without the change in ownership? We have already argued that ownership *does* matter because consumers in general will be better served. Also, for political reasons, privatisation may be a necessary accompaniment to competition. The additional liberalisation of entry into telecommunications announced in February 1983 would not have been politically feasible if the transfer of British Telecom to private ownership had not by then been in process. Furthermore, competition policy is (or certainly could be) more effective against a private company than against a nationalised industry.

Alternative ways of increasing market pressure are politically limited. The benefits of privatisation derive partly from the ability to diversify and redeploy assets, unconstrained by nationalisation statutes. These statutes might be relaxed without transferring ownership, but rival firms and taxpayers fearing government-subsidised competition or uncontrolled expansion would undoubtedly oppose this. Again, efficiency might increase if governments refrained from intervening in the industries, but as long as the industries are nationalised, such self-restraint is implausible. The industries might be asked to act commercially, but nationalisation itself delays inevitable adjustments to market forces. The substantial reductions in overmanning in BA and the nationalised manufacturing industries could surely not have been achieved if the intention to privatise had not already been expressed.

Nationalised industries were deemed appropriate vehicles for a wide variety of social policies. But most consumers' interests were adversely affected, and nationalisation often proved inadequate for the social purposes too. It is now necessary to reform the industries while meeting social needs. This is always a politically difficult exercise, and impossible with nationalisation. Privatisation properly designed makes it

possible to decouple the two tasks, and to focus social policy
more effectively.

IV. Competition

Competition is the most important mechanism for maximising
consumer benefits, and for limiting monopoly power. Its
essence is rivalry and freedom to enter a market. What counts
is the existence of competitive threats, from potential as well as
existing competitors. The aim is not so-called 'perfect' competition; rather, one looks for some practical means to introduce or increase rivalry. The relevant comparison for policy is
between the level of competition that could realistically be
created, and the present state of the nationalised industry.

Certain features of nationalisation need attention whatever
the ownership form finally adopted. The artificial restrictions
on entry embodied in the statutory monopolies granted to most
of the earlier nationalised industries should be removed.
Government-controlled resources (e.g. wayleaves and radio
spectrum; airspace, routes, and landing rights; harbour
facilities; mineral rights on land and sea; etc.) should be made
equally available to new entrants, without favouring the
incumbent nationalised concerns.

The starting structure for the successor private company or
companies is extremely important. In some cases, different
parts of the industry could compete if formed into horizontally
separate companies. Resources or assets could be transferred
to potential entrants. Vertically separating the industry into
different companies would also generate rivalry at the inter-
face. If, for example, British Telecom's International division were separated from the Inland division, each would
encourage alternative sources of supply (including self-
supply).

Splitting up an organisation might involve sacrificing
economies of scale or scope. Increased costs of production or
transacting may offset the gains from increased competition.
This argument is dubious for present nationalised industries,
since they have been determined largely by political or
administrative, not market, forces. However, in the absence
of competition, one cannot know in advance precisely what

industry structure will prove most efficient. Therefore, as far as possible, the future growth of the industry should not be fixed by the pattern established at flotation. Companies should be allowed to expand or contract, diversify or specialise, as market forces dictate. Where there are very few existing outside competitors, or none at all, the starting structure should be designed to create effective competition. When in doubt, smaller rather than larger successor companies should be created, and allowed to merge thereafter, subject to rules of competition policy discussed below.

V. Regulation and competition policy

Even the introduction of such competition as is feasible may still leave the incumbent with significant monopoly power in some industries. How should this be dealt with? Government will no longer have the direct and indirect control associated with nationalisation, but alternative means of influencing or regulating conduct are available (besides the promotion of competition).

One favourite idea is to influence the successor company's prices by limiting the profits earned, expressed as a rate of return on capital. The US has had much experience of this; the result has generally been higher rather than lower prices. Some defects are well-known: disincentives to efficiency, a 'cost-plus' mentality and expensive enforcement. Other defects are gradually becoming better understood: the vulnerability to 'capture' of the regulatory commission by the regulated industry, and the associated tendency to limit competition among incumbents and to restrict new entry. In fact, US regulation embodies a philosophy similar to nationalisation, with similar effects. Rate-of-return regulation should not be thought of as a relevant accompaniment to privatisation.

There is considerable pressure for efficiency audits or value for money audits, on the grounds that monopoly industries will have inadequate incentive to increase efficiency. Without sanctions for non-compliance, such audits are likely to be ineffective. However, if they are used for setting tariffs and controlling investment plans, the system essentially amounts to rate-of-return regulation, itself defective for the reasons

just indicated. Pressure of competition and the firms' own incentive not to waste resources are likely to be more effective
inducements to efficiency than the creation of a government
nanny.

Another possibility is to limit prices directly by means of
explicit tariff restrictions. For example, it is proposed that the
price of a bundle of telecommunications services should not
increase by more than X percentage points below the retail
price index (the RPI-X formula) for a period of five years.
This could be applied to any set of services, perhaps weighted
as in the bills of a representative consumer. The level of X
would, in practice, be the outcome of bargaining between BT
and the Government; an exhaustive costing exercise is not
called for.

The purpose of such a constraint is to reassure customers
of monopoly services that their situation will not get worse
under privatisation. It 'holds the fort' until competition
arrives, and is inappropriate if competition is not expected to
emerge. It is a temporary safeguard, not a permanent method
of control. The one-off nature of the restriction is precisely
what preserves the firm's incentive to be efficient, because the
firm keeps any gains beyond the specified level. Repeated
'cost-plus' audits would destroy this incentive and, moreover,
encourage 'nannyish' attitudes towards the industry.

A preferable alternative to detailed regulation of costs,
profits or prices is greater reliance on competition policy.
Predatory competition should be discouraged, both to curb
monopoly power and to allow new ownership structures to
emerge after privatisation. In the UK at present, potential
anti-competitive practices have to be considered in turn by
the Office of Fair Trading, the Monopolies and Mergers
Commission and the Secretary of State. In the case of hitherto
nationalised industries a stronger and speedier policy is
required. The main aim should be to protect existing and
potential competitors likely to be at a disadvantage when
competing with a dominant incumbent, who in the past has
generally had the advantage of statutory protection, and who
even now probably has significant legal and other advantages
(e.g. rights of way). Certain practices (e.g. price discrimination, refusal to supply, full-line forcing) should be explicitly

prohibited if they are used by the dominant incumbent to eliminate or discipline specific competitors. Parties adversely affected should be able to sue in the Courts, perhaps for triple damages.

The 1983 Bill privatising British Telecom exhibits some awareness of the problem. Present monopoly control has been supplemented by an Office of Telecommunications, and BT's licence will require published tariffs and prohibit predatory price discrimination. However, encouraging future entry and reliance on competition policy instead of regulation have yet to be as firmly established as would be desirable.

VI. Non-commercial obligations

Nationalised industries provide various services which are uneconomic at present prices and costs. Not all are necessarily uneconomic and some could be made viable by a private company or companies operating with increased efficiency. However, there will also be attempts to raise certain prices and/or reduce certain services. Since a main aim of privatisation is to guide resources to the most highly valued uses, the companies should not be prevented from doing so. Nevertheless, it may well be felt socially desirable or politically necessary to ensure that certain prices or services are maintained (e.g. in rural areas).

Procedures for establishing non-commercial obligations need to be clearly specified. Each privatisation act should define which services are potentially of social concern. Any company claiming that such a service is uneconomic should be required to provide relevant financial data to support its case, accompanied by a request to withdraw unless a subsidy is provided. A specified public body (e.g. a local authority) will then consider whether the case is plausible, whether another operator is willing to provide the service, and whether a subsidy should be provided.

Where should this subsidy come from? One of the prime aims of nationalisation was to facilitate cross-subsidies from more profitable services. However, cross-subsidisation largely hides the extent of the subsidy and opens the door to political pressures. Also, it inevitably entails restrictions on competition so as to protect the source of funds: cross-subsidisation and unrestricted competition are mutually incompatible. For these reasons, economists have long recommended that explicit public subsidies should be provided in preference to cross-subsidies.

What if the government is unwilling to do this? Explicit subsidies have admittedly not proved politically popular to date. Other possibilities have to be explored. In telecommunications it is currently envisaged that BT will charge an access fee to other networks; this will be used to finance emergency services, call-boxes, and certain loss-making services in rural areas. This amounts to a tax on telecom operators to support particular socially sanctioned outputs. So long as the scope of these 'social' services is narrowly defined, stringent tests of loss-making are applied, and the access fee is applied to all relevant operators, the tax will remain low and competition should not be seriously damaged. Such compromises may well have to be worked out for many cases of privatisation in which protection of particular consumers is deemed important. They will reduce total net benefits to consumers; but political realities have to be faced. Unless safeguards are provided for adversely affected interest groups, privatisation itself could well be jeopardised. Once again, the design of the privatisation scheme is crucial.

Privatisation is often opposed on the grounds that it leads to unemployment. But even state-owned firms cannot in practice finance overmanning over long periods. Large-scale redundancies have already occurred in those which have failed to match international competitors' efficiency. Where the effects of privatisation promise to be severe, generous redundancy payments should be made. However, remaining employees' prospects will be brighter in privatised industries, which have a superior ability to adapt, diversify and grow.

VII. Priorities

We have argued that a nationalised industry should be privatised if the net benefits to consumers from doing so are positive. Many industries will meet this criterion, yet it would be impossible to privatise all of them at once, if only because

of the constraints imposed by the parliamentary timetable.
Which industries should then be given priority? Leaving
aside political considerations, our criterion indicates those
industries where the consumer benefits of privatisation are
greatest. How can this be determined?

First, other things being equal, a larger industry offers
larger potential scope for savings. That is, if costs and prices
can be reduced by an average of x per cent, an industry with a
turnover of £2 billion offers twice the potential benefit of an
industry with a turnover of £1 billion. Table 1 lists the
nationalised industries in order of turnover. It shows that the
largest three industries (electricity, telecommunications, and
gas) account for nearly half the total turnover in the nationalised sector. At the other end of the list, there is relatively little to be gained by privatising the smallest seven industries,
whatever percentage gains each one could generate, since
together they account for less than 6 per cent of total turnover in the nationalised sector. Of course, other things are
not equal, and the industries offer significantly different
scope for generating benefits, as we show in a moment.
Nonetheless, the criterion of size must be constantly borne in
mind. For example, to match a 1 per cent saving in capital
employment in the electricity industry, it would be necessary
to achieve a saving of 2 per cent in telecoms, 5 per cent in
coal, 13 per cent in steel, or 24 per cent in posts.

Second, industries will offer less scope for savings if they
have already been subject to severe remedial action, and more
scope if they are as yet relatively untouched. The last column
of Table 1 shows the percentage changes in manpower over
the last two years. By this criterion, the 'manufacturing'
nationalised industries (British Steel, BL, Rolls-Royce,
British Shipbuilders) plus British Airways and the bus companies probably have relatively small further savings to offer
compared to the other industries, particularly since press
reports suggest that yet more redundancies are already in
train.

Third, benefits to consumers are likely to be greater in so
far as competition rather than monopoly is likely to pre-
dominate. Competition could come from multiple ownership
in the same industry, from abroad, or from rival products.

Table 1. Nationalised Industries,[1] year 1981/2

	Turnover £m	Capital employed (CCA basis) £m	Workforce thous	Percentage change in workforce since 1979/80
Electricity Industry[2]	8,057	32,605	147	− 8
British Telecom	5,708	16,099	246	+ 2
British Gas	5,235	10,955	105	0
National Coal Board	4,727	5,891	279	− 5
British Steel	3,443	2,502	104	−38
BL	3,072	1,521	83[3]	−31
British Rail	2,899[4]	2,746	227	− 7
Post Office[5]	2,636	1,347	183	0

British Airways	2,241	1,338	43[6]	−24
Rolls-Royce	1,493	992	45	−23
British Shipbuilders	1,026	655	67	−18
S Scotland Electricity Board	716	2,817	13	−5
National Bus Company	618	508	53	−16
British Airports Authority	277	852	7	−7
N Scotland Hydro Electric	270	1,981	4	−3
Civil Aviation Authority	206	162	7	−2
Scottish Transport Group	152	157	11	−17
British Waterways Board	16	50	3	−2
Total	42,792	83,178	1,627	

1. These are the organisations classed as nationalised industries in the public enterprise division of the Treasury, as reflected in HM Treasury (1983) with the addition of BL and Rolls-Royce.
2. Including CEGB, Council and Area Boards. Figures for CEGB alone are £6,364m, £23,357m, 55,000, —11 per cent.
3. UK only; overseas approximately 22,000.
4. Including government contract payments £810m.
5. Including Giro and postal orders.
6. Reportedly 37,500 as at March 1983.

DEMAND PROSPECTS

	Good	Bad
Single	A Electricity distribution (Area Boards and Grid) Telecoms (local) Gas distribution Airports	B Rail Post (or possibly C?) Waterways
Multiple	C CEGB (excl. Grid) Telecoms (excl. local) Gas production Coal British Airways	D Steel BL Rolls-Royce Shipbuilding Buses

SUPPLY PROSPECTS

Figure 1. Classification of Nationalised Industries
Post-Privatisation[c]

However, in order to ascertain which industries, or parts of industries, are susceptible to competition it is necessary to examine more closely the demand and cost conditions under which the industries are likely to operate.

These ideas may be clarified by conceiving of each nationalised industry as located in a simple two-by-two matrix. Demand prospects for typical services and products are classified as Good or Bad, depending on long-term trends, and supply prospects are classed as conducive to Single or Multiple (competing) ownership depending on developments in technology. This of course over-simplifies the situation, but the contrasts between the industries are great enough for the divisions to be useful.

Figure 1 shows our own conjectures as to the quadrant in which each industry would be located *if appropriately privatised*. These are not necessarily the same quadrants as the one in which the industries would currently be placed. As we shall shortly argue, privatisation may well be necessary in order to shift an industry from an 'inferior' quadrant to a 'better' one, i.e. to one which offers greater benefits to consumers (and, often, to employees also). In some cases, too, it is appropriate to place different parts of an industry into different quadrants (e.g. electricity production and distribution). We now consider each quadrant in turn—for convenience, in the order D, C, A, B.

(i) *Quadrant D*

Industries in this quadrant need present no problems of monopoly power, since multiple ownership is quite feasible within the UK. Moreover, the manufacturing industries among them—British Steel, BL, British Shipbuilders, and Rolls-Royce—are already subject to international competition, which secures prices as low as can be expected, given the current excess capacity on a world scale. Operating efficiency —or lack of it—in the UK industries is a relatively minor factor in determining prices. Labour monopoly power has surely been much reduced. There may be expansion as the depression ends, but there will probably be increasing competition from superior sources abroad, so these industries are always likely to occupy quadrant D. Thus, consumers in these manufacturing industries will gain little *directly* from privatisation.

Consumers will, however, gain indirectly from privatisation, notably as taxpayers. Private owners will be more willing and able than the government to identify and rectify inefficiencies and to exploit new opportunities. Privatisation will reduce the liability to losses and free resources for better use elsewhere. It should not be deferred merely to get the industries 'into the black', by further subsidies, so that a 'respectable' flotation price can be achieved.

Of all the nationalised industries, bus operations are least suited to the scale of operations which nationalisation implies. Nevertheless, the prospective gains are greater from encouraging competition than from privatisation. An important element of NBC is long-distance traffic. Here deregulation occurred in 1980, leading to increased competition, better service, and lower prices. Further gains would follow from removing further obstacles to competition (e.g. by facilitating access to favourable terminal locations). In urban areas—the principal short-distance markets—quite different conditions prevail. The incumbent operators are owned by local authorities, and to a much lesser extent by NBC, and entry is still toughly regulated. Here, there would be a large gain from deregulation, not least in the redistribution of bus resources towards the more favourable routes. Methods of subsidy should also be changed to stimulate competition so as to promote efficiency among all kinds of operators (e.g. by shifting subsidies to users, not paying them to producers).

In sum, privatisation of the manufacturing industries in quadrant D will yield positive but small net benefits to consumers, so a high priority is not indicated. In the bus industry, preference should be given to facilitating competition where it is at present restricted.

(ii) *Quadrant C*

Industries in this quadrant are characterised by good long-term demand prospects. They happen to be very large, and (with the exception of British Airways and British Telecom) are relatively untouched as yet, so they presumably offer considerable scope for improvements in efficiency. They need present no significant problems of monopoly power, because multiple ownership is viable. Thus they are prime candidates for privatisation.

Interestingly, however, none of the industries is organised as if it were in quadrant C at present. The CEGB and British Telecom are each a single organisation (though Mercury should begin to offer a challenge to the latter). The NCB is a single organisation whose prospects in the absence of privatisation are somewhat dim. British Airways is part of a multi-ownership industry, but again its prospects without privatisation are unclear. Currently, these industries would probably be put in quadrants A, B and D respectively. Privatising them involves recognising that, wholly or partly, they could belong to quadrant C, and that benefits for both consumers and employees can be secured without generating severe problems of monopoly power. However, careful attention needs to be given to their structure after privatisation.

In the case of the CEGB, the national grid should remain in public ownership for the present, perhaps as a common carrier. (It might be integrated with the Department of Energy.) The generating stations should be sold to separate buyers, so as to establish competition in production. Firms would be allowed to bid for a group of stations (and coal mines) so as to achieve economies of integration, but sufficient independent entities would be created to make competition workable.

Privatisation of the British coal industry would follow a similar pattern. Consumers would benefit directly from the lower prices due to competition, including the removal of restrictions on imports. The prospects for the British coal industry itself would also be greatly improved. There are currently very dramatic differences in costs between different pits. Resources of capital and labour would be reallocated so that the more efficient pits—which would command the highest prices on privatisation—would expand. There would also be benefits from a severe reduction in the monopoly power of labour. The relatively low capital–labour ratio (£21,000 capital employed per man in 1981/2) could profitably be increased. Because long-term trends in demand are favourable to coal (particularly when synthetic fuels become viable), and because Britain has many favourably placed locations for coal mining, the industry could once again become an expanding one. Employment could then increase in the British coal industry as a whole. In practice, privatisation seems necessary to secure these benefits. Of the pits which are presently extra-marginal, some would become viable as a result of more efficient management. Widespread closure of the least efficient pits would necessitate a generous policy to cope with social adjustment. As noted earlier, a merit of privatisation is that it divorces the problem of industrial development from that of discharging society's debts arising from the past.

The 1983 Bill enabling the privatisation of British Telecom does not envisage the restructuring of British Telecom. The present analysis would indicate the creation of several successor companies. Local distribution (which we place in Quadrant A) presents the chief monopoly problem. The Bill does explicitly recognise the need for developments in competition policy to prevent the exploitation of a dominant position, and the Government has concurrently announced limited measures to facilitate competition from new entry, though more could be done. Overall, most of the industry is prospectively in quadrant C.

The British Gas Corporation is already subject to competition in the discovery and extraction of gas. It has hitherto held a favoured position as sole buyer; this has recently been discontinued. Competition and efficiency would be further increased if some of the extremely valuable existing contracts were auctioned to new entrants, if the production side of the Corporation were completely separated from the national grid and local distribution, and if restrictions on gas exports were removed. Whether privatisation of gas production would create direct as well as indirect benefits for consumers is not clear.

No special steps are necessary to achieve a competitive market structure for British Airways, though fewer restrictions on routes and allocation of airport landing slots on a more competitive basis would facilitate competition. However, as with the manufacturing industries, it is not clear that the further gains to consumers from privatising BA would be substantial. Thus, in quadrant C, the prime candidates are the CEGB, British Telecom, and the NCB.

(iii) *Quadrant A*

The industries in this quadrant are characterised by good demand prospects but the supply prospects do not favour multiple competing ownership. Local distribution systems for electricity, gas, and telephones are characterised by high sunk costs. With the possible exception of telephones, they do not face much immediate technological challenge, and will be sustainable as local monopolies. Consumers are therefore at risk.

Cannot the market process be used even if successor entities are sustainable monopolies? Some have argued for auctioning franchises to private bidders, thereby encouraging competition for the monopoly privileges. Franchising would transfer the value of the inherent monopoly power to the seller—in this case the government. This benefits the taxpayer, but does little to help the consumer. There are practical snags, too, in awarding the franchise to the bidder offering the lowest price to consumers, as witness experience in the US with franchising cable TV. It is difficult to specify in advance the appropriate pattern and quality of output, and the costs of negotiating and monitoring contracts are substantial. Furthermore, it is difficult to sell a franchise on the premise of sustainable (natural) monopoly alone. Bidders will usually demand statutory monopoly privileges, which will create formal exemption from risks of entry and engender a position from which to exact further concessions from governments. Though the franchising option is not ruled out, it needs far more analytic attention before positive recommendations can be made.

This does not mean that nothing can be done to generate benefits for consumers in these industries. Restrictions on new entry can be removed, so as to pare down the monopoly to a minimum. This has recently been done for gas and electricity, but entry into local telephone networks (e.g. by cable TV companies) is still highly restricted.[d] Dividing utility distribution systems into regionally independent units would create market pressures on supplies of factors of production, not least in providing alternative opportunities for hiring and rewarding management talent, and would facilitate competition on the production side. Between airports, there is some, but not much, scope for direct competition for customers. It would be quite feasible, and beneficial, to organise the more important airports as separate entities.

To summarise, privatising the industries in quadrant A will pose problems in curbing monopoly power. It would be more fruitful to encourage competition by removing restrictions on entry and restructuring the industries, even if the successor companies remain as nationalised, municipal or other public bodies.

(iv) *Quadrant B*

The industries in this quadrant have declining demand prospects while their supply conditions favour a single organisation. Monopoly power may be a problem in some services, but it is generally not severe because the reason for the decline in demand is the emergence of substitutes preferred by consumers. Nationalisation was seen as a means of resisting decline: it led to continued injections of new capital and the financing of losses. The aim of privatisation would be to facilitate the movement of resources out of these industries and/or use existing resources more fully by developing new products and services. However, social and political problems will accompany the withdrawal of services. Privatisation schemes will need to be designed with careful thought to non-commercial obligations.

As far as rail operations are concerned, British Rail would remain in quadrant B after privatisation. These operations are not easily divisible below reasonably-sized and geographically separate sectors, such as the old regions. No-one is likely to want, or to be able, to emulate such successor railway supply companies, so their monopolies will be technically sustainable. However, demand is adverse, and will increasingly be so. This particular combination of circumstances BR shares with British Waterways. But BR is marked off from the other nationalised industries by the exceptionally high alternative use value of its assets. Its territory is immense, and in many parts very valuable indeed. Privatisation here would indeed be called an asset-stripper's paradise, not just for selling land, but for all the myriad deals which can be constructed, based on locational advantage.

In the case of a declining industry of high alternative use value, asset-stripping is very much in the general consumer's interest. However, railways are perhaps the most politically sensitive of all the nationalised industries. Wholesale withdrawal of services would not be politically acceptable. A practical compromise therefore presents itself. Successor companies could be floated which, in return for command over assets, would have to bind themselves to a minimum programme of rail output. This output would be heavily passenger-oriented and would, in effect, be financed by profits from other activities. Because of privatisation, the required output would be achieved in a much more economical way than at present, thereby freeing up many stations, marshalling yards, and miles of track. The alternative use value of these assets is so great that a quite considerable passenger output could be insisted upon. The

Serpell Report thought it necessary to curtail the rail network severely in order to achieve financial viability. With the present approach, a much higher rail output could be attained. Thus privatisation would open up social solutions not possible under nationalisation.

Demand for postal services is probably decreasing, partly because of more direct competition from telecommunications. However, there are attractive market possibilities in new forms of collaboration with new techniques. In fact, though most would now place the Post Office in quadrant D, there are opportunities for its eventual emergence in quadrant C. Mainly because it is so labour-intensive—capital employed is the lowest of all Table 1's industries at £7,360 per man—there is considerable scope for labour substitution and redeployment. The basic distribution network has great potential for development outside traditional Post Office work. A useful form of privatisation would be a successor national company, or several regional companies, which essentially would franchise the local operations to individual small groups. One could therefore expect not only an improvement in postal services, but also a willingness to diversify into such services as security and delivery work.

VIII. Conclusions

Privatisation is not merely a matter of selling shares in a nationalised industry. The underlying intent is to improve industry performance by increasing the role of market forces. To achieve this, other devices for promoting competition must also be adopted. Each act of privatisation must be part of a whole scheme tailored to the particular conditions of each industry.

The following general considerations should guide policy:

- Privatisation schemes should be designed to maximise net consumer benefits, measured primarily by lower prices and improved quality of service, rather than stock-market proceeds. A futures market for shares would facilitate flotation.
- The promotion of competition—by removing artificial restrictions on entry, making resources equally available to

potential entrants, and restructuring the existing industries —is the most effective means of maximising consumer benefits and curbing monopoly power.

- Stricter competition policy is preferable to rate-of-return regulation, efficiency audits and related forms of government 'nannying'.
- Clear ground rules should be laid down concerning the criteria for providing uneconomic services and the sources of finance for these.
- Compensation should be paid for serious transitional unemployment, though in the longer run employees' prospects will be enhanced by privatisation.
- Priority should be given to privatising those industries where consumer benefits are likely to be greatest. Potential benefits will depend upon the size of the industry, whether it has already received attention, and whether competition rather than monopoly is likely to ensue.

The scope for privatisation is substantially greater than is commonly believed. Consumers would benefit, directly or indirectly, from appropriately designed privatisation schemes in industries covering over four-fifths of the presently nationalised sector. In the remaining industries, notably buses, airports, and local distribution of electricity, gas, and telephones, the main benefits would derive from restructuring into smaller units and facilitating new entry.

The announced intention to privatise British Airways and the manufacturing industries has already helped to increase efficiency, and privatisation should not be delayed merely to increase the proceeds from flotation. Nevertheless, these industries are no longer first priorities. Greater benefits to consumers would derive from privatising the Central Electricity Generating Board (excluding the national grid), British Telecom, the National Coal Board, British Rail, and the Post Office. Apart from British Telecom, these industries are seldom thought of as candidates for privatisation. However, the bulk of the consumer benefits that can be expected to follow from privatisation could be achieved by appropriately designed policies for these five industries alone.

EDITORS' NOTES

a. This issue is discussed in Part VI.
b. A review of the evidence is provided in the Introduction.
c. British Telecom has been privatised since this article was written.
d. More details are provided in the article by Vickers and Yarrow in Part IV.

2

PRIVATISING PUBLIC ENTERPRISES: AN ANALYSIS OF THE GOVERNMENT'S CASE*

David Heald and David Steel

I. Introduction

The Conservative Party has never believed that the business of Government is the government of business.

(Nigel Lawson, November 1981)[1]

The present Conservative Government[a] has invested more political capital in putting this belief into practice than any of its predecessors. During the first two sessions of this Parliament no fewer than eight statutes were enacted empowering Ministers to privatise public enterprises by selling assets or shares and by relaxing statutory monopoly powers. Progress in implementing these provisions was more limited but, by the third anniversary of the Government's accession to office, two public enterprises had been sold entirely, two had been converted into companies with 50 per cent private shareholding, various state shareholdings had been sold, and restrictions had been lifted on entry into two industries. Moreover, two further Bills, one of them dealing with two major industries, were well on their way to the statute book and at least three further sales were planned for the 1982/3 financial year.

In comparison, the achievements of earlier Conservative Governments look paltry. The 1951–5 Government de-

---

*This article was first published in *Political Quarterly*, 1982, 53. Reprinted by permission of the authors.

David Heald is a Lecturer in Management Studies at the University of Glasgow.

At the time of writing this article, David Steel was a Lecturer in Politics at Exeter University; he is now Assistant Director of the National Association of Health Authorities in England and Wales.

[1] *Hansard*, vol. 1 (8th Series), col. 440.

nationalised only iron and steel, which had barely been nationalised, and road haulage; and in neither case was the process complete. Although ambitious plans had been mooted before 1970, the Heath Government achieved no more than marginal changes in the size of the public sector of industry by selling the state management districts and the two state-owned travel agents.

The present Government's determination to 'roll back the frontiers of the state' and to free market forces reflects the shift that occurred in the 1970s in the intellectual mainspring of Conservative thinking. Its adherence to the post-war Keynesian/interventionist consensus had been successfully challenged by monetarism and by the revival of support for the free market as a more reliable instrument than elected governments for securing economic goals. These doctrines have had a major influence upon the economic strategy of the Government since 1979 and, significantly, some of their most enthusiastic advocates, such as Sir Keith Joseph, Mr Norman Fowler and, more recently, Mr Nigel Lawson, have held those offices most closely concerned with public enterprise.

The aims of this article are to examine the ideas that lie behind the Government's belief in privatisation[2] and to assess the extent to which its specific proposals are likely to realise these aspirations. However, it is necessary first to outline the Government's programme and its progress in putting it into practice.

II. The privatisation programme

The Government's programme to privatise public enterprise has two main elements: *denationalisation*—the sale of an enterprise's assets or shares; and *liberalisation*—the relaxation or abolition of statutory monopoly powers. As far as the former is concerned, the extent of denationalisation varies. In some cases the entire assets of an enterprise or all of its shares are being sold. This has already happened in the

---

[2] The term 'privatisation' is now used frequently to refer to government action to restrict the activities of the public sector generally. In this article, however, our concern is with public enterprise alone although many of the arguments discussed apply also to other parts of the public sector.

cases of the Radiochemical Centre (renamed Amersham
International) and some of the National Enterprise Board's
subsidiary companies, such as Ferranti, International Com-
puters, and Fairey Holdings. It is also destined for British
Gas's oil interests and some of the subsidiaries of British Rail
and British Steel.

In other cases the Government is converting public corporations into Companies Act companies and then selling a
proportion of each company's shares—in most cases about
50 per cent—thereby creating a hybrid company. These new
companies will raise their capital from the capital market and
will be freed from any form of control by Ministers other
than that applied to all companies. The only cases so far in
which this process has been completed are British Aerospace
and Cable and Wireless[3] but it is in progress for three others
(British Airways, the British Transport Docks Board, and the
oil-producing side of the British National Oil Corporation).
It was also intended for the National Freight Corporation
(although the Government planned to retain at most only a
very small shareholding). This was converted into a company
in October 1980, but the recession, which hit the road
transport industry very severely, caused postponement of its
flotation and the Government eventually sold the company to
a consortium of its employees, backed by a group of major
banks.

The second element in the privatisation programme has
been liberalisation. The Government has already acted to extend competition significantly in the bus and telecommunications industries, and marginally in relation to the postal
service. In addition, legislation which will abolish British
Gas's monopoly rights over the purchase of North Sea gas
and its sale to industry and compel it to dispose of its gas
showrooms to the private sector[b] has passed its Commons
stages. Mention should also be made of two other developments which, although not strictly part of the privatisation
programme, are related. First, there are two enterprises—the
British National Oil Corporation and British Telecommunications—in which the Government has been considering

[3] In the case of Cable and Wireless the first stage of the process was not needed as
it has always been constituted as a Companies Act company.

introducing private capital by the issue of revenue bonds, without affecting the control of the enterprise (although, in both cases, its enthusiasm for this option is waning in favour of fully-fledged privatisation). Secondly, the 1980 Competition Act extended the terms of reference of the Monopolies and Mergers Commission to include the operation of the nationalised industries.[4]

By April 1982 the Government had announced *firm* proposals for over twenty enterprises. The only industries not covered were coal, electricity, and shipbuilding (and in the last two cases Ministers had declared their intention to introduce privatisation plans). Some of the enterprises involved, such as Amersham International, the British Sugar Corporation, and even the British Transport Docks Board, may be regarded as of minor importance in relation to the public sector of industry generally. A few others are only marginally affected. For example, the Post Office's letter monopoly has been relaxed only in areas such as express mail and the transfer of mail between document exchanges. As far as British Rail is concerned, privatisation is planned only for its subsidiary activities such as hotels, shipping, and property, but the fact that some of these activities are or have been profitable has serious implications for the rail business itself. In most cases, however, there can be no doubt about the importance of the enterprises concerned or about the impact that the Government's proposals will have upon them.

In legislative terms the Government's record in obtaining endorsement of its proposals is impressive and reflects its large majorities in both Houses of Parliament. However, its progress in actually implementing its plans has been much slower than it intended. In particular, with only a few exceptions, its sales have been delayed, in most cases by a considerable period. The most serious obstacle which the Government has encountered in implementing its proposals has been the poor financial health of many of the enterprises involved.

[4] In addition, the 1980 Civil Aviation Act, in an effort to move towards freer competition and less state intervention in the air transport market, made changes in the duties of the Civil Aviation Authority, putting greater emphasis on the interests of users and requiring that restrictions should be minimised. This was not directed specifically against British Airways but it has affected its operating environment significantly.

From the Government's point of view, it is unfortunate that its programme should have coincided with the most severe recession since 1945. This has had very serious consequences for the finances of enterprises such as British Airways and the National Freight Company. In some cases this has caused the indefinite postponement of flotation; in others it has led the Government to proceed with great caution. The management of new issues is always difficult and it was anticipated that the novelty of this type of operation and the Government's decision to impose various restrictions on most of the sales, for instance to limit foreign purchases and to secure wide dispersal of ownership, would exacerbate these problems.

It is not surprising, therefore, that the Government decided to proceed first with three of its best prospects: British Aerospace, Cable and Wireless, and Amersham International. In one sense these sales were highly successful in that they were heavily over-subscribed (British Aerospace by 2.4 times; Cable and Wireless, 4.6; and Amersham International, 24.6). However, such over-subscription, together with the premium at which the initial dealing took place, suggests that the selling prices could have been fixed at a higher level and that assets have been disposed of at less than market value.[c] Indeed, this aspect of the Amersham sale in particular caused the Government considerable embarrassment and its methods of selling shares were criticised by the Public Accounts Committee in April 1982. It also noted that, in the case of British Aerospace, the Government's objective of securing a wide dispersal of ownership, which had been one of its main reasons for deciding to sell the shares at a fixed price rather than by tender, had been undermined by a dramatic 83 per cent fall in the number of shareholders in the ten months following the sale.

The 'success' of these early sales will have encouraged the Government to proceed with some of the more difficult enterprises in its portfolio. Ironically, however, it may now encounter more serious opposition from another source: the industries themselves. So far, neither management nor unions have made much impact. In the first two years of the programme, only the British National Oil Corporation (BNOC) and the National Enterprise Board publicly opposed the

Government's plans and in the latter case the Board's objection was restricted to the time-scale for selling its assets. Indeed, there is evidence that some Board members regard denationalisation as the only means of escaping the harsh financial controls being exerted by the Government and the unsympathetic climate in which they currently operate. Moreover, the Government has brought in new chairmen, for instance in British Airways, British Steel, and BNOC, who are known to be sympathetic to privatisation.

Nor has trade union opposition had much effect. Indeed, in five cases employees have become directly involved in denationalisation schemes: the 'employee shares' in British Aerospace, Cable and Wireless, and Amersham were very popular; the National Union of Railwaymen has become a shareholder in Gleneagles Hotels, the company established to run three former British Rail hotels in Scotland; and a consortium of employees, backed by three of the four unions involved, has bought the National Freight Company.

However, during the next two years a more concerted challenge looks likely to be mounted. In a number of cases, unions have taken or have threatened industrial action. In particular, at British Gas, the Government faces determined opposition from both management and unions. The latter oppose privatisation in principle, whilst the former seem more concerned about the break-up of a highly successful organisation, part of whose success depends upon the integrated nature of its operations. Knowing that its ability to resist the Government on a political matter is limited, British Gas has challenged Ministers to privatise the entire corporation. The Government has rejected this course of action and a battle of wills therefore seems inevitable. The financial strength of British Gas, its Chairman's reputation for toughness, and the potential leverage open to its employees if they decide to take industrial action all point to this battleground as the crucial test of the Government's strength of purpose.[d]

III. The Government's arguments

No official statement of the Government's case for privatising public enterprise has been published.[e] However, such a case can be assembled from ministerial speeches and from books and pamphlets which are known to have been influential (such as those which were on the reading list issued by Sir Keith Joseph to his officials on his arrival at the Department of Industry in May 1979; see Bosanquet, 1981). Four general arguments recur: three, concerning economic freedom, efficiency and pay bargaining, relate to both elements of privatisation—denationalisation and liberalisation; the fourth, concerning public sector borrowing, to denationalisation only.

Before examining each of these arguments in turn, two general points need to be made. First, a significant—but largely unvoiced—motive for the Government in promoting privatisation is its desire to respond to the expectations of its natural constituency by providing enhanced profit opportunities for the private sector. In addition, knocking the nationalised industries is a popular public pastime and dislike for nationalisation is very strong among Conservative voters. It is difficult to assess the importance of such factors relative to the arguments of principle considered in the rest of this section. However, neither the expectations of private business nor the anti-nationalisation sentiments of much of the electorate are new. In order to understand why the present Government attaches more importance to privatisation than its predecessors and has shown greater determination in putting its proposals into practice, it is necessary to examine its case carefully.

Secondly, not all the arguments which will be discussed here apply in each case of privatisation. Indeed, the urgency attached by the Government to reducing public sector borrowing has led it to act first in relation to some enterprises about which its general arguments are least convincing.

(i) *Privatisation will enhance economic freedom*

The Government's case

The consumer is sovereign in the private sector. In the public sector he is dethroned by subsidy or monopoly.

(Sir Geoffrey Howe, July 1981)[5]

[5] The speech was widely reported in the Press in this form but, interestingly, the full text qualifies both parts of the Chancellor's assertion.

This assertion by Sir Geoffrey Howe sums up the first strand in the Government's case: that public enterprise threatens economic freedom. In so far as public enterprises enjoy statutory monopoly powers or are able to use their market strength to compete 'unfairly', they limit consumers' freedom of choice. In addition, the very fact of public ownership impinges upon economic freedom because the government is depriving individuals of income or capital and forcing them to hold 'implied shareholdings' which they might not privately choose. Individual freedom is therefore fostered by extending competition and by reducing the public sector so as to allow individuals to keep a higher proportion of their wealth in the form they themselves choose.

Discussion

Arguments such as these have had a major influence upon the Government's proposals. The liberalisation of route licensing in the bus industry has increased consumer choice by facilitating the entry of private operators, for instance in providing express coach services, and the consumer is in the process of being offered an array of telephones and other telecommunications devices by British Telecom and its new competitors. Similarly, the proposed sale of British Gas's showrooms[f] was in response to criticism from the Monopolies Commission that British Gas had abused its market strength, for instance to prevent manufacturers supplying other outlets. The sale of public assets and shares is also reducing the extent of the public's 'implied shareholding'.

However, a number of important caveats need to be registered. Not all of the Government's proposals will increase competition. Some, such as British Steel's joint venture with Guest, Keen and Nettlefolds PLC in rod and steel bar production, and the merger between Seaspeed and Hoverlloyd, former competitors in the provision of cross-Channel hovercraft services, will have the opposite effect. The strangest case relates to British Rail's Sealink subsidiary. The Government considered a bid from Sealink's major competitor, European Ferries, which is run by Mr Keith Wickenden, a Conservative back-bencher. This bid, which would have given European Ferries 80 per cent of the cross-Channel market, was eventually rejected by Mr John Biffen, the then Secretary of State for Trade, on the advice of the Monopolies Commission. If the Government had been serious about competition, it would never have considered it, removing the need for an eight-month inquiry.

The impact of privatisation upon competition depends upon the circumstances of each case. The Government's view rests upon the virtues of atomistic competition. However, market forces themselves can lead to accumulations of private power. It is highly questionable whether freedom is more threatened by British Telecom operating under a statutory monopoly than by some subsidiary of ITT on the basis of regulated or unregulated monopoly. Nor is experience of public regulation of private enterprises very encouraging in terms either of its effectiveness or of its economic side-effects.

There is also the question of the effect of competition upon the quality and range of service provision. With the protection provided by limitations on new entry, public bus operators have been able to maintain a comprehensive network of services through the practice of cross-subsidisation. Although this is in principle regarded as an undesirable practice, it has played an important role in supporting the 'social' network, particularly as considerable difficulties have been experienced in implementing schemes, as under the 1968 Transport Act, in which either central or local government pays the operator a subsidy for specific routes. Competition on profitable routes will severely curtail the ability of public operators to continue to cross-subsidise. It is not surprising therefore that many Conservative local authorities have shown great reluctance to take advantage of the most radical provisions of the 1980 Transport Act which allow them to establish 'trial areas' in which all restrictions on entry would be abolished for an experimental period.

If the Government is genuine in its desire to promote competition, it is also essential that it adopts a more relaxed approach to the external financing requirements of those public enterprises which remain in existence. This argument has been stressed repeatedly by British Telecom in its attempts to persuade the Treasury to allow it to raise money privately so that it can undertake the investment needed to enable it to compete effectively in its rapidly changing and expanding market. Unless public enterprises have proper access to external finance, the new era of greater competition will be a sham.

There are also more fundamental objections to this strand in the Government's case for privatisation. It is based upon a very limited definition of economic freedom which takes this to mean solely the absence of government intervention in the market. Advocates of a more active role for the State stress the positive contribution which government action can make in promoting individual liberty. Also the 'implied shareholding' argument is compelling, even on its own terms, only on the assumption that the allocation of investment funds determined by the operation of the capital market is viewed as socially optimal. For example, the social returns in maintaining an indigenous steel industry might be higher than the private returns. Moreover, this argument does not provide a justification for the Government's apparent preference for retaining a substantial share in most of the enterprises that are being privatised.

(ii) *Privatisation will increase efficiency*

The Government's case

Nationalised industries are immunised from the process of spontaneous change which competition and fear of bankruptcy impose upon the private sector.

(Sir Keith Joseph, January 1980)[6]

The second argument in favour of privatisation concerns efficiency. It is argued that public enterprises are intrinsically less efficient than private enterprises because they are insulated from the disciplines of the capital and product markets. They do not have to compete for capital in the open market, nor do most of them have to meet consumers' wishes in order to remain in business. With the sanctions of bankruptcy and takeover removed, and with no private shareholders to satisfy,

---

[6] *Hansard*. vol. 977, col. 921.

managers of public enterprises have little incentive to promote efficient use of the resources at their disposal.

In any case, their efforts to do so have frequently been frustrated by government intervention in pursuit of macro-economic and income redistribution objectives. As a result, nationalisation, far from promoting the efficient allocation of resources in the economy as its proponents have claimed, has had the opposite effect. Nor have the attempts by successive governments since 1961 to overcome these problems by setting financial objectives and guidelines for decisions on prices and investment been successful, partly because the enterprises have not been offered adequate rewards for compliance and partly because governments have been able to override their own rules in response to political and macro-economic pressures.

Privatisation is advocated as a solution to all these problems. The abolition or relaxation of statutory monopolies promotes efficiency through competition in the market-place; denationalisation restores market disciplines; and partial denationalisation will, by introducing pressures to attract and maintain private capital, increase incentives to operate efficiently and make government intervention more difficult because of the private interests involved.

Discussion

The influence of these arguments can be detected in much of the Government's programme. Thus liberalisation in the telecommunications industry and the ending of British Gas's near-monopoly in the sale of gas appliances are examples. Similarly, efficiency arguments have been used to justify most of the cases of total and partial denationalisation. In the latter case, the new hybrid companies will raise new capital from the capital market and will have no impact upon the Exchequer's finances except through any new equity capital to which the Government chose to subscribe in order to maintain the public stake. Although a substantial public shareholding will remain, the Government has made it clear that it will not monitor the companies' affairs, nor will it intervene except in very special circumstances, such as an attempt to alter a company's articles of association so as to permit a higher proportion of foreign ownership.

Only experience will tell whether these intentions, which are not statutory and in any case cannot bind future governments, hold in the face of political and economic pressures. The history of the nationalised industries certainly provides many examples of 'self-denying ordinances' which have been quickly forgotten when it suited Ministers to do so. It remains to be seen how effective private shareholders will be in exerting pressure should a government attempt to use its stake in these new hybrid companies in order to influence managerial decisions. Indeed, this scepticism is shared by one of the leading advocates of privatisation, Stephen Littlechild, who has argued (1981) that joint ownership can be useful only as a transitional measure: '. . . as long as ultimate control lies with government, one cannot realistically hope to avoid all the problems . . .' (p. 14).

Moreover, all government involvement cannot be eliminated without constitutional limitations which, although championed by some right-wing economists, have not been taken up by the present Government. The fact is that all the important public enterprises operate in sectors such as defence and energy, which, for one reason or another, impinge upon wider public interests for which Ministers are responsible. Thus, quite apart from the need to establish an effective framework of control for those enterprises which will remain in public ownership for the foreseeable future, it seems likely that it will not be as easy as Ministers claim to dismiss the need for establishing a proper pattern of relations with hybrid companies.

Although efficiency arguments have featured prominently in most ministerial statements, it is notable that the first candidates for privatisation have been enterprises, such as British Aerospace, Cable and Wireless, BNOC, and British Gas, whose performance has not been the subject of much criticism. This reflects the importance of other factors (notably the desire to reduce public sector borrowing). However, the record of such enterprises also casts doubts upon the Government's belief that public enterprise is inevitably inferior. The evidence on the respective merits of public and private enterprise is far from conclusive.[g] Surprisingly little effort has been devoted to careful study of this question, partly because of the serious methodological problems which

have to be overcome. Those studies that have been undertaken, however, do not point to a clear-cut superiority on
either side and suggest that ownership may well be a factor of
fairly limited importance in determining efficiency. One by-
product of privatisation, therefore, may be the generation of
evidence which is useful in throwing light on this question.

(iii) *Privatisation will ease the problem of public sector pay*

The Government's case

> [Where nationalised industries] have the nation by the jugular vein,
> the only feasible option is to pay up.
>
> (The 'Ridley Report', 1978)[7]

The problem of pay bargaining in the public sector has been
prominent in Conservative Party debate since the conflict
with the miners in 1974, which precipitated the fall of the
Heath Government. The problem centres around the absence
of an effective budget constraint. Whereas trade unions in the
private sector know that an excessive pay award may lead to
bankruptcy, no such constraint exists in the public sector.
This has led many Conservatives to believe that it is impossible to withstand pay claims in those sectors in which
workers have the power to hold the nation 'by the jugular
vein' and that the problem can be solved only by removing
access to Exchequer funds. Denationalisation potentially has
this effect; liberalisation also contributes to the solution of
this problem by making it more difficult for managers to pass
on excessive pay increases to consumers by raising prices.

Discussion
Although this argument has often featured in discussions of
privatisation, it has not been dominant. So far, denationalisation has not been proposed for those areas in which either
militancy or the potential for leverage is greatest. Indeed, it is
notable that two industries not so far affected are the very
ones in which these problems are most acute—coal and elec-

[7] This view was expressed in 1978 by a Conservative study group, chaired by
Nicholas Ridley MP, whose unpublished report was leaked to *The Economist*,
27 May 1978.

tricity. It remains also to be seen whether partial, and even total, denationalisation does remove the safety-net of the Exchequer in the minds of trade unionists or whether other means of regulating pay will be needed. Recent examples of companies that have been privatised, and indeed that have always been privately owned, suggest that it is by no means easy to break the expectation of access to Exchequer funds. In any case, unless privatisation is taken very much further than is at present envisaged, these solutions will have only a very limited effect upon the wider problem of public sector pay.

(iv) *Denationalisation will reduce public sector borrowing*

The Government's case

Why should they [nationalised industries] be a demand on our resources? . . . Why shouldn't they contribute to the nation's resources instead of being a drag on them?

(Adam Butler, December 1979)

The Government's determination to arrest monetary growth has led it to pay great attention to reducing public sector borrowing. Denationalisation contributes to this process in two ways: the sale of public assets produces a direct gain to the Exchequer, and the creation of hybrid enterprises enables the Government to exclude their external finance from the PSBR. Under present conventions, the borrowing of the nationalised industries is included in the PSBR regardless of its source. In contrast, although practice is rather confused, the borrowing of companies (irrespective of the proportion of their shares held by the State) has in the past usually been excluded. Thus the external finance from non-government sources of Rolls-Royce, although wholly owned by the State, has never been included in the PSBR. The Government has not made a clear declaration of its intentions in this respect as far as the new hybrid companies are concerned. However, it appears that the new test will be the question of whether effective control has passed out of the Government's hands.[8] There remains considerable doubt about the precise percentage

[8] Further information on present practice and on the Government's intentions for the future can be obtained from p. xx and Appendix 18 of Select Committee on the Treasury and Civil Service (1980–81).

at which an enterprise leaves the PSBR: British Aerospace is out at 48 per cent, but a 30 per cent figure was considered necessary for Gleneagles Hotels.

Discussion

The rationale for the Government's stress upon monetary policy and for its preoccupation with the PSBR lies outside the scope of this article. However, given the importance attached to the PSBR, denationalisation has appeared an attractive option, especially as an alternative to making cuts in public spending. In this respect, the Government's preference for such action is not new. Despite its ideological commitment to public ownership, the last Labour Government chose to sell shares in BP as a substitute for even greater spending cuts in its budgetary package made necessary by the conditions attached to the IMF's loan in 1976. However, such a precedent does not constitute an adequate defence of this policy. It is not normally regarded as good commercial practice either to sell capital assets to fund an ongoing revenue deficit or to sell shares under a publicly declared deadline. More important, the short-term gain to the Exchequer from any sale needs to be set against the adverse long-term consequences which result from the loss of future dividend streams and of capital gains.

Two examples provide particularly clear illustration of the issues involved. The Government's decision to compel British Gas to sell its offshore oil interests and its stake in the onshore Wytch Farm oilfield will, for the sake of a short-term reduction in the PSBR, result in the loss of a substantial stream of profits in the future. Moreover, highly profitable British Gas has a large negative external financing limit which means that it actually hands over cash to the Exchequer. Perhaps even more striking is the case of the British National Oil Corporation. The sale of a majority stake in its oil-producing business will mean that the Government will lose not only its future profits but also its entire cash flow since at present BNOC's bank account is the Treasury in the form of the National Oil Account. All its revenues thus go to the Exchequer, thereby reducing the Government's need to borrow.

The proceeds from the privatisation of nationalised industries and public shareholdings have so far been very small: £767 million cash over three years.[h] There have been fewer sales than intended and the benefit to the Exchequer has been limited because of the need to provide certain companies with new capital and to fund deficiencies in pension funds. Several of the items counted towards the target for special asset sales have been dubious, such as the forward sales of oil by BNOC and the disposal of oil and other stocks. Even on the definitions used, special asset sales over these three years reduced the combined public expenditure planning total by only 0.0045 per cent.

The Government has been setting explicit targets for the 'special sales of assets' as a method of reducing the PSBR. These were set at £1000 million for 1979/80, £500 million for 1980/1 and £50 million for 1981/2 (all in 1979 survey prices). The actuals were, respectively, £999 million, £356 million, and − £92 million (all in cash). The near-achievement of the 1979/80 target was almost entirely dependent upon the receipts to BNOC from advance payments for oil. This simply shifted cash flow forward, thus causing the negative figures for 1981/2 when these transactions unwound.

However, there are two tiers to the privatisation of public sector assets. In some cases, including British Rail and British Steel, the proceeds have been remaining within the businesses, even if effectively offset by equivalent reductions in Exchequer finance. The benefits in these cases of privatisation to the PSBR are therefore indirect. It is significant that, because of the sums involved and the profitability of the enterprise, the Government's power to force British Gas to make disposals is accompanied by a requirement that the proceeds be paid to the Exchequer.

To date, the impact on the PSBR of reclassifications has been modest. British Aerospace and the National Freight Company have been taken out. Only that part of Cable and Wireless's external finance which came from the Exchequer was ever included. The Radiochemical Centre was entirely outside. Furthermore, if denationalisation leads to a rationalisation of activities, there may be other budgetary implications for the Exchequer in the form of redundancy payments and unemployment pay, both of which would push up the PSBR.[9]

If the Government succeeds in selling a majority stake in BNOC's oil-producing business and British Gas's offshore oil interests, its record will look very different.[i] However, in the present state of the oil market, these assets may not realise their true value, particularly as the Government has indicated that it will impose restrictions on overseas purchases and prospective buyers will know that the Government is anxious for a quick sale before the General Election.

This link between privatisation and the PSBR raises the wider question of the Government's concern about 'crowding out'.[10] The Treasury has maintained that higher nationalised industry investment, a method of reflation with support from both the CBI and the TUC, would not lead to higher output. Without becoming too embroiled in the macro-economic debate, it is worth making two points. First, such a policy focus on the PSBR suggests that investment by British Aerospace (a public corporation) leads to crowding out, but investment by British Aerospace PLC (a hybrid company) does not. This proposition invites scepticism, if not disbelief. Given the Government's macro-economic policy stance, the operation of such PSBR rules has real economic consequences. The collapse of the North Sea gas gathering pipeline project was closely linked with the Government's insistence that it could not be a British Gas project and that consortium financing must involve no charge on the PSBR. Moreover, if crowding out of the private sector is a genuine concern, sale of the public sector's most lucrative assets, thus channelling private savings into ex-public oil, land, and shares, would seem a strange way of relieving the pressure on private manufacturing.

[9] This point is made in Peacock and Shaw (1981). Interestingly, this study was commissioned by the Centre for Policy Studies and a first draft was presented to a seminar organised by the Prime Minister's Policy Unit and chaired by Professor Alan Walters, the Prime Minister's economic adviser.

[10] The arguments on crowding out are set out on pp. xiv–xix of Select Committee on the Treasury and Civil Service (1980–81).

IV. Conclusion

We have also embarked on the long and complex process of returning state-owned enterprise to private ownership . . . Legislation has
been passed or is under way to denationalise many . . . concerns.
We are restructuring corporations . . . with a view to returning
them or parts of them to private ownership as soon as we can. This
will take time, and it takes a lot of money. That is the price of the
folly of public ownership.

(Margaret Thatcher, February 1981)

The Queen's Speech of November 1981 reaffirmed the
Government's commitment to privatisation. A considerable
amount of legislative time in the 1981/2 session has been
devoted to privatisation and, during the first few months of
1982, the Government took various steps towards implementing some of the schemes for which it had already received
legislative endorsement and drew up new proposals (for
example to enable private firms to generate electricity as a
main business).[j]

Without doubt, therefore, the public sector of industry will
have been further reduced by the time of the next General
Election. For various reasons, however, it is extremely difficult to predict exactly how far privatisation will have pro-
gressed. The Conservative Party's 1979 Manifesto provides
no guidance. It referred only to denationalisation of three
enterprises—British Aerospace, British Shipbuilders, and the
National Freight Corporation—and to liberalisation in the
bus industry. The Government has already moved much
further than this. This development has not been greeted by
the chorus of protest from the press or from the House of
Lords which might be expected if a Labour Government had
attempted to push through nationalisation measures outside
its manifesto commitments. Also it seems likely that its most
recent proposals, particularly in the energy field, will receive
more concerted opposition than has been mounted to date.
Nevertheless, the opposition has remained curiously subdued
and ineffective.

The future of the privatisation programme is bound up
with the Government's economic strategy for the remainder
of its term of office. As long as its present policies are retained,

its ability to sell public enterprises will be curtailed by the effects of continued recession upon their financial health. The adoption of reflationary policies could have one of two effects upon privatisation. It could be downgraded in importance or even abandoned as part of the Government's efforts to return to the centre ground of British politics. Alternatively, its importance could grow as an attempt to mollify those of the Government's supporters who were critical of its change of direction and as a unifying force for all Conservatives, among whom hostility towards public ownership is almost universal.

Our prediction is that privatisation will remain an important element in the Conservative Party's programme during the 1980s. Indeed the logic of ministerial arguments in favour of privatisation makes it difficult to conceive of a limit until all public enterprises have been transferred to private ownership if they are profitable or closed down if they are endemically unprofitable. Practical considerations will, of course, prevent the adoption of such policies in full and will dictate the speed with which they are implemented, but there can be little doubt about the direction of Conservative policy towards public enterprise.

Nor is it easy to predict what will happen if there is a change of government at the next election.[k] Labour's Alternative Economic Strategy envisages further nationalisation, but the extent of its commitment both to reverse privatisation and to extend public ownership will depend upon the outcome of the current struggle for power between the Parliamentary Labour Party and the Party Conference. Moreover, the creation of the SDP and its alliance with the Liberal Party make it unlikely that the Labour Party will be in a position to implement these policies in full.

The SDP has been critical of most of the Government's privatisation proposals designed to change the existing mix. One of its leaders, Roy Jenkins, has argued the case for a stable mix while at the same time displaying his hostility towards public ownership, claiming that there is: 'mounting evidence from all over the world that full-scale state ownership is more successful in producing tyranny than in producing goods. . . . More successful nations are those which embrace a mixed economy and follow it with some consistency of purpose, not forever changing the frontiers.'[11] However, in the future the SDP may well argue that it is better to leave things as they are rather than to incur further disruption.

British experience in this field is unusual, not only in respect of the extent to which the frontier between public and private enterprise is a matter of political controversy, but also the shallowness of the terms in which most of the debate is conducted. Politicians prefer slogans such as the 'tyranny' of state ownership and the 'vandalism' of privatisation; academics for their part have failed to generate data upon which reasoned argument could be based. In recent years, the critics of public ownership have begun to articulate their case more effectively. Their opponents should not only scrutinise these arguments carefully but also build an equivalent case in favour of public ownership in which attention is focused upon its objectives and the means of putting them into practice. Thirty years of consensus have tended to produce complacency among those who advocate a positive role for the public sector in industry. No longer, however, can they rely upon the status quo to defend their beliefs.

[11] Reported in *State Enterprise*, no. 2, July 1980.

EDITORS' NOTES

a. Since this article was first published in 1982, the pace of the Government's privatisation programme has continued. See also Steel and Heald (1984).
b. The last of these proposals has been superseded by plans to privatise British Gas as a whole.
c. See also the article by Mayer and Meadowcroft in Part VI.
d. The Government has now introduced proposals to privatise British Gas as a whole.
e. The speeches by John Moore MP included in Part I now provide a comprehensive statement of the Government's case. The issues raised are similar to those discussed by the authors of this article.
f. This proposal has been superseded by plans to privatise British Gas as a whole.
g. See the readings in Part II and also the Introduction.
h. See the Introduction for an up-to-date assessment.
i. Both these proposals were subsequently implemented; see the Introduction.
j. Subsequently implemented as the 1983 Energy Act.
k. In 1983 the Conservative Government was returned for a second term.

3

WHY PRIVATISE?*

John Moore (1983)

I. Size and importance of present nationalised industries

Privatisation is a key element of the Government's economic strategy. It will lead to a fundamental shift in the balance between the public and private sectors. It is already bringing about a profound change in attitudes within state industries. And it opens up exciting possibilities for the consumer; better pay, conditions, and employment opportunities for the employees; and new freedom for the managers of the industries concerned. Yet, the rationale underlying the programme is poorly understood. The Government's motives are frequently misinterpreted. We are accused of sacrificing the nation's assets for short-term gain and of selling the family silver to pay current debts. Nothing could be further from the truth. The Government's privatisation strategy is justified on economic and business criteria as well as making sense in political terms. If the present momentum is maintained, it will help provide a remedy for some of the ills that have beset UK industrial performance in recent years.

Why do I believe this? The performance of nationalised industries is of major importance to the performance of the UK economy as a whole. The industries account for about a tenth of the UK's gross domestic product, roughly a seventh of total investment in the economy, and around a tenth of the retail price index. They employ some 1½ million people, many of whom are extremely able. They dominate certain sectors of the economy, in particular the transport, energy, communications, steel, and shipbuilding sectors. Their actions directly affect every individual in the United

* This article reproduces a speech made at the annual conference of City of London stockbrokers Fielding, Newson Smith at Plaisterer's Hall, London Wall on 1 November 1983.

John Moore MP was the Financial Secretary to the Treasury.

Kingdom and they affect every firm both as suppliers and as customers.

The effect of the nationalised industries' dominant position can hardly be over-emphasised. The industries' actions permeate industrial life in Britain. If those nationalised industries which are monopolies exploit their position; if the industries are run as bureaucracies and not businesses; if they lack responsiveness to their markets, the effect is felt throughout the economy.

It is worth examining the reasoning that led to the original establishment of nationalised industries. The businesses that were appropriated had in many cases been founded by the great Victorian entrepreneurs. They would not even have been created, let alone have flourished, if there had not been a free market. But the act of nationalisation was first and foremost a political act. It was believed that nationalisation would increase the equality of income and wealth and advance the general prosperity of the nation. The outcome has been entirely the opposite. Unfortunately, the original proponents were strong on idealism but weak on practicalities. They shunned the entrepreneur and replaced him by the bureaucratic centralist. They believed that by placing the management and workers in public enterprises in a position of responsibility and trust, they would be so imbued with a sense of the public good that their actions and aspirations would naturally reflect what was best for the country.

Herbert Morrison (1933) set out what he saw as the major theoretical benefits of nationalisation. These benefits included the following:

[i]   The quality of service will tend to advance and the price charged will tend to fall.
[ii] The industry itself will be more efficiently and economically conducted.
[iii] The board [of the nationalised industry] and its officers must regard themselves as the high custodian of the public interest.

In essence it was considered sufficient to take the industries into state ownership, provide no economic or financial criteria other than a requirement to break even after full depreciation 'taking one year with another', and to leave them to it. 'Arm's length' was the order of the day.

Unfortunately, experience over many years shows that the industries, left to their own devices, will not automatically work efficiently for the national good. The commanding heights of the economy have been handed over to large remote monoliths that may be strong on paper plans but are weak on actual performance. Herbert Morrison concluded that 'the full healing powers of socialism cannot be applied until all the large industries and services are planned and organised for social ends'. We should all perhaps be thankful that this theory was never put to the test.

Because those who nationalised the industries had great faith in the enterprises they were creating, they were prepared to entrust to them extensive monopoly power. It was often considered that the 'public interest' was best served by having a monopoly supplier. Competition was somehow 'wasteful' and costly to the detriment of both the consumer and the taxpayer.

It is, however, a great mistake to believe that all the nationalised monopolies are in any sense natural monopolies. They were in many cases artificial monopolies. Natural monopolies are few and far between. Because of the integrated nature of the networks, it may make economic and business sense at the present time to organise regional and national monopolies to carry out the transmission and distribution of water, gas, and electricity, to provide local district telephone services, and to carry away sewerage. But activities such as electricity generation, the production and marketing of gas, coal production and sale, telecommunications (other than local district services), bus transport, sewerage treatment and disposal are in no sense natural monopolies. The monopolies in these areas were created (not natural) and it is by no means self-evident that they are necessary or even beneficial. The public would not tolerate state monopolies in clothing or food. Imagine—Nationalised Food: no Sainsbury's, no Tesco, no Co-op, no neighbourhood grocer! Just one state-controlled concern.

II. Industries' comparative performance

Has the lack of competition been justified? Have the industries fulfilled the trust that was placed in them? I am sorry to say that by any criteria, their performance has been disappointing. Although much was claimed for nationalisation, little has been achieved. Since the mid-1960s, the nationalised industries' total return on capital employed has been significantly and consistently below that of the private sector even after allowing for the impact of subsidies. Since the early 1970s, the industries' aggregate returns on capital have been around zero.

The industries' long-term record on prices has also been contentious. Herbert Morrison had high hopes that nationalisation would cause prices to fall. But it is all too easy for monopolies to lose control of current costs knowing that the consumer will pick up the bill. Historical comparisons show that nationalised industry prices have regularly increased more rapidly than the retail price index.

Because of the industries' position in the public sector, governments have found it difficult at times to resist the temptation to intervene in industries' pricing policies. This has had perverse effects on nationalised industry prices with periods of artificial price restraint—reflecting a misplaced counter-inflation strategy—followed by the inevitable painful period of catch-up. More specifically, government intervention has in some cases seriously distorted the true market position. For example the British Gas Corporation's monopoly purchasing and selling rights allowed it in the short term artificially to try and avoid the effects of the OPEC oil shocks on energy markets. But how short-sighted. The OPEC influence affected all fuels and all countries. As a consequence of the decisions on gas, electricity (which was not so protected) suffered a substantial but artificial deterioration in its competitive position especially for off-peak sales. This contributed to the problems of excess capacity in the electricity industry, and to the coal industries' surplus production and stocking problems. Gas shortages developed at times forcing the BGC to turn away new business in industrial markets and adding to the pressures to import more gas. These are not academic issues. Domestic consumers turned for example from electric night-storage heaters to gas not realising that no government could allow the industries to sustain the artificial gas price indefinitely. To my mind, all this illustrates vividly the serious and costly consequences of government intervention in state industries. Government is not blessed with any special powers of foresight or economic intelligence that enable it to set energy prices accurately. The results in recent years have been endless distortions which have caused considerable pain for different categories of customer. We have taken steps to begin to rectify the true underlying market position in energy by not shirking difficult decisions on gas pricing, and by opening the door to competition. We are now looking closely at further ways of increasing competition and introducing privatisation into the energy sector.

The industries' performance on both productivity and manpower costs has also been disappointing. Public sector trade unions have been extraordinarily successful in gaining advantages for themselves in the pay hierarchy by exploiting their monopoly collective bargaining position. Herbert Morrison's dreams of employee responsibility are a caricature of the true position. Although it cannot be justified by productivity, most of the large industries' employment costs per employee increased faster than the national average over the period 1970/1 to 1982/3 and in many cases much faster, without corresponding increases in productivity. For example, employment costs per employee in the gas industry rose 38 per cent more than the national average, in the coal industry by 21 per cent, and in the telecommunications and electricity industries by 18 per cent.

In certain cases direct comparisons can be drawn between the performance of nationalised industries and their private sector counterparts. Be it in civil aviation, rail catering, ferry and hovercraft services, or the sale of gas and electrical appliances and contracting, the comparisons are unfavourable to state industries. The message is clear. Public enterprises perform relatively poorly in terms of their competitive position, use labour and capital inefficiently, and are less profitable.

The nationalised industries have also unfortunately not been very good at satisfying their customers. A National Consumer Council Survey published in 1981 said that standards of service provided by many of the nationalised industries were clearly falling short of customers' expectations. They found a pervasive discontent with declining standards. Many respondents expressed the view that they were captive consumers—prices rose as standards dropped and there was little that they could do to reverse the trend. Services often did not seem to match needs or expectations. Anecdotes recounting examples of poor service from nationalised industries are legion.

The overall performance of the major nationalised industries was extensively reviewed in an academic study published in 1981 (Pryke, 1981). The author, previously an enthusiast for nationalised industries, concluded the following:

Although the picture is not wholly black, most of the industries display serious inefficiency because they do not use the minimum quantities of labour and capital to produce the goods and services that they provide. Furthermore, resources are being misallocated because of the widespread failure to pursue the optimum policies for pricing and production. Far too many of the nationalised industries produce at a loss, engage in average cost pricing or practice cross-subsidisation. In general, the nationalised industries' performance has been third rate though with some evidence here and there of first class standards.

My judgement is that the nation cannot tolerate a third-rate performance for a significant proportion of its productive capacity.

III. Public sector constraints

Why has the industries' performance been so disappointing? I do not believe that the industries' management and workers are at fault. They do their best but are faced with an impossible task. The odds are stacked against them. Not only are the industries constantly at risk from political and bureaucratic interference, the managers must at times wonder what it is they are supposed to be managing. Are the industries businesses or social services? Social and commercial objectives intertwine to the detriment of both. Tell any able manager to create and build up a prosperous efficient company and he will know what to do. Tell him at the same time to carry out a host of non-commercial functions and he will get hopelessly muddled. The commercial and social objectives then both suffer.

A host of other reasons contribute to nationalised industries' poor performance. For example, companies in the public sector have to abide by public sector rules. Their borrowing, because it is underwritten by the Government, is indistinguishable in market terms from other forms of public sector borrowing. It is a significant component of the PSBR. This has major consequences. The Government's prime responsibility is to the economy as a whole, and unfortunately, there will be times when the needs of individual state industries have to be subordinated to macro-economic requirements. And it is no answer to say 'let's pretend the industries are not in the public sector'. The fact is that as long as financial markets perceive that the Government, as owner, stands in the last resort between an industry and its creditors, genuine risk capital is not—and never can be—available to the industries. The industries' financing flexibility in the public sector is thus heavily constrained.

Financing constraints spill over to the industries' investment programmes. Problems of allocation constantly emerge both within the public sector and between the public and private sectors. Finance available to the Government—whether for current or capital expenditure—is not open-ended and has to be shared over many competing programmes. The claims of state industries—which may be absolutely justifiable in commercial terms—have constantly to be viewed against the totality of public expenditure. Does it really make sense for politicians to be called upon to judge whether investment in new steel-making plant is better or worse than building a new hospital, or than social security and defence expenditure? The net result of our present system is that political considerations—often short-term in nature—have in the past loomed larger than commercial considerations. Depending on the state of the economy, feast or famine will alternate. The location of investment, for example, can become more significant than its intrinsic merits with all too visible eventual consequences.

Not only an industry's finance and investment are heavily constrained by exogenous factors and by the political process; the same can be true of matters such as the location of its headquarters, the structure of its balance-sheet, its accounting principles, and the time-frame within which decisions are taken. In these circumstances, is it any wonder that the companies chafe at what they see as unwarranted restrictions on their freedom of action, and perform less well than their private sector counterparts? Yet, as long as the industries are in the public sector, public money is at stake and public accountability must be preserved. The requirements of Parliament stand paramount; the Government's annual financial cycle must be obeyed; the Ministers must be held supreme over the industries' chairmen. This is clearly unavoidable in a democracy, but is it the best way to run a business? It is no fun managing an industry when large amounts of the working day can be taken up with answering the queries and quibbles of a stage army of second-guessers in Whitehall.

At the end of the day the heart of the matter is that a nationalised industry does not have to succeed in order to survive. Even if left to their own devices, the industries have no real incentive to improve their performance or to strive for greater efficiency. If the Government stands behind the industries and is viewed as possessing a bottomless purse, it is no wonder that inefficiencies flourish and market responsiveness does not stand very high in an industry's scale of priorities. Nationalisation and the Morrisonian concept have in effect failed to provide the stimuli that are needed. The consumer, the taxpayer, and the industries themselves have all suffered as a result.

How have governments attempted to grapple with the poor performance of nationalised industries? What solutions have been brought forward? Major White Papers were published in 1961, 1967, and 1978, which set out an increasingly stringent control framework. Industries were urged to adopt marginal cost pricing; controls on investment appraisal were introduced; new investment programmes were required to meet a specific rate of return comparable to that achieved in the private sector; external financing limits, financial targets, and performance aims were imposed; and comprehensive corporate planning and monitoring procedures have been set up.

One of the principal reasons for frequent changes in the control framework of the nationalised industries has been the lack of success of each successive control mechanism. Old control mechanisms rarely die, they only fade away. The original idea was that the industries should break even, taking one year with another. This had to be superseded, because they didn't break even. The system that all their capital investment should be subject to rigorous discounted cash flow appraisal, keeping up with the trends and fashions of the time, also ran into difficulties. Large proportions of the investment programme were never subjected to this critique, and those that were subjected to it invariably failed to hit the targets. The imposition of an overall rate of return on the total investment programme was an attempt to grapple with the inadequacies of a system that only ever appraised a proportion of an industry's investment. This too failed to deliver the goods. Only recently, with the emphasis on External Financing Limits, financial targets, and performance aims, has there been any improvement in overall discipline. But even this system is subject to severe strain, as all too often industries return to the Government, cap in hand, and demand more money.

What has been the purpose of all these changes? It is revealing that, although there are some differences in emphasis, the governments since the early 1960s have followed the same evolutionary course. The arm's-length relationship has been progressively eroded and increasing discipline has been applied to the industries. No government has felt able to leave the industries to their own devices. To what end? In essence, governments of either major party have attempted to compensate for the lack of market forces by imposing surrogate market forces on the industries. Governments have systematically set about creating a set of external stimuli, that, in the absence of real competitive forces, tried to provide pressure similar to that normally provided by market mechanisms.

Although the attempts to apply bureaucratic controls to the industries have met with some success, they clearly have not provided a long-term solution. In practice, attempting to control the industries' conduct administratively does not deal with the core problems that result from state ownership and monopolistic structure. Privatisation and competition replace the surrogate market with the real market and bring the control philosophy that has evolved over the years to its logical conclusion.

IV. Benefits of privatisation

The advantages of privatisation are many. It brings clear benefits to the companies concerned. Managers are set free to manage and new opportunities are opened up. It is no surprise to me that companies which have been privatised to date are trading extremely successfully in the private sector. For example, Cable and Wireless's pre-tax profits have more than doubled since privatisation. Associated British Ports raised profits from £1.5 million to £6.8 million in the first six months as a private company, Amersham's profits are up by a third despite fierce overseas competition, and the National Freight Company is said to be likely to make a profit of about £5 million this year compared to last year when the company barely broke even. In all these cases, turnover is up and share prices have increased substantially to the benefit of both employees who hold shares and non-employees.

The companies have revelled in their new-found independence. Their balance-sheets have been geared to the particular needs of the business and their finance can now be drawn from the normal capital markets rather than from the Government. Commercial investment can increase and a completely new set of financial criteria operates attuned to the company rather than to the needs of the PSBR. The Finance Director of Britoil has recently isolated three principal benefits to his firm from being in the private sector: freedom of action, lack of second-guessing by civil servants, and a need to take greater account of the way the market perceives the company. It is no wonder that Britoil's profits in the first few months of trading were comfortably above the prospectus forecasts and that the company is now generally reckoned in the City to be well-placed to take advantage of future opportunities.

And it is not just the companies which have benefited. Attention is too seldom focused on the benefits that privatisation can bring to those who work for the companies concerned. Trade union leaders, when they oppose privatisation on doctrinaire grounds, rarely take time to consider the best interests of their members. Only in nationalised concerns, for example, are employees debarred from owning a stake in the businesses in which they spend their working lives. It is fortunate that the employees directly involved in privatisations have recognised the potential benefits.

Special offers and preferential treatment for those employees who want to acquire shares in their own company have been key features of all privatisations to date. Around 100,000 employees have taken advantage of the opportunities that have been offered representing around 90 per cent of the total eligible workforce. A staggeringly high proportion.

Employee participation has been particularly noteworthy in the case of the National Freight Corporation. As a public enterprise, academic studies suggested that the organisation was not performing as well as comparable private sector concerns. The run-up to the sale in 1981 was frankly unpromising, with the markets taking a sceptical view. Then the workforce mobilised itself. They persuaded commercial banks to lend them £57 million. With this, and money of their own, they purchased the company.

What has been the result? Well over 9,000 employees, together with 1,300 pensioners, took up shares, subscribing an average of over £700 at £1 a share in January 1982. The value of their holding has now more than trebled to £3.40 a share. The Chairman's report last year said that the improved results were due largely to changed management attitudes and a well-motivated workforce. This does not surprise me since the average shareholder-worker has already received substantial dividends and an increase of over £1,600 in the value of his capital. Changes have occurred across the whole spectrum of NFC's activities. Not only has the company taken the opportunity to move into new markets but the workers-turned-owners have been quoted as saying that they now turn off unnecessary lights and take better care of vehicles and other equipment than previously. Comments like 'Repairs cost the firm money' summarise a major change in perspective.

Benefits to the employees and managers of privatised firms go much wider than the chance to acquire a stake in their own company. It is very difficult within the public sector to devise sensible financially-based motivation packages customised to the needs of individual firms. For example, we have done what we can to appoint top-class managers to run state industries but I readily admit that remuneration has to be settled within an overall framework that may not be fully appropriate in individual cases. Privatisation sets managers free to manage. It makes it possible to link pay to success and to provide appropriate rewards.

I believe that overall pay bargaining can be carried out much more responsibly and easily in companies freed from government interference. We have consciously tried to place responsibility on the management of nationalised industries and to make it clear that pay negotiations are matters for them and their employees. But public sector trade union experience of previous administrations has given their leaders a taste of political power without responsibility. They are all too ready to seek to involve the Government in the interests of their political objectives if not in the interests of the members. Privatisation decisively breaks the political link.

It also enables pride in work and job satisfaction to be increased. It is unfortunate but true that nationalised industries are held in low esteem. Their perceived lack of drive, low consumer-responsiveness, and general willingness to exploit their monopoly position have conspired to give them a bad press. It is no wonder that employees' morale is low. And yet many able people work for and run the nationalised industries. It is institutional constraints and lack of motivation that conspire to blunt the overall performance.

It is a fallacy to believe that nationalisation preserves jobs. For example, in the fifteen years from 1963 to 1978, employment in the gas industry dropped by 19 per cent, in electricity by 22 per cent, and in coal by no less than 51 per cent. Nationalisation has in fact destroyed jobs. Private sector firms faced with secular decline for their products continually search out new opportunities to replace lost business. They have no option. Contrast nationalised industries. Their statutory straitjacket limits their means of adjustment. They struggle on and try and turn their backs on the real world. In the end, circumstances force abrupt and traumatic change. But too late. Jobs

are lost forever. Nationalisation may create a spurious sense of
security but it is not a means of ensuring continuing employment.

Competition, on the other hand, breeds jobs. It forces
modernisation and technological change. To take an example,
since 1972, employment in the telecommunications industry in
the USA has increased twice as rapidly as comparable employment in British Telecom. Competition can also influence
demand. In any UK High Street, banks compete with banks,
shoe-shops compete with shoe-shops. Each employs staff. If
the State took over control, competition and jobs would vanish
overnight.

Great entrepreneurs would never flourish if they were
faced with the constraints imposed on managers in the
nationalised industries. Nationalisation stifles flair and
imagination and blunts business skills. And yet these qualities
are essential if new products are to be developed, new
markets sought, and new jobs created.

No government in a democracy can forever turn its back on
the market. Unless nationalisation produces mechanisms for
ensuring that goods and services are produced of a kind that
customers want at a price that customers will pay, there is no
long-term future for the output that is being produced. If, for
example, poor productivity and poor control of costs cause
prices to rise beyond the level that the market will stand,
either subsidies have to be sought or customers look elsewhere in cases where they have freedom of choice. A spiral of
unprofitability sets in; it may be tolerated for a while; but
then abrupt structural changes are necessary. Far better to
ensure that the company concerned constantly adjusts to its
markets and is enabled to seek new openings to compensate
for lost opportunities. Privatisation forces this to happen.

Although it is clear that privatisation can bring substantial
benefits to both employees and the companies concerned, the
main prize, if competition can be increased, is for the consumer. On its own, privatisation is not the cure for all
ailments. We are not so naive as to think that an unrestrained
monopoly in the private sector would be less inclined to exploit its position than the monopolies in the public sector.
The key here is to ensure that greater competition goes hand

in hand with returning industries to the private sector. And where competition is not practical or is slow to develop, regulation or franchising can ensure that the harmful effects are minimised whilst at the same time promoting efficiency and benefits to the consumer.

Governments have done what they can to make the public sector more consumer-orientated and more responsive to customers' needs. There is a network of Consumer Councils and performance aims have been set for a number of industries. But the overall impact on customers has been minimal and the standard of service in some areas has been little short of disgraceful. It is only the spur of privatisation and competition that has made British Telecom increase the range of telephones it offers to its customers, that has encouraged British Rail to use innovative marketing, and has pushed British Airways into being one of the world's best airlines. I am afraid that the typical public sector attitude has been to put the customer rather low in its order of priorities. Lack of competition breeds a take-it-or-leave-it attitude where, to be truthful, customers can be rather a nuisance. It has always struck me as rather revealing that the phone numbers of British Gas showrooms are not listed in public telephone directories and it is impossible for customers to obtain them. Would it be conceivable for Currys or Comet to run their business in this way?

The potential benefits to customers from privatisation bear constant repetition and emphasis. The National Consumer Council in its latest annual report comments that it is not self-evident that a simple change from public to private monopoly will help consumers. The Council says its task must be to try to ensure that privatisation brings a genuine increase in competition and choice for consumers. The Council is pushing at an open door. The primary objective of the Government's privatisation programme is to reduce the power of the monopolist and to encourage competition. As the programme moves into the heartlands of the public sector, maximising competition will become of dominant importance. No state monopoly is sacrosanct. We intend through competition and privatisation to open up the State sector to the stimulus of competition and reverse the creeping bureaucratisation of the last thirty-five years. The long-term success of the privatisation programme will stand or fall by the extent to which it maximises competition. If competition cannot be achieved, an historic opportunity will have been lost.

I have emphasised the benefits which competition through privatisation will bring. You may ask what about British Telecommunications—the largest enterprise well on the way to the market?[a] Some have argued that we are simply privatising a monopoly. But the changes are much greater than our critics care to admit. Mercury has been licensed to provide an alternative network and—local difficulties apart—is already starting to have some impact on certain trunk call charges. Responsibility for the approval of apparatus for connection to BT circuits is being removed from BT although the process of writing standards is going more slowly than we would like. Competition in the supply of equipment from large PABXs to cordless telephones is being introduced and will be enhanced as the standards become clearer. The use of private circuits leased from BT for the provision of value added network services is now allowed under a general licence—at the last count some sixty projects were underway. Providers of cable television will be able to provide local services in conjunction with BT or Mercury and the provision of mobile telephone services by two consortia (one including BT as a partner) has been agreed. Progress is being made. In addition, technology is developing fast in the communication area and in the longer term might be expected to reduce the present market dominance of BT anyway.

These moves will continue. At the same time, it is clearly essential to ensure that privatisation does not erode essential services. An advantage of privatisation is that it forces into sharp relief a distinction between activities which are commercial and activities which are not. The confusion I have referred to earlier is ended. If uncommercial activities merit support, subsidies should be direct, contractual, and specifically targeted. Why should commercial companies not compete regularly for the subsidy, in the same way as they compete for customers? This ensures that subsidy levels are kept as low as possible and yet also encourages efficiency and customer satisfaction.

V. Conclusion

Competition is an extraordinarily efficient mechanism. It ensures that goods and services preferred by the consumer are delivered at the lowest economic cost. It responds constantly to changes in consumer preferences. It does not require politicians or civil servants to make it work.

We have over the next four to five years an historic opportunity to reform key areas of the British economy. For too long, outdated and unrealistic concepts and ideas have been allowed to hold sway. There has been an absence of radical thinking and a too-ready acceptance of present practices. The privatisation programme is coherent, and well thought-out. It holds substantial advantages for the management of the industries, their employees, the consumer, and the taxpayer. And it also, of course, brings benefits to the PSBR and furthers our objective of reducing the size of the public sector. But these important by-products are secondary to the main theme. Our main objective is to promote competition and improve efficiency. Less government is good government. This is nowhere truer than in the state industrial sector. Privatisation hands back, to the people of this country, industries that have no place in the public sector. Long may the process continue.

EDITORS' NOTE

a. British Telecom was subsequently privatised in 1984.

4

THE SUCCESS OF PRIVATISATION*

John Moore (1985)

I. Extension to natural monopolies

Privatisation has proved of such major benefit over the last five years, we have decided that it is right to extend it progressively to the so-called 'natural monopolies'. These are the monopolies where economies of scale and barriers to entry are such that it would be artificial, wasteful, or impractical to break them up. The cheapest means of producing or supplying a commodity in these circumstances may well be a natural monopoly. We believe that it is possible to privatise natural monopolies in such a way that their customers, their employees, and the economy as a whole will all benefit. The privatisation of British Telecom, with its virtual present monopoly of domestic telecommunications, showed the way. Gas, airports, and, possibly, water are next. Let me explain why.

Conventional wisdom was that monopolies were so powerful, so prone to take advantage of their customers, so liable to become fat and inefficient, that the only safe place for them was in the public sector. Only politicians and civil servants could be entrusted with monopoly power because only they would exercise it with restraint, justice, and good sense. What nonsense this proved to be! Experience over the last forty years has surely taught us that, from the customer's point of view, the State is just as likely to abuse a monopoly position as a private owner. And worse, when it does, despite ministerial responsibility and parliamentary accountability, the customer has little effective redress. Contrast the security given by effective regulation such as provided by the Office

* This article reproduces part of a speech made when opening Hoare Govett Ltd's new City dealing rooms on 17 July 1985.

John Moore MP was the Financial Secretary to the Treasury.

of Telecommunications (OFTEL), the Monopolies and Mergers Commission (MMC), and, as a last resort, the right to challenge abuse directly in the Courts.

Although the size and extent of natural monopolies have clearly to be constrained to what is truly 'natural', I firmly believe that where competition is impractical privatisation policies have now been developed to such an extent that regulated private ownership of natural monopolies is preferable to nationalisation. Those who criticise the decision to privatise utilities as being a Treasury-inspired fund-raising exercise have just not considered the facts.

Firstly, privatisation increases productive efficiency whether or not a monopoly is involved. Pressures from shareholders looking for a return on their investment—considerably enhanced when these shareholders are also managers and employees—give a clear incentive to privatised companies to organise their internal affairs as efficiently as possible and seek the maximum competitive terms from their suppliers. The enhanced competition amongst suppliers, as well as benefiting the privatised company, also benefits the UK economy as a whole. Suppliers who fight others for orders are likely to compete more aggressively in overseas markets and also be more likely to seek out technical innovation.

Secondly, the extraordinary success that privatisation now has in creating a wide distribution of shares produces shareholder pressures quite unlike those faced by nationalised industries or conventional companies. The existence of large numbers of shareholders who have both paid for their shares expecting a reasonable return *and* are customers interested in good service at a fair price is an irresistible combination and a powerful lobby in favour of both efficiency and price restraint. Giving people shares free in these companies—as some have suggested—would completely negate this effect.

Thirdly, private sector companies able to draw on capital markets to finance efficiency or expansion face circumstances different from those faced by industries in the public sector. We have been able to find the finance to allow nationalised industries to invest in worthwhile projects and their chairmen said last year that the present levels and patterns of investment spending were broadly consonant with the proper development of their businesses. The industries have however not always been as fortunate and I do not blame them if they think that the financial markets are likely to be a surer source of funds over a period of time than the political capital market funded by public sector borrowing.

Maybe surprisingly, the counterpart of private sector finance is a continuing discipline which in practice may be far more effective than that which can be applied in the public sector. State-owned industries escape scrutiny by analysts and bankers, and may fall into the habit of thinking that they have the Government available in the last resort to bail them out. This tends to undermine financial disciplines, financial control, and internal accounting techniques. Privatisation brings with it fundamental improvements in these key areas.

Fourthly, the establishment of OFTEL shows how regulatory arrangements can be developed which are tough, transparent, and provide full protection to customers as well as other businesses. Some regulation has, however, in the past had an undeservedly bad reputation when used insensitively and we have deliberately set out to learn from the experiences of others. We will avoid regulators becoming too associated with any particular company in order to pre-empt 'regulatory capture'. We will ensure that the regulatory regimes which are adopted will encourage efficiency, and we will make certain that regulation does not stifle innovation and technological advance. I am confident that this can be done.

II. Conclusion

Our future policy on privatisation in the UK is quite straightforward. We will continue to return state-controlled industries to the private sector. We will encourage competition where appropriate but where it does not make business or economic sense we will not hesitate to extend the benefits of privatisation to natural monopolies. When this is done, we will ensure that they are subject to tough, transparent, effective regulation to the benefit of their customers and the economy as a whole. We will continue to offer incentives to employees and seek their participation in the success of the companies in which they work. We will structure the sales to give the greatest possible incentives to wider share ownership. And we will use the sale receipts to further our overall economic strategy.

By the end of this Parliament we hope that, subject to parliamentary approval where necessary and satisfactory market conditions, at least another eight major state businesses will have been transferred out of state control and into the private sector in the full sense. These include the activities of the National Bus Company, British Airways, Shorts, Unipart, Rolls-Royce, Royal Ordnance, the British Airports Authority, and the British Gas Corporation. If this programme was achieved in full it would mean that, since the programme started in 1979, the proportion of GDP in the hands of state industries would have dropped from 10½ per cent to around 6½ per cent. Over 600,000 jobs would have been transferred to the private sector. In the course of two Parliaments, we would have nearly halved government involvement in state-owned business and liberated a substantial portion of economic activity from suffocation by the State. I have no doubt that the successful conclusion of this Parliament's programme will produce an irreversible shift in attitudes and achievement which will bring lasting benefits to the United Kingdom.

Part II

THE COMPARATIVE PERFORMANCE OF THE PUBLIC AND PRIVATE SECTORS

5

THE COMPARATIVE PERFORMANCE OF PUBLIC AND PRIVATE ENTERPRISE*

Richard Pryke

I. Introduction

The nationalised industries' performance was unsatisfactory during the 1970s. However, the same can be said of much of the private sector. Poor management and low productivity are by no means confined to public enterprise, and financial assistance, which has had such an adverse effect on the efficiency of the nationalised concerns, might—in the absence of public ownership—have been afforded to private firms in the way that it has abroad. Moreover, for many of the industries the alternative to state ownership is not competition under private ownership but private monopoly operating under public regulation. Hence many of the weaknesses which appear to spring from public ownership could be the result of monopoly. It is therefore a matter of judgement as to whether the ownership of the nationalised industries by the State helps to explain why they have, in general, performed so badly. In a book of mine (Pryke, 1981) I concluded that public ownership has had a deleterious effect but this was at best no more than an informed opinion (and in an earlier survey of the industries (Pryke, 1971), which covered the period up to 1968, I reached a different verdict).

II. Like-with-like comparisons

In order to throw some much needed light on the effect of ownership *per se* what are required are comparisons between

* This article was first published in *Fiscal Studies*, 1982, 3, 2.

Richard Pryke is a Senior Lecturer in the Department of Economic and Business Studies at the University of Liverpool.

state and private undertakings which are in competition with each other or are at least engaged in the same type of business. Numerous comparisons of this type have been made in other countries, although many of them are vitiated by the failure to allow for differences in operating conditions or in the composition of output. However, very few comparative studies have been made for Britain. This is surprising as there are a number of places where public and private enterprise are engaged in the same activity and three of the most important areas will be examined in this article. They are:

- *Civil aviation*. Here British Airways (BA), which is of course publicly owned, can be compared with British Caledonian (BCal), which is in private ownership. BCal is the only private operator of any size that is, like BA, almost exclusively engaged in scheduled operations. The only other private concern which might have been included in the comparisons is the now defunct Laker Airways. However, this had a large charter side, made extensive use of other organisations for tasks which BA and BCal perform for themselves, and had a very long stage length. During 1980 BCal and British Airways had almost identical stage lengths and, although they do not for the most part operate over the same routes, appeared in many ways to be remarkably similar. The most obvious contrast is that BA, with over 53,000 employees, in 1980 was far larger than BCal, which had fewer than 6,500. However, British Caledonian is probably large enough to obtain the limited economies of scale that are available in airline operation.

- *Short sea ship and hovercraft services*. The Railway Board has two subsidiaries[a] which operate on the short sea routes. First, there is Sealink UK (SLUK) which provides shipping services to France, Belgium, Holland, Ireland, the Channel Islands, and the Isle of Wight. Most of the continental routes are operated in conjunction with the French National Railways and Belgian and Dutch state-owned shipping concerns. Sealink's principal private enterprise rival, and the only one for which financial information is available, is the shipping side of European Ferries (EFL) which controls Townsend Thoresen. EFL provides competitive services for passengers and road vehicles to the continent and Northern Ireland. In most other areas SLUK is either in competition with B and I, which is owned by the Irish Government, or does not face direct competition, e.g. to the Channel Islands and for the movement of railway wagons and containers. It is therefore with EFL that Sealink UK will be compared. The second of the Railways Board's subsidiaries provides hovercraft services to France in partnership with the French railways. Comparison can readily be made between BR Hovercraft (BRH) and Hoverlloyd, the only other hovercraft concern, which was owned by Swedish interests. BRH and Hoverlloyd have, however, now been merged.

- *The sale of gas and electric appliances and contracting.* The British Gas Corporation (BGC) and the Electricity Boards (EBs) sell appliances—principally from their showrooms— install appliances and engage in contracting. BGC has managed to retain most of the market for gas appliances but, because the retailing of gas appliances is much the same as that of electrical goods, it is possible to throw light on BGC's performance—and on that of the EBs—by means of comparisons with Currys and Comet which are, respectively, the largest and second largest electrical groups in private ownership. Currys is very similar to the showrooms but Comet employs a different marketing strategy and places less emphasis on quality of service, relying almost exclusively on charging bargain prices. There is also some useful information which covers other private multiple and discount chains. The Office of Fair Trading has, for instance, published a study of the London Electricity Board's shops which provides details about a sample of private electrical retailers. This and other material can and will be used to extend the comparisons between the showrooms and the two biggest private groups.

III. Performance compared

In the areas that have been investigated, and on the basis of the comparisons which I have made, public enterprise has performed relatively poorly in terms of its competitive position, has used labour and capital inefficiently and has been less profitable. In most cases the public activities have been losing money over a long period. This is a comprehensive denunciation but the evidence seems clear.

In 1964 EFL, or rather its predecessors, started operating out of Southampton and was already running, with a single ship, from Dover to Calais. Between 1964 and 1980 the number of tourist vehicles which it carried on this route soared up from 84,000 to just under 400,000. Meanwhile carryings by Sealink UK and the French Railways across the Straits of Dover fell from 312,000 to 301,000, of which SLUK's share was 208,000. If all the relevant routes are taken together—and their rates were remarkably similar—the traffic carried by EFL and Sealink was, during 1980, as shown in Table 1.

Table 1. Traffic carried by EFL and Sealink on their Continental Routes and between Scotland and Northern Ireland

(1980, thousands)

	EFL	SLUK and partners	SLUK's share
Passengers	5,850	9,048	4,506
Tourist vehicles	1,083[1]	978	500
Lorries and trailers	476	375	223

1. Includes a small number of coaches.

Passengers were the only type of traffic where the Sealink partnership had a lead over European Ferries, and SLUK's share was substantially smaller even for passengers; and in every relevant geographical sector except Scotland–Ulster. If attention is confined to those sectors and types of traffic where SLUK and EFL were in competition it is found that the latter's turnover was some 80 per cent greater. Moreover, turning to hovercraft, Hoverlloyd's receipts were almost a third greater than those of BRH during 1980.

Between 1971 and 1980 the Electricity Boards maintained their share of sales by all radio and electrical goods shops at about 18 per cent. But this gives an exaggerated impression of their success since the small independent retailers were rapidly losing ground. In 1971 Currys had a market share of 7 per cent but by 1980 it had risen to 12 per cent, although this owed something to the acquisition of another group. Meanwhile Comet had built up its stake from virtually nothing to around 9 per cent. No figures are available for the EBs' share of total expenditure on electrical contracting, but it seems likely that the Boards have lost ground. Over the period 1971–80 their volume of work fell by around 25 per cent. However, it should be noted that this decline occurred during the first part of the period and that, although the Boards' share of sales by radio and electrical shops declined between 1971 and 1977, it recovered thereafter.

BGC continues to sell a very high proportion of all gas appliances, and British Airways retains its premier position but, because of the way in which air routes are assigned, it has not had to face competition from another British operator over most of its network, and the Gas Corporation's dominance owes more to its monopsony power than to its competitive ability. When, during the early 1970s, BGC became concerned at the increasing interest which independent retailers were beginning to pay to the gas appliance market it put strong pressure on manufacturers to grant it larger preferential discounts and used other tactics to maintain its position. Hence BGC's predominance does not upset the conclusion that the public enterprise activities with which we are concerned have had a relatively poor competitive performance.

Nor does there seem much doubt that nationalised industries make comparatively inefficient use of labour and capital. British Airways uses its aircraft less intensively than BCal.[b] In 1980 BA's planes averaged 6.8 flying hours per day whereas BCal's flew for 8.2 hours, which was 21 per cent longer. BCal's labour productivity was also higher since it produced 15 per cent more capacity tonne kilometres per employee and 6 per cent more load tonne kilometres. (The slightly greater proportion of charter work at BCal has been taken into account by notionally increasing the size of British Airtours, which is BA's charter subsidiary, until non-scheduled operations represent the same proportion of capacity at both airlines.) Although the contrast between BA and BCal is not very sharp, further estimates for the productivity of different groups of workers confirm that it exists.

Similarly, productivity appears to be higher at European Ferries than at Sealink. During 1980 EFL's turnover per employee was 24 per cent higher even excluding those at SLUK who were engaged on work for BR and who were employed at its workshops on tasks which, in EFL's case, are undertaken by outside concerns. European Ferries also uses its capital more productively. As measured by turnover (during 1981) per pound of the net replacement value of ships (at the beginning of the year) EFL had a lead of 41 per cent.

According to the Monopolies Commission turnover per worker at gas showrooms is substantially less than at comparable retail groups, and in the one Electricity Board for which information is available—the South of Scotland—retailing turnover per pound of staff expenditure was, during 1979/80, about 15 per cent lower than at Currys. Moreover it is clear that electricity showrooms have high costs. One simple yardstick of costs is to express all operating expenditure, including depreciation but excluding expenditure on appliances, as a proportion of the latter item. During 1978/9 this cost mark-up stood at 38 per cent for the EBs whereas it was only 28 per cent at Currys. In 1980/1 a sample of multiple and discount stores in London had a cost mark-up of 20 per cent but for the London Electricity Board showrooms it was 42 per cent. The London Board has exceptionally high costs, but the figure for the Electricity Boards as a whole was around 34 per cent in 1978/9, as against 19 per cent for the private electrical shops in London. (The cost mark-up for the EBs is lower than the one given previously because of the exclusion, for purposes of comparability, of the costs of hire-purchase administration and bad debts.)

As might be expected the public enterprise activities under discussion have been relatively unprofitable and have in most cases been running at a loss for many years. During 1980/1 the EBs lost £12 million on their retailing and contracting on a current cost accounting basis and after allowing for the opportunity cost of loans to hire-purchase customers, as estimated from the yield on Treasury bills.[1] This loss represented 7 per cent on net capital at current cost, excluding HP lending. At no time from the mid-1970s have retailing and contracting earned a true profit. The Electricity Boards have been less profitable than Currys and Comet. Between 1976/7 and 1978/9 the EBs' profit margin on their retailing—profit as a proportion of turnover—averaged −1 per cent, after allowing for the cost of HP loans but on a historic cost basis. Currys which is almost wholly engaged in retail work had a margin of +5 per cent, and Comet one of +4 per cent. In London, which is a particularly difficult area for electrical shops of all types, the London Electricity Board's showrooms have had even less success than private multiple and discount stores. When hire-purchase charges and costs are excluded the Board had a profit margin of −15 per cent between 1977/8 and 1980/1, whereas for a sample of multiple and discount stores the figure was +2 per cent. Very little information is available for contracting but it appears that here too the Electricity Boards have been less profitable than private concerns. Turning to gas, BGC's retailing and contracting sustained a loss of £22 million after allowing for HP costs and on a current cost basis. There has not been a profit since the early 1970s.[c]

Results at Sealink UK and BRH have been just as dismal. SLUK showed a £3 million profit in 1980. However, at current costs Sealink UK, and the BR harbours that it uses incurred a joint loss of £9 million; and with depreciation at replacement cost SLUK must have made a loss almost every year from 1973. It even had a loss on a historic cost basis between 1974 and 1976. EFL's financial performance has been markedly superior. During 1980 it made a profit of £14 million, at historic cost, and between 1972 and 1980 EFL's profit margin averaged 15.4 per cent compared with SLUK's 2.1 per cent. Over this period European Ferries' operating profit and depreciation on vessels was just equal to its capital expenditure on ships, when they are both restated at 1980 prices. But at SLUK capital expenditure exceeded the profit

---

[1] All references to financial results relate to profits after depreciation but before tax and interest, except for the opportunity cost of HP loans where it is made clear that this has been deducted.

and depreciation by about £90 million. One possible weakness of these comparisons is that SLUK operated in sectors
where EFL does not compete. During the earlier part of
the period SLUK's continental car ferry services made the
largest profits but in 1980 a loss, at historic cost, was earned
on that part of its business where it was in competition with
European Ferries. Moreover, if an organisation's existing
pattern of operations is unprofitable it needs to be modified,
but SLUK has been persistently less profitable than EFL.
Similarly BRH was consistently less profitable than Hoverlloyd. Between 1972 and 1980 BRH only twice showed an
operating profit, with depreciation at historic cost, whereas
Hoverlloyd did not make a loss. Hoverlloyd's profit margin
averaged 10 per cent over the period 1976–80 but BRH's
figure was −16½ per cent and, disregarding interest,
Hoverlloyd had a cumulative cash flow surplus of £6 million,
at 1980 prices, as against BRH's deficit of £24 million.

During 1980/1 BA lost about £180 million at current costs,
and even before its current financial crisis the airline was,
taking one year with another, doing little more than breaking
even. British Airways has, over the relatively short period for
which meaningful comparisons can be made, been less profitable than British Caledonian. The first year in which British
Caledonian obtained the great bulk of its revenue from
scheduled operations was 1976/7 and Table 2 shows the
profit margins, in the most nearly comparable years, for the
two airlines since that time.

Table 2. Operating Profit as a Percentage of Operating Revenue
for BA and BCal

Financial year	BA %	BCal %	Financial year
1977/8	3.6	9.1	1976/7
1978/9	5.4	10.1	1977/8
1979/80	1.0	5.0	1978/9
1980/1	−6.0	5.2	1979/80

Over this period profits at historic cost have averaged only 1 per cent of BA's turnover as against 7.3 per cent at BCal. The figure would have been somewhat higher if the part played by charter work had been as small as at British Airways, because BCal's charter operations have been financially unhealthy.[d]

IV. Public enterprise advantages

Although the performance of the public enterprise activities that are under investigation has been relatively poor they have had a number of important advantages over their private counterparts.

Because of the availability of rail connections SLUK and BRH are particularly convenient for those passengers who are not travelling by car. About 40 per cent of the passengers who use the continental services which are operated by SLUK and its partners arrive by rail and this explains why passengers are the one type of traffic where the partnership's carryings are greater than those of EFL (see Table 1). Despite Hoverlloyd's success in obtaining passenger traffic through the provision of coach links, BRH carried twice as many foot passengers during 1980, but Hoverlloyd was far more successful in attracting car traffic for which both organisations were competing on the same terms. In 1980 Hoverlloyd's revenue from private vehicles and their occupants was nearly 50 per cent greater (although as we have seen its total turnover was only around a third higher).

British Airways has the advantage that it is mainly based at Heathrow whereas BCal operates from Gatwick. Its use of Gatwick is a historical accident. At one time it was largely a charter airline and Gatwick was the natural airport for charter operations. When more recently BCal might have wanted to transfer to Heathrow it has been effectively prevented from doing so by the substantial investment required and the difficulty, because Heathrow is so congested, of obtaining permission. Gatwick is, however, a second-rate airport because only a limited number of destinations can be reached from it. Hence those passengers from abroad who, in the absence of a direct service, have to fly into London and then out again tend to use Heathrow. Moreover, Gatwick is less favourably situated than Heathrow because it is much less convenient for those travelling by road from central London, or from the Midlands and the North. Thus where passengers have a choice between Gatwick and Heathrow the majority will use the latter, and something like 70 per cent of British Caledonian's services, as measured in terms of passenger kilometres, operate in competition with services from Heathrow. Hence, other things being equal, there is relatively little traffic for BCal to carry. In this situation it could opt for a frequent service and good load factors by using small high-cost aircraft. Or it could provide a much restricted service with large low-cost planes and hope to obtain high load factors. Or, alternatively, it could pursue a middle course by somewhat restricting its frequency and by using planes which, although smaller than those employed by its competitors at Heathrow, are too large for the available traffic. This is the policy which British Caledonian appears to have adopted. In 1980 the aircraft on BCal's scheduled services provided about 20 per cent fewer tonne kilometres of capacity per kilometre flown than BA's, but despite this British Caledonian had a load factor on its scheduled services of 54.9 per cent compared with BA's 60.5 per cent.

Although British Caledonian's inferior load factor is partly due to being based at Gatwick, it appears that its marketing has not been particularly effective, whereas this has long been one of BA's strong points. It is significant that business traffic, where relatively little promotion is required, accounts for an unusually high proportion of British Caledonian's work and that, on those routes where it is competing with another carrier which uses Gatwick, they tend to have higher load factors. This provokes the question of whether BCal's difficulties in filling its aircraft may not be wholly attributable to poor marketing. However, there is no doubt that it is a disadvantage to use Gatwick. When during 1973/4 the Dutch airline KLM was flying to Amsterdam from both of the London airports its carryings were much heavier from Heathrow, and BA has lost more than 20 per cent of its traffic on the Madrid and Barcelona routes to Iberia because it has switched to Gatwick, whereas the Spanish airline continues to use Heathrow.

Because BCal's aircraft are smaller and emptier than those of British Airways, the private airline is operating under a considerable handicap, albeit one which is in part the result of its own weakness at marketing. The fact that BCal's load factor is relatively low explains why its productivity lead over British Airways is significantly higher in terms of capacity tonne kilometres per employee (15 per cent) than in terms of load tonne kilometres per worker (6 per cent). Moreover there are considerable economies of scale for aircraft: small planes tend to be relatively expensive to buy and to fly per unit of capacity. Labour productivity should be significantly higher if large planes are used since the amount of maintenance and service work, and the number of cockpit staff, do not increase in line with the capacity of the aircraft. Hence, BCal's relative efficiency is greater than its 6 per cent lead over British Airways, as measured by load tonne kilometres per worker, would appear to suggest because, even if its marketing had been excellent, it would still have had to use smaller planes and/or to produce more unused capacity.[e]

The Gas Corporation's retailing activities benefit from its failure to charge their full costs to its appliance marketing account. The cost of remedial work to appliances that are under guarantee is charged to its main gas account; all of the Corporation's advertising expenditure is debited to gas; and only a quarter of the showrooms' overheads is allocated to retailing, because their division between this activity and the collection of payments for gas is based on the estimated distribution of the number of hours worked by shop staff, though it is evident that the great bulk of the space is devoted to appliances. According to the Monopolies and Mergers Commission (1980), 'the allocations made in drawing up the appliances marketing account amount in effect to subsidies from the sale of gas account' (p. 99). The size of these subsidies is not known but it could well amount to £20 million, in which case the loss on BGC's retailing and contracting would have amounted to over £40 million in 1980/1.

The electricity industry's accounts are also misleading. It is the practice of most of the Boards effectively to transfer part of the costs of selling certain appliances, which they regard with favour, from their retailing to their main electricity account. In the London Electricity Board, which is the only place for which details are available, the chosen appliances include cookers, storage radiators, water heaters, freezers, and space heaters. The main argument by which this financial support is justified is that the use of these appliances helps to improve the Board's load factor. This, however, cannot be true of all these appliances since together they account for the great bulk of domestic sales; and it is difficult to see why the Board, if it believes that more of the selected appliances should be sold, confines its financial support to its own shops. If their costs were not so high they would not need so much support, or at least it would be put to better use; which is a further reason why it is difficult to take the Board's arguments seriously. Moreover, the subventions to the retailing account must in the main constitute an advantage which the London Board's shops enjoy but is denied to its competitors even though they too handle the chosen goods and, with the exception of cookers and storage radiators, accounted for the great bulk of the market. In London the cross-subsidy from electricity to retailing amounted to over £600,000 in 1980/1, and represented 4 per cent of its shops' turnover.[2] Mention should also be made of the marketing advantage which the Boards must derive from having a large proportion of the population visit their showrooms in order to pay their electricity bills.

V. Private enterprise advantages

Because of the considerable advantages which our public enterprise activities have enjoyed their performance is even worse than it looks, unless their private counterparts have for some reason been correspondingly blessed or the public activities have been handicapped to such a degree as to negate their advantages. However, what are relevant here are those disadvantages which do not arise because of the activities' ownership by the State. If efficiency and profitability have suffered for this reason, then so much the worse for public ownership. Our public activities do not appear to have been

---

[2] This subsidy has been eliminated in the preceding comparisons between the London Electricity Board and its competitors.

working under any special handicaps of the type that would be relevant except possibly that SLUK has, in recent years at least, operated ships that carry container and railway wagons under contracts with BR and Freightliners which enable it to do no more than recover its costs including interest and depreciation at historic cost. However, because SLUK's profitability has been so poor, it seems unlikely that these arrangements have in general served to depress its profits and in poor years, like 1980, they must have boosted them.

BCal is the only private activity that appears to have enjoyed any special advantages. It was able, as a result of licensing decisions, to begin operating on four major long-haul routes during 1980, viz. to St Louis, Atlanta, Dallas, and Hong Kong. This led to a substantial increase in capacity (17 per cent) and, since British Caledonian managed to avoid the employment of much extra labour, to a significant increase in productivity. Because of these new routes BCal was therefore able to achieve higher efficiency without making workers redundant, an opportunity which was not open to British Airways. Another favourable factor is that although air fares have, under the IATA system, been largely dependent on distance those to Africa and South America are relatively high. Since African and South American routes form a substantial part of BCal's route network, it has probably had the benefit of a higher fare structure than British Airways.

VI. Mismanagement

It must be concluded that public enterprise activities which are being investigated have, despite substantial advantages, had a relatively poor performance. British Caledonian is the only counterpart concern to have been favoured by fortune but British Airways has enjoyed advantages which must have been as great and may well have been greater. Why is the public enterprise record so dismal? The proximate explanation is that the activities in question have been badly run. A full examination of the way in which the activities have been managed cannot be presented here, if only because of the space at my disposal. However, let me briefly cite some of the most striking and important evidence of managerial failure and, what amounts to the same thing, long-standing weaknesses which have not been tackled.

SLUK and the electricity showrooms have been neither prompt nor successful in reacting to market developments. After Thoresens had demonstrated that lorries could successfully be carried along with cars in multi-purpose vessels EFL promptly constructed boats of this type for its routes across the Straits of Dover; but SLUK and its partners did not and, although the train ferries which operated between Dover and Dunkirk could accommodate lorries, they were for various reasons unattractive. By 1971 the partnership only had one multi-purpose ship operating across the Straits whereas EFL had four and, as a result, was able to establish what it described in 1974 as 'a commanding position in the conveyance of commercial freight traffic out of the port of Dover' (Select Committee on Nationalised Industries, 1974, p. 286). Until 1979 EFL and the Sealink partnership had a price-fixing arrangement, but when it broke down SLUK let itself be undercut and then made a series of price reductions which caused confusion. This helps to explain why, during 1980, the partnership's car traffic across the Straits of Dover fell by 7 per cent, whereas EFL's rose by approaching 50 per cent. However, this was also due to the arrival of EFL's new ships, which were its response to the increasing competition from hovercraft. These new ferries have cut the journey time between Dover and Calais from 1½ to 1¼ hours whereas SLUK's new ships still take 1½ hours and, despite their slower speed, consume as much fuel.

The EBs were slow to adapt to the much greater degree of competition that developed in the retailing of electrical goods. At one time they were sold at prices fixed by manufacturers but, after the end of resale price maintenance, this system gradually broke down. The showrooms either continued to charge the recommended prices or gave smaller discounts than other shops. The Consumers' Association found, in 1975, that 'showrooms often charged full price'. Their prices averaged 88 per cent of those recommended by manufacturers whereas for Currys, and for electrical shops as a whole, they averaged only 79 per cent, with the discount retailers even lower at 75 per cent. The showrooms have now become more competitive, but an investigation by the Association in 1980 showed that they still tended to be more expensive than the multiple stores and discount sellers.[3]

Public enterprise has been prepared to go on operating sections of its business at a loss and has failed to rationalise its pattern of operations. Some showrooms are widely unprofitable—not one in the London Electricity Board makes a profit—and the Monopolies and Mergers Commission (1980) found that 'one in four [gas] showrooms had a turnover, in 1978, of less than £25,000 (equivalent to the sale of just over two cookers per week)' (p. 20). During 1980/1 Currys' sales revenue per shop was 50 per cent higher than that of the EBs in England and Wales and approaching twice that of BGC's showrooms. This must help to explain its greater profitability since retailing tends to be most profitable at those EBs where the turnover per shop is greatest.

That SLUK's operations are in want of rationalisation is evident from the proliferation of short sea routes and the (inefficient) provision of too much capacity. Whereas EFL operates from Dover to Calais and Zeebrugge, SLUK and its partners operate between Dover and Calais/Boulogne/Dunkirk, between Folkestone and Calais/Boulogne/Ostend, and between Newhaven and Dieppe. The last route has been consistently unprofitable and it is difficult to believe that the provision of so many services from Folkestone and Dover, which are only seven miles apart, serves any useful purpose. What it does is to spread traffic thinly. During 1980 SLUK's car ferries, and those of the French railways, made well over twice as many trips between Britain and France across the Straits of Dover as EFL's and they only carried sixteen tourist vehicles per crossing compared with EFL's forty-eight. Similarly, Hoverlloyd consistently achieved higher load factors than BRH. It offered a very frequent service over one route whereas BRH provided a less frequent service to two destinations. Hence Hoverlloyd was able to cancel lightly loaded flights without causing its passengers any great inconvenience.

BA's principal weakness has been overmanning. The problem was belatedly recognised by management and in 1978 the

[3] *Which?*, April 1975 and May 1980.

Chairman declared that 'The blunt fact is that British Airways, in comparison with its major competitors . . . is in certain areas . . . over-staffed by any form of measurement that we can introduce' (Select Committee on Nationalised Industries, 1978, p. 3). A manpower survey revealed that employment could be cut by around 15 per cent. However, it was planned that BA should grow into its excessive workforce. The intention was to double traffic by the mid-1980s and transform BA into a low-cost airline catering for a mass market. This plan may from the beginning have been over-optimistic and BCal adopted a far more cautious strategy. In any case the rise in oil prices and the world recession soon put pay to BA's hopes. But management was slow to recognise this and manpower rose, instead of falling slightly as had been planned. Only when profitability had collapsed was action taken, though BA should emerge a more efficient airline.

VII. The importance of ownership

Granted that the public enterprise activities that are under scrutiny have been badly run the question arises as to why this is the case. It could be chance: some undertakings are well managed and flourish; others are badly managed and languish. The activities which I have selected happen to be of the latter type. This could be the answer but it seems unlikely. The National Freight Corporation displayed weaknesses similar to those shown by the showrooms, BA, and SLUK.[4] Another possible explanation for our activities' lack of success is that they have long been big and bureaucratic while their private counterparts are still at an entrepreneurial stage. However, this explanation does not entirely fit the facts because BRH was no larger or older than Hoverlloyd but was markedly less successful. Moreover, it does not appear to be true that large established concerns within the private sector are, as a general rule, less competitive than their small rivals. Marshall's picture of industry as a forest where old trees are replaced by new ones does not correspond with reality.

---

[4] See Pryke (1981), Chapter 7.

The most likely explanation for the poor performance of the public enterprise activities is that they are in public ownership. It could have had a harmful effect by inducing the belief that the activities should act as social services and take the national interest into account. BGC told the Monopolies Commission that it maintains unprofitable showrooms 'for public service and social reasons'; and both the Corporation and the EBs face, or at least believe that they would face, considerable difficulty in closing down their loss-making outlets because of resistance from customers and local pressure groups. British Gas feels that it should do no more than cover the costs of regular servicing (which, unlike on-demand work, is included in the contracting account) and has expressed concern that higher charges might deter consumers from having appliances serviced with consequent adverse effects on safety, a fear that had previously been voiced by the King Committee. SLUK had to buy its latest ships from a British yard, whereas EFL went abroad, and in the mid-1970s the Government was reluctant to sanction the withdrawal of the Heysham–Belfast car ferry service.

However there are some activities which do not regard themselves as social or national services. BA seems to regard its remit as being wholly commercial and SLUK has complained strongly at government interference which has in any case been limited to a few isolated instances. Moreover, it is doubtful whether BGC's claim that it is acting as a social service is more than a convenient excuse for inertia. There are alternative ways in which BGC and the EBs could provide facilities for cash payment and advice in those places where showrooms are unprofitable. The one organisation might, for instance, employ the other on an agency basis, or a local shop might be used. Furthermore the difficulty of closing unprofitable showrooms has not prevented Eastern Electricity from building up a retailing organisation which matches Currys, and there have been opportunities for BGC and the EBs to adopt a more commercial approach. The Prices and Incomes Board recommended in 1970 that the gas industry should undertake a thorough examination of the viability of its showrooms, and should close down those that could not be made profitable. In the following year, the Government told BGC to compete more fairly and make progress towards earning a full commercial rate of return on retailing and contracting. If BGC really wanted to promote the servicing of appliances, it would print a warning on gas bills stating that it is dangerous not to have them maintained.

It is therefore difficult to believe that public ownership has caused managers to believe the activities are social services, though this is sometimes a convenient excuse for commercial failure. What public ownership does is to eliminate the threat of take-over and ultimately of bankruptcy and the need, which all private undertakings have from time to time, to raise money from the market. Public ownership provides a comfortable life and destroys the commercial ethic. But, whatever the reason may be, the record of the activities which I have been investigating does suggest that public ownership leads to performance which is relatively poor by private enterprise standards.

NOTE ON SOURCES

My principal sources were:

Annual Reports, including Curry's report to its employees;
Civil Aviation Authority *Annual Statistics*;
Monopolies and Mergers Commission (MMC), 1979, 1980, 1981b, and 1981c;
Monopolies Commission, 1974;
Office of Fair Trading, 1982;
Price Commission, 1979.

I have also relied on information gained through interviews and correspondence, etc., and would like to thank Jonathan Aylen for help and a copy of his valuable memorandum (1973).

EDITORS' NOTES

a. Sealink was subsequently privatised in 1984; see the Introduction.
b. More comparisons of airline efficiency are given by Ashworth and Forsyth in Part III.
c. In recent years a profit has been shown.
d. Subsequently British Airways' profitability has improved; see the article by Ashworth and Forsyth in Part III.
e. See the article by Ashworth and Forsyth in Part III.

6

THE COMPARATIVE PERFORMANCE OF PUBLIC AND PRIVATE OWNERSHIP*

Robert Millward

I. Introduction

At first blush it is remarkable how little work has been done by economists on a subject so popular and contentious in the political arena. At second blush there is perhaps little surprise given the huge pitfalls of a conceptual and measurement variety and the difficulty, at least in this country, of finding the two species in coexistence in the same product area. The recent surge of cost studies has, belatedly, drawn on the wide variety of institutional forms in certain industries in North America. Even so the coverage is patchy. Electricity has been well studied and there has been some work on water supply, railways, urban transport, and airlines. In these areas output is generally subject to user charges. This paper therefore focuses on areas of a 'semi-commercial' nature so that health and education are not covered, though the temptation could not be resisted of including an area both fecund in its variety of institutional forms and one where economists seem to have found their true home—refuse collection. There is a problem in specifying what is meant by performance and how it is measured. There is, on the other side of the coin, a problem in knowing what can be deduced from those things that can sometimes be measured, that is relative costs and relative profitability. In addition this paper reconsiders some of the earlier comparative studies in the USA (cf. Peltzman, 1971;

* This article was first published (in slightly extended form) in Lord Roll (ed.), *The Mixed Economy,* 1982, Macmillan, London and Basingstoke; Holmes and Meier, New York; it appears here by permission of the publisher.

Robert Millward is Professor of Economics at the University of Salford.

De Alessi, 1974) which carried conclusions about the relative inefficiency of public ownership in electricity and the claim of one writer (Spann, 1977) that the relative inefficiency of public provision is reasonably well substantiated.

II. Relative cost efficiency

If we are to deduce anything about managerial efficiency from observations of differences in unit costs as between public and private firms, the crucial issue is knowing whether factors other than management efficiency are being held constant. There are three major issues:

- In considering the costs of producing particular output levels or a constellation of different products, it is in the present context immaterial whether such output levels or some particular products are not worth producing by some other criterion such as profitability or social net benefit. If postal service to the Scottish Highlands is one of the activities of the public firm, it is immaterial whether this activity is profitable. What we want to know is whether a private firm can do this more cheaply than a public firm. Similarly the cost studies treat the prices paid for inputs as the appropriate input cost rather than any shadow cost figure. If the ruling wage rate overstates the true cost of labour in some particular locale with high unemployment, where true cost is defined by some externally given social accounting method, this would be ignored unless both private and public firms in question had been explicitly subsidised to the precise amount. This clearly involves an assumption that an efficient management is one which treats the cost of an activity as the cash cost to the firm.

- Both the quantitative and qualitative dimensions of output have to be carefully defined. Thus Californian private electric utilities have conceded that their costs are higher than publicly owned electric companies but argue that their territories are more difficult to serve (Neuberg, 1977, p. 310, footnote). Even so, the coexistence in the USA of large numbers of public and private firms in the same industry in the same state clearly makes comparisons rather easier than a comparison of CEGB with private electric companies in other countries. The procedure in the cost studies has been to estimate, across the sample of firms, the way in which costs vary with topography, volume of sales, number of consumers, quality dimensions, etc., and then to estimate whether, allowing for the general movement of costs with these variables, it is still the case that observed unit costs in private firms differ significantly from public firms (for example measured by a shift in the cost function).

- The implications of the above two points for input prices need perhaps explicit mention. Since firms can face different fuel prices, wage rates, interest rates for reasons other than their being public or private, then input prices, when the data are available, are treated as additional variables in the cost function, separate from the mode of ownership. This approach is particularly useful when for example a public firm (like CEGB) is not allowed full choice in its source of fuel. On the other hand public firms might be paying higher prices for inputs precisely because they are public and some of the differential *may* be due to the absence of pressure on management to bargain. There is some evidence that in this country, allowing for normal cyclical movements, in the early 1970s wage inflation in public industry rose significantly above that in manufacturing for the first time in the post-war period and that this also manifested itself in wage levels (Dean, 1975 and 1977). The particular reason for this movement has not yet been pinned down. Similarly, new evidence in Canada has pointed to significantly higher wage and salary levels in the public sector, after allowing for differences in grades, qualifications, sex, race etc.[1] Any tendency for public firms to employ, at high input prices, a larger volume of inputs than is typical in that industry will be reflected in the cost function estimates for public firms, but whether this is due to weak management as opposed to say government policy will not be reflected. Finally, there is the thorny question of capital costs. Where data have been available, annual capital costs have often been approximated as depreciation

---

[1] See Gunderson (1979) but note also Hammermesh (1975).

of the firm's capital stock plus a cost of capital times that depreciation. It is sometimes suggested that public firms have a lower cost of capital than the private sector and that the appropriate figure to use is the rate of profit earned in the private sector. Since, however, realised rates of profit in the public sector have been, at least in this country, affected by government policy, then the use of higher figures would overstate the cost of capital to the *enterprise*. If, again therefore, an efficient management is one which treats the cost of an activity as the cash cost to the firm, then, in cost studies purporting to reflect differences in managerial efficiency, the cost of capital should be treated like topography, etc.—that is, exogenous to management. A remaining difficulty is that current differences between firms in cost of capital may not be the same as the differences in force in the past. Since in most of the cost studies the data relate to a cross-section of firms for one year, any differences in unit costs may be reflecting in part differences in the cost of capital in earlier years.

III. The cost of electric power in the USA

Adding the normal problems of data availability to the above requirements reinforces the difficulties of making efficiency comparisons between the UK public corporations, with virtually national monopolies of their products, and 'similar' private firms. Whilst the US electric utility industry has been described 'as close to perfection in public–private comparability as any other imagineable real world case',[2] it does contain problems arising from the size distribution of firms. Most of the research studies in this industry discussed in this paper refer to cross-sections of data drawn from within the period 1964–72 and sampled from a basic population which included all but the smallest of firms.[3] Outside the basic population hundreds of municipal generating systems thrive

[2] Yunker (1975, p. 66), also for data on the size distribution of firms. The problems of comparing British public firms with 'similar' private firms in other countries are well discussed in Pryke (1971).

[3] Sales of less than $1 million in 1970 (De Alessi, 1974b, p. 11, footnote). Note that the remaining basic population includes firms involved in gas as well as electricity and Meyer (1975) excludes such multi-purpose firms from his sample.

on the low cost of capital afforded by preferential treatment with respect to corporate and bondholder liability for income taxes. The possible resource misallocation arising from this has been pointed out by Wallace and Junk (1970), but there is no question here necessarily of managerial inefficiency. Indeed in so far as there are public firms in the basic population with similar characteristics and in so far as the estimate of their cost capital includes before-tax interest payments, the size of their capacity will look large relative to firms with the same apparent cost of capital; the results may to this extent be biased against management in public firms. A rather more difficult issue is that some municipals continue generating rather than buying in power simply because of the bitter rivalry between municipals and private wholesaling producers. In so far as management is not the driving force behind this rivalry the cost differences again cannot be attributed to them.

In this period there were sixty-seven federal projects, involving largely hydro-electricity, producing 12 per cent of the nation's power, wholesaling about half of this to other utilities. Of the 536 municipal firms in the basic population, slightly more than half were not involved in generation, 40 per cent generated less than 0.5 million megawatt-hours per firm per annum, 6 per cent generated between 0.5 and 4 million leaving six firms generating between 4 to 30 million. Municipal firms generated only 5 per cent of the nation's electricity though they purchased a similar amount for resale. The 210 private firms in the basic population produced 77 per cent of the nation's power and their distribution amongst the above size categories was 13 per cent, 20 per cent, and 36 per cent with the remaining 3 per cent generating 30 to 50 million megawatt-hours.

Yunker (1975) examined the allegation that public firms were inefficient by estimating costs as a function of output and the number of customers for 1969. Concerned at the different size distributions in the public and private industries, he restricted attention to private and municipal firms producing 0.5 to 4 million megawatt-hours per annum and further restricted to firms with at least a thousand customers since some firms sell to only a very small number of business or government users. Looking at the remaining twenty-four public and forty-nine private firms his equation suggested costs were lower in public firms but the results were not statistically significant. He concluded therefore that there was no evidence that private firm costs were lower than public firm costs. Yunker had not however controlled for input prices nor for the differing proportions of generation/transmission/distribution in each firm. Meyer (1975) also lacked data on input prices which he felt might vary regionally. He therefore attempted a partial offset by grouping the basic population geographically, excluded firms which were not engaged in all three functions and then random sampled thirty public and thirty private; a review of size of firms by volume of generation indicated that the composition of the public and private samples were quite similar. He found that from observations for each of the three years 1967, 1968, 1969 the cost structures of the two types of firm were significantly different in all the different functions. Generating costs per megawatt-hour declined with the number of megawatt-hours and were generally lower for public firms. Total transmission costs were primarily determined by the number of customers with the results pointing to lower costs for public firms. The percentage of sales to resale customers was not found to affect either transmission or distribution costs. Neither were distribution costs per megawatt-hour affected by the split of sales between residential and non-residential but they were affected in a complex way by both output and the number of customers, but Meyer did not identify the pattern of the difference between public and private. In each of the above estimates he excluded maintenance costs which were found, separately, to be primarily determined by plant size, and maintenance costs per megawatt of capacity[4] were significantly lower in public firms. Similar separate estimates of (a) sales and account expenses and (b) general and administration expenses again pointed to lower costs in public firms.

The work of Yunker and Meyer was important in being the first[5] attempt to assess relative cost efficiency in electricity,

[4] He was forced to use net investment in plant as a proxy for capacity.

[5] Note that Moore's (1970) main purpose was that of examining the effects of regulation but he did find that there was no significant difference between private

but the estimates related simply to *operating costs* embracing therefore only labour, fuel, and raw materials. Data deficiencies were the main problem but it does mean that, in addition to the problem of input prices, the results have significance only if the similar size composition of firms in the two samples controls precisely for differences in capacity and technology, that is for capital costs, and if Meyer's public sample included the federal projects. Neuberg (1977) overcame some of these problems in his detailed study of distribution where he also argued that some of the complex features of customer characteristics and location could be picked up by allowing for miles of overhead distribution line (S_2) and the square mileage of the territory (S_3). From the basic population of firms he excluded the federal projects and some twenty-five private firms not involved in distribution and then conducted a questionnaire survey of the remaining private firms and a sample of the municipal firms, finishing up with data from ninety private firms and seventy-five municipal firms for the year 1972. Costs embraced distribution proper, sales, customer accounts and a proportion of general and administrative expenses. The main result for costs per ultimate customer was, in log form and rounding out some of the figures:

$$\log C_n = 6.1 - 0.40 \log \gamma + 0.01 \, (\log \gamma)^2 + 0.25 \log \frac{S_1}{\gamma} - 0.09 \, D$$
$$+ \, 0.92 \log \frac{S_2}{\gamma} + 0.97 \log \frac{S_3}{\gamma} + 0.30 \, P_L$$

where γ is the number of ultimate customers, S_1 is megawatt-hours of electricity, P_L is the wage rate, and D takes a value of 1 for public and 0 for private. The F and t tests were significant at the 1 per cent level or better except for the coefficients on S_3 and the dummy variable.[6] Other models explored showed that when the last three variables are omitted and operating costs only considered (cf. Meyer) the dummy coefficient is significant at the 1 per cent level with the shift factor on costs per customer such that public firms are

and public firms in excess capacity (ratio of peak demand to total capacity), labour per plant, and the cost of building plant, all of which are indirect indications that cost efficiency is not less in public firms.

[6] Both Neuberg and Meyer found the cost equations for the two samples were significantly different using Chow tests.

roughly 23 per cent cheaper. This figure falls to 15 per cent when capital costs are included. When S_2, S_3, and P_L are re-introduced the figure is 9 per cent as shown above and this is significant at the 9 per cent level. Wage rate levels in public firms may therefore be different from those in private firms. On the other hand Neuberg's use of a common interest rate across all firms in his calculation of capital costs may work the other way if the public firms' actual cost of capital is— rightly or wrongly—lower than the private firms'. Pescatrice and Trapani (1980) restricted themselves to generation data for the years 1965 and 1970. They were able to estimate a cost of capital[7] for each firm and in addition explored differences in generating technology. For the latter they argued that for two firms whose capacity was similar in age and broad technical method, the extent to which one firm had introduced newer vintages would be reflected in unit costs. From the basic population they therefore excluded firms for whom adequate data were not available and who were not generating exclusively by coal, gas or oil. For each of the re-maining thirty-three private firms and twenty-three municipal firms, they calculated a weighted average age of equipment (L). The basic approach allowed some flexibility in the form of the coefficients on output and on input prices. Since number of customers is not important in generation the rounded results, for 1965, may be shown in the form of (the log of) costs per million megawatt-hours:

$$\log C_P = 1.43 - 0.01 \log Q + 0.014 (\log Q)^2 - \frac{1}{L} [0.01$$
$$+ 0.002 \log P_L + 0.001 \log P_K - 0.0003 \log P_F]$$
$$+ 0.25 D + \log P_L (0.05 \log P_L + 0.04 \log P_K$$
$$- 0.16 \log P_F - 0.02 \log Q) + \log P_K (0.07 \log P_K$$
$$- 0.20 \log P_F - 0.01 \log Q)$$
$$- \log P_F (0.03 \log Q - 0.18 \log P_F)$$

where Q is million megawatt-hours, L is the index of age of equipment, P_L is the wage rate, P_K the cost of capital, P_F the price of fuel, and D takes a value of 1 for private firms and 0 for public firms. The U shape of the unit cost curve was

[7] The sum for each firm of interest and dividend payments divided by the sum of nominal debt and equity capital. Real capital employed was measured as the undepreciated value of the plant in 1958 dollars.

found to be significant as it was in Neuberg's estimates of distribution cost per customer. The shift factor indicates that costs are roughly 25 per cent lower[8] in public firms with a *t*-statistic of 1.86; for 1970 the results were 43 per cent (2.32). A potential source of this difference is the contents of the square brackets which is a measure of technical progress, comprising a neutral[9] technical change of 0.01 and price-induced changes which in the periods covered led to higher fuel use. Measured at the mean prices in each sub-sample, the rate of technical progress in public firms was shown to be considerably higher than that in private firms.

In summary then, and subject to the general problems of cross-section cost functions, the evidence is pointing to costs being lower, rather than higher, in public firms. Finally that part of De Alessi's study (1977) which related to the level of prices paid for wholesale electricity by distributing firms who bought in some of their supplies has some bearing on the concern expressed earlier that standardising for input prices may obscure managerial inefficiency which manifests itself in bargaining. His data base was the selling price in 1969 of non-federal wholesaling firms (145 private and sixty-four municipal) not financially associated with the buyers. De Alessi's hypothesis was that municipal buyers have less incentive to bargain and more incentive to conclude convenient agreements. Estimating the selling price as a function of the size and ownership mode of the selling firm, regional variables to pick up demand effects and input price variations, the number of customers, and whether the buying firm had multiple sources and whether it was public or private, he found however that the prices paid by public firms were not *ceteris paribus* significantly higher than those paid by private firms.

IV. Overmanning in water utilities

Crain and Zardkoohi initially (1978) examined data available from the American Water Works Association, on 1970 cost

---

[8] At the sample means private costs exceeded public costs by 23.5 per cent in 1965 and 32.9 per cent in 1970.

[9] The coefficient was not significant.

figures embracing operation, maintenance, administration, and depreciation.[10] There were twenty-four private utilities left after those with inadequate data were excluded. Similar considerations restricted the public sample but the final number was limited to eighty-eight firms because of difficulties of getting comparable data on cost of capital, and in addition any public firm larger than the largest firm in the private sample was excluded. All coefficients were significant on t and F tests at 5 per cent or better. On the pooled sample the shift factor on costs per million gallons of water (Y) per annum (C) was such that private firms had 25 per cent lower costs than public firms. The cost structures of the two separate samples were found to be significantly different and may be presented as follows:

Public $\log C = 0.93 - 0.24 \log Y + 0.67 \log P_L + 0.33 \log P_K$

Private $\log C = -1.97 - 0.14 \log Y + 0.84 \log P_L + 0.16 \log P_K$

Thus returns to scale are such that a doubling of output reduces unit costs by 14 per cent in private firms but 24 per cent in public firms. However, the output ranges in the sample of firms are never such that the absolute level of unit costs in public firms falls below that in private firms. Doubts about these results arise from the exclusion of the large public firms from the sample; if some of the smaller public firms have embryonic features of the large ones, results may be biased against public firms.

Setting this aside, what is the source of the unit cost differences in the above? Since a Cobb–Douglas production function was used, it can be shown[11] that these results imply that the elasticity of labour (capital) with respect to output is higher (lower) in public firms than private firms. Thus a given

[10] The meaning of the depreciation figure and the size and structure of the basic population are not discussed in the article.

[11] If a_1 and a_2 are the coefficients on capital and labour respectively in a Cobb–Douglas production function then the coefficient on the log of output with respect to the log of unit costs will be $\dfrac{1}{a_1 + a_2} - 1$, the coefficient on P_L will be $\dfrac{a_2}{a_1 + a_2}$ and the coefficient on P_K is $\dfrac{a_1}{a_1 + a_2}$. Hence $\dfrac{1}{a_1 + a_2} = 0.76$ for public and 0.86 for private.

The elasticity of output with respect to labour is $a_2 = 0.88$ public and 0.97 private.

increase in output entails a proportionately larger (smaller) increase in labour (capital) in public firms. In a further exercise restricted to seventy-eight of the above firms who could supply data on the value of capital stock, Crain and Zardkoohi (1980) estimated an equation for the capital/labour ratio for the pooled sample as follows:

$$\frac{K}{L} = 149.5 - 126.5D - \frac{P_L}{P_K}(59.3 - 6.7D) + Y(0.016 - 0.016D)$$

where D is equal to 1 in public firms and 0 in private firms and where only the coefficients on Y were significant and the one on DY was significant only at the 12 per cent level. That element in the capital/labour ratio which is independent of output is small and does not differ significantly as between public and private firms. Crain and Zardkoohi concluded that[12] there is some suggestion that the capital/labour ratio responded more to output increases in private firms and whilst the private firms may be over-capitalised, the public firms are overmanned and the latter factor is the source of the relative cost inefficiencies.

Some further doubts about this result will be discussed in Section VII, 'Competition and Regulation'.

V. Refuse collection in Canada, Switzerland, and the USA

Government ownership or regulation in electricity and water can sometimes be seen as a method of exploiting economies of scale and of contiguity without monopoly profits. Refuse collection has similar features, probably of a smaller magnitude, but in addition there is the concern to impose minimum despatching speeds for garbage to avoid public health danger, though the enforcement of minimum levels is by no means universal. The cost components would normally cover fuel, maintenance, labour, and capital costs; the incidence of billing and disposal costs would vary with the institutional arrangement whilst the inclusion of taxes and licences varies across studies. Public provision is to be found in 37 per cent of US communities in metropolitan areas

---

[12] The authors assert but do not demonstrate that marginal costs and the marginal product of capital (labour) appear to be absolutely lower (higher) in public firms.

(Savas, 1977) and is financed through municipal revenue with income from citizens taking the form usually of a local tax rather than a user charge. One result of this is that cost data have to be sought for services rather more integrated into general municipal costs than electricity and water and with varying accounting practices.

In studying the private sector, the focus is on the user charge levied or the contract price. In the USA at one extreme are areas where collection is completely unregulated firm/household agreements; then there are cities where user charges are regulated and/or hauling licences stipulated. Citizens can self-haul in such cities, as they can even in some cities where area franchises are granted to private firms, thereby allowing some exploitation of economies of contiguity. In the Edwards and Stevens (1978) study of private firm collection prices per household in seventy-seven cities in the USA for 1975 no significant differences were found between these various agreements. The 318 cities initially contacted in a mail and telephone survey were reduced to the final sample on grounds of availability of data and to firms providing only once-a-week kerb-side service. The significant differences arose between the above group of arrangements and a further group which included franchise cities where self-hauling was not permitted and cities where households have no choice in service levels and are serviced by private firms with exclusive area contracts with the municipality paying the contractor. The lower prices found in this latter group were attributed to economies of contiguity and scale. Within this second group the contract cities were cheaper mainly due to the contractor not bearing billing costs; whether the contract was negotiated or determined by competitive bidding had no significant effect on prices.

The degree of detail of private sector arrangements in the Edwards and Stevens study has not often been matched in studies which compared private to public, where the latter, in the majority of cases, has been found to be more expensive. With exclusivities in area coverage associated with public provision, the various dimensions of 'output' become vital. Edwards and Stevens had controlled for frequency and location of service and included in their cost equations variables for household density, temperature, rainfall, average income levels, and wage rates (but not for other input prices), but none of these variables proved significant. Other relevant variables would be the volume and type of garbage and how, if at all, it is separated, topographic variations, seasonal variations, the split between residential/commercial, households per pick-up point, and distance from disposal site.

Thus the one US study which found public provision cheaper lacked much of the relevant information. Of the sixty-three collectors in Montana in the early 1970s,[13] there were twenty-seven from whom Pier, Vernon, and Wicks (1974) obtained data on costs, covering only, however, labour and capital. The only other variation across firms they could control for was number of pick-ups. More localised studies can sometimes implicitly standardise for several variables though obviously at a cost in terms of generality. Savas (1974) reports a comparison for 1968/9 between the New York Department of Sanitation and firms who were carrying similar garbage (putrescible waste and rubbish— Class I firms) and who were privately owned, levying user charges on contracted customers, the details of which were monitored by the Department of Consumer Affairs. The cost data for the public firm excluded taxes, licences, garage space, and profit margin, and an adjustment to reflect these items was made to the private sector quoted maximum charges. The costs per ton came out at $17 for the private sector (of which $10 was labour cost) and $40 for the Sanitation Department. The latter however serves residential users involving less volume per pick-up than the private firms serving commercial users—and this might partly, though certainly not wholly, explain the higher manning per truck and labour costs of $32 per ton. The private sector on the other hand has a more scattered population and despite this is able to get a better truck utilisation.

The problem of differing customer groups is not found in Savas's study (1977) of Minneapolis which, from 1971, for purposes of residential refuse collection, was served by the

---

[13] Pier *et al.* (1974) join Bennett and Johnson (1979) in not stating the date to which their data refer.

Sanitation Division in one area and in another area by a consortium of private firms on the basis of five five-year contracts. The latter spelt out frequencies and related service characteristics so that comparable requirements were made of both groups. Cost per ton for the Sanitation Department (overheads excluded) was some 10 per cent higher in 1971 than the contract income per ton (with monitoring costs not attributed) and costs expressed per household were 15 per cent higher (but see comments in the later part of this paper). A similar superiority of private producers appears in Bennett and Johnson's study (1979) of residential refuse collection in their home county of Fairfax, Virginia, one-third of which is serviced by the Solid Waste Division (SWD); in other areas householders must[14] contract individually with one of a set of twenty-nine competing firms. The average user charge for the twice-weekly service came out at $85 per household per annum with all but two of the firms charging less than $100. Suspicious of cost data from municipal authorities, and knowing that households were charged for refuse collection on a fee basis (a flat amount plus a part related to property value), Bennett and Johnson based their cost estimates on the SWD's assertion that fee income covers their costs (excluding taxes but including disposal charges also levied on the public firms). The cost for households with average property values came out at $126 for a once-weekly collection, the difference with private firms being largely mitigated from the householders' point of view by the charge being allowable against state and federal taxes. What we do not know in this study is the significance of SWD serving the area at greatest distance from the disposal site.

Finally, two studies are of significance for their national coverage. From mail and telephone questionnaires Kitchen (1976) assembled data for forty-eight Canadian municipalities for 1971 on operating costs plus depreciation. He included most of the variables mentioned at the beginning of this section and found that costs were significantly higher in public provision though the varying private sector arrangements were not identified. As in other studies, economies of

---

[14] The authors do not clarify in what sense householders 'must' contract—nor under what regulatory framework, if at all, the private collectors operate.

scale were found to exist once one got to the stage where larger equipment could be used. On the other hand increased population density actually raised costs, probably, Kitchen hypothesised, because of its association with multiple dwelling units and traffic congestion. For his key output variable population had to be used so that tonnages would only be picked up by the variable, persons per family. The cost of capital was not included on either side of the equation, thereby possibly under-estimating the efficiency of those firms with low costs of capital who took full advantage of this in their capacity plans. Furthermore the method of wage payment and the size of vehicle capacity *were* included which, from the point of view of public/private comparisons, are items which one would like to see reflected simply in the cost curve.

Pommerehne and Frey's sample of 103 Swiss cities embraced half the Swiss population. The costs (including all capital costs) of residential refuse collection were calculated for cities in 1970 that did not collect industrial and residential refuse jointly and also could supply, through questionnaires, necessary supplementary data to published sources. Forty-eight of the firms were private and their costs were measured by the user charge or contract fee. A final form chosen for output was weight in thousand tons (A), topography was controlled by a measure of height differences within each city (C), and distance of disposal site from the centre of the city (E) was included. One of their main results for (the log of) costs per ton collected in francs may be presented as follows:

$$\log C_s = 1.03 - 0.82A + 0.31A^2\ 10^{-6} + 0.10B + 0.49C - 0.19D$$
$$+ 0.30E + 0.05F - 0.07G + 0.05H - 0.36I - 0.03J$$
$$+ 0.12K$$

where the coefficients on G and H (seasonality variables for tourist traffic), I (the number of pick-ups per street kilometre), J (the number of households per pick-up point), and K (snowfall variable) were not statistically significant. F took a value of 1 if the service was largely financed by user charges (zero otherwise). The positive coefficient is suggestive of other indications (Hirsch, 1965; Savas, 1976 and 1977; Young, 1974) that user charge arrangements are more costly, including even public provision; the coefficient is not significant in this model but it is when costs are expressed per household. All other coefficients were significant. Unit costs are declining over a wide range; eventually economies disappear, a tendency often associated with the density of cities, a factor revealed in Pommerehne's and Frey's other models of costs per household. B takes a value of 1 when collections are more than twice-weekly (zero otherwise). Finally the coefficient on the dummy ($D = 1$ when private, 0 for government) indicates a shift factor on costs per ton such that private provision is some 20 per cent cheaper. The authors have in this model deducted from the private price an estimated 7 per cent profit margin (overall costs including interest charges). Whilst this can be defended, the more general problem is the lack of data on cost of capital and wage rates across firms. All the signs are however that private costs of refuse collection are lower than municipal costs.

VI. Tariff structures in US electricity

Some of the earliest work on public/private comparisons in the USA related to features of tariff structures but since they predated the cost studies their results can now be viewed in a new light. Peltzman's approach (1971) was that the constellation of outputs and tariffs of public firms reflected political considerations. For a firm serving differing customer groups, he hypothesised there was one tariff structure which maximised profits but lower profit levels were consistent with varying combinations of prices to the different groups. He assumed that managers of public firms were interested in the continued existence of the enterprise and of their jobs, the vehicle for which was political support. *Ceteris paribus*, lower prices would raise votes. Moreover, though the cost of supplying group A might be greater than the cost of serving group B, price differences would not completely reflect this since a lower and lower price for group B might gain less votes than were being lost from group A. Thus Peltzman expected price differences between customer groups to be less than in private firms and also to be less closely related to cost differences.

His sample for 1966 was non-federal firms each serving at least 10,000 customers, excluding private firms serving more than one municipality—though the private firms remaining tended to operate in cities with larger populations. So far as the *level* of tariffs is concerned he found public to be significantly lower and asserted that this difference was due to their preferential tax treatment which was 'a manifestation of an overall political incentive to low rates' (Peltzman, 1971, p. 136). The possibility that public firms had lower costs was never mentioned. Meyer (1975) calculated for 1969 average revenue per kilowatt-hour of residential, small commercial, and 'other', where consumption levels per consumer were similar in private and public firms, and suggested that the lower price found for public firms was consistent with his cost estimates; for the resale group of customers the public price was only one-third of the private but part of this may have been due, given block tariffs, to considerably higher consumption levels for the public firm's customers. (For large commercial see later discussion.) Similarly some of De Alessi's results (1975, cf. above) take on a new light given the cost studies. He had hypothesised that management in public firms would not bargain hard in obtaining selling prices and found that, after standardising for other variables, the shift factor for the ownership dummy was such that public firm prices were some 30 per cent lower. This is however quite consistent with the cost differences revealed in other studies.

There is however rather more convincing evidence that the tariff structure of public firms is less differentiated with respect to customer groups and less reflective of differences in costs as between groups. Peltzman suggested that the cost per kilowatt-hour for a firm supplying a group of consumers with particular cost characteristics would be equal to the system-wide unit costs less amounts that get bigger the larger is the ratio of that group to the total customer population. He then regressed prices on system-wide unit, operating and capital costs and variables to reflect the varying proportions of residential/non-residential and, within each, high consumption/low consumption. For private firms he found that the prices of high consumption residential customers were significantly related to these variables whereas the public firm prices were not; a similar result emerged for non-residential customers. In confirmation of this De Alessi (1975) found that the 1966 selling prices of municipal wholesaling firms were less significantly related to regional variables than were the prices of private firms. Indeed by putting the price of one group as an independent variable in the price equation for the other group, Peltzman found that his residential and non-residential prices were highly and significantly inter-correlated for public firms but not for private firms. Thus costs of particular groups are reflecting themselves in the overall tariff structure rather than the price of particular groups. Suggestive evidence on the same lines can be found in Peltzman's other work[15] on liquor prices in state-owned and private stores.

Independently of cost differences, one might expect that, since electricity is non-storable and consumers can change monopoly area suppliers only inconveniently by shifting residence, firms will operate price discrimination. On the grounds that private firms are more geared to maximising their owners' wealth and less geared to the ballot box than public firms, more price discrimination might be expected in private firms.[16] Peltzman hypothesised that, given the same average price and standardising for differences in the number of customers and their income levels and any regional effects, a more enthusiastic execution of price discrimination would raise the volume of kilowatt-hour sales per customer. The results indicated significantly higher volumes for private firms. He also found that private utilities tended to have a larger number of rate schedules but this result was not standardised for other variables. De Alessi's careful examination (1977) of rate schedules in 1970 involved allowing for regional differences in income and state regulation, for differences in city sizes, for the residential/non-residential mix, and for different sources of power, by the selection of matching pairs of municipal and private firms. He finished up with twenty pairs and found that public firms had significantly lower numbers of peak schedules and of total schedules.

In summary, private utility tariff structures seem to be more profit-orientated than those in public firms. There is

[15] Towards the end of the 1971 article.

[16] Mann and Siefried (1972) paradoxically treated evidence of public electric utility prices being affected by income levels, after standardising for costs and other variables, as indicative of inefficient non-profit tariff structures.

however a problem in attributing this exclusively to political factors. Since the attenuation of property rights in public firms could lead to scope for more managerial discretion, then the results are consistent with the ease of managing simple tariff structures (De Alessi, 1974b). Alternatively, thinking of the British context, the fares and tariff structures of the UK nationalised industries were, historically, deeply influenced by the nationalisation Acts which were consistently interpreted to require uniform fares and tariffs across different geographical areas and customer groups, to a large extent independently of cost characteristics. Whilst the short-run manipulation of these prices for electoral purposes does occur, the attribution of their long-run structure to similar electoral issues is to obscure their use as tools of wider economic and social policies—whatever views we, as economists, have about such policies. Some rather more discriminating tests of the electoral versus management inefficiency versus social welfare maximising models are required (cf. Millward, 1978).

VII. Competition and regulation

The performance of public firms may of course be affected by whether or not they face competition. The performance of private firms may be affected by the degree to which their prices and profit rates are regulated. Considering regulation first, this carries the implication that cost differences between public and private may be reflecting inefficiencies in private firms occasioned by regulation as much as any inefficiencies in public firms arising from the mode of ownership. Whether one would expect regulation of private firms to be active; whether, if active, it would be effective is still a matter of some dispute. Attention here is restricted to those few studies which have linked the question of regulation to private/public comparisons. De Alessi (1974, 1977) has argued that regulation of monopoly rents is likely to be active because regulators are under pressure from vested interests (buyers, consumers, potential entrants). In so far also as regulated firms can minimise interference by moderating prices and profit rates, then some of this intervention may be effective. He, however, expects it to be weak because regulated firms are well placed to collude and have an incentive to influence regulators, who in any case have little vested economic interest of their own in acquiring the full information needed for effect—the latter point being particularly apposite for regulation by independent commissioners each of whose job-related sources of income are usually equal.

To the extent that regulation prescribes a permitted average rate of return above the cost of capital and to the extent that this constraint bites in being lower than the unconstrained average rate profit, the Averch–Johnson (1962) effect involves an extension of the rate base. Starting from an unconstrained profit-maximising output and capital stock per man, the imposition of a prescribed lower rate of return will reduce actual profits and the latter can therefore be increased by raising the capital/labour ratio (overcapitalisation). It has already been recorded (cf. above) that in the Crain and Zardkoohi study, the capital/labour ratio in private water utilities was not significantly related to the relative prices of capital and labour. This, and its responsiveness to output increases, is suggestive of overcapitalisation. Since, however, overall unit costs were lower in private utilities than public firms they conclude that any inefficiencies due to private firm overcapitalisation are less than the overmanning inefficiencies associated with the mode of ownership. One doubt about these results has already been expressed arising from the exclusion of large public firms from the sample. A further query is that the coefficient for public firms linking changes in the capital/labour ratio to changes in output is precisely zero—which certainly calls for, but does not get, any explanation.

In Pescatrice's and Trapani's study (cf. above) of electricity generation, fuel, as well as capital and labour, was treated as an explicit input and some rather more complicated tests of regulation were required. The focus was that of the response of demand for inputs to changes in the prices of inputs. The standard response for a cost-minimiser can be translated into a response measured in terms of an input's share of total cost. In particular the data enabled own and cross-price elasticities of demand for inputs to be calculated and the signs of these are the crucial guide. In a standard cost-minimising framework a rise in the price of a factor leads to reduced usage. Since, for public firms in the sample, the relevant elasticities were found to be negative in both 1965 and 1970 then in a comparative static sense the evidence is consistent with their being cost-minimisers. On *a priori* grounds with three inputs, the signs of the cross-elasticities are not predictable so the finding that they were generally positive neither adds nor detracts from the result.

Similar signs emerged for the private utilities but this does not rule out the importance of regulation. Pescatrice and Trapani demonstrate that a firm for which the regulatory constraint (λ) is binding will so choose its inputs that their marginal rate of substitution is equal not to the normal input price ratio but to a ratio which replaces the cost of capital (P_K) by a lower shadow cost (P_K'). The regulated firm behaves as if it were minimising the cost of some given output using as the shadow cost of capital:

$$P_K' = P_K - \frac{1}{1-\lambda}(S - P_K)$$

measured as an average of actual rates earned by a firm during the current and previous two years and λ was allowed to take certain illustrative values between 0 and 1. A rise in P_K' would of course be expected to lead to reduced usage of capital and this is borne out in the results.[17] A rise in the price of labour will initially cut the profit margin and thereby reduce the firm's rate of profit below the permitted level. The firm would in such circumstances be permitted to raise prices and a restoration of the rate of return necessitates a contraction of capital as well. The impact on the usage of labour (contrast the standard case) and fuel is not known. Thus the prediction is that the cross-elasticity between capital usage and the price of labour will be negative. The results however for both 1965 and 1970 were a positive elasticity. A rise in the price of fuel would also be expected to lead to reduced usage

[17] A rise in P_K, as opposed to P_K', will have no effect for the regulated firm as long as P_K is less than S since the gross profit margin is unaffected. For other discussion of the regulated firm see Averch and Johnson (1962), Courville (1974), and Spann (1974).

of capital; for 1970 the elasticity was positive but for 1965 it *was* negative. Finally we should note that their general findings were not particularly sensitive to variations in the value of λ.

In summary, the evidence that some of the cost differences between public and private firms may be due to the effects of regulation on private firms is lacking substantial support at present. Another 'market structure' effect may however eventually prove more decisive. The cost efficiency of firms might be greater if they are facing competition. One would expect this for private firms; for public firms the *a priori* effect has not been explored in the literature in any depth. Where government has built comparative yardsticks into the supervisory process or where government is sensitive for other reasons to cost-inflated prices then again one might expect some difference in performance when competition is present. Meyer's analysis (cf. above) of the degree to which lower public firm costs were reflected in lower prices stumbled over the problem that for large commercial users private and public average revenue per kilowatt-hour was the same. Since sales per large commercial customer by private firms were double those of public firms, the block elements in tariff structures could thereby be offsetting the lower unit costs. The average revenue was however noticeably lower than any other customer group (except resale) and Meyer felt that the large commercial customer's ability to set up his own generating capacity was a sizeable threat. Rather more pointedly Savas's report on refuse collection in Minneapolis, as we have already seen, showed the private firms with lower costs in the first year of a scheme of segregated areas—which had replaced a scheme where public and private dealt in different kinds of refuse. From 1971 the two sectors were performing similar functions and the City Sanitation Division's cost inefficiency, relative to the private sector, quickly diminished such that by 1975 costs per ton were only 1 per cent higher and costs per household were actually 1 per cent less. The city cost per ton had risen in constant 1967 dollars from 25 in 1966 to 32 in 1969 and then fell to 23 by 1975.

Finally there are Primeaux's more detailed findings which drew on 1964–8 data concerning municipal firms only. Addressed in part to the question of whether the conferment of area monopoly status on electricity suppliers (whether public or private) was necessary, he used an apparently not well known fact that there were a number of cities (forty-nine in 1966 with a population exceeding 25,000) where competition between utilities existed—mainly municipal versus private. In some cases customers cannot switch after committing themselves to one firm; in others a switch at any time is possible. For each of the municipal firms so positioned he selected one other municipal in the same state, of the same size and with the same power source and excluded from the non-competitive group any firm which did not adequately match the competitive municipal firm for whom it was the nearest approximation. He then (1977) regressed costs (excluding taxes) per thousand kilowatt-hours on sales, capacity, fuel costs, consumption per consumer by customer group, cost of purchased power, market density, a variable for firms using internal combustion, and several regional dummies. From the use of a further dummy he concluded that competition significantly changed the unit cost curve from being downward sloping to being upward sloping. In a further study (1978) he excluded firms which did not generate electricity and estimated an equation for capacity utilisation (actual annual kilowatt-hours divided by maximum possible). The competition dummy did increase excess capacity but not by a statistically significant amount. Moreover, and more importantly, the 1977 study had shown that the whole unit cost curve though changing its slope was shifted downwards, by competition, by a factor of roughly 10 per cent.

There would seem to be some scope in the transport area for examining the performance of public firms relative to private firms and relative to the market structure. To date however there are no studies of which I am aware controlling for both the mode of ownership and the type of market structure. The public firms within the sample of fifty-eight US urban bus transit systems examined by Pashigian (1976) had monopolies of their particular service. After controlling for total vehicle mileage travelled, he found that profit margins were less in publicly owned systems, a pattern consistent with the hypothesis that in such areas the systems are unattractive to unsubsidised private firms because they would be intolerably regulated, especially where marginal costs lay below average costs. As with most profit data, little can be deduced about managerial efficiency in publicly owned transit systems though Pashigian has some interesting points to make about the impact on routes, fares, and profits of voters who are non-users. Whilst the study by Caves and Christensen (1978) of the experience of Canadian railways in the period 1956–75 does not allow an examination of performance with and without competition, the finding that the publicly-owned Canadian National did not have higher unit costs than Canadian Pacific is supportive, now in a competitive context, of the broad pattern from electricity. The regulatory framework applies to both railroads and had become increasingly restricted to the transport of prairie grain and flour. The authors compared total factor productivity in the two firms for each year and since the two output categories of passenger and freight were weighted by cost elasticities and the different inputs were weighted by cost shares—revenue shares would have partly reflected the regulated fare structure—the comparison is, in principle, similar to a unit cost study. Canadian National factor productivity was some 10–15 per cent lower than Canadian Pacific in the period 1956–64. Canadian Pacific was experiencing however a substantial decline in passenger volumes. During the next two years CN productivity caught up and in the period 1967–75 its factor productivity was higher, the size of the superiority being bigger the more one allowed for differences in the composition of freight ton-miles.

VIII. Conclusions

Many studies have to rely on cross-sections of firms for only one year, coverage of areas is patchy and in general the subject is in an embryonic state. One of the problems of using *ex post* data is that it tells us nothing about the way problems have to be faced *ex ante* with all its uncertainties. The *perception* of costs and revenue could be different in the two modes and this itself might be obscuring anything that can be deduced about managerial efficiency. Subject to these provisos the following conclusions seem warranted.

- If managerial efficiency is higher in private firms, one would expect there was a good chance of this being revealed in unit cost studies. This paper has analysed the results emerging for firms in North America involved in 'semi-commercial' operations but finds, overall, no broad support for private enterprise superiority. In US electricity the evidence seems to suggest that unit costs are lower in public firms whether or not one controls for differences across firms in wage rates, cost of capital and area covered. The possibility that this difference is attributable to the effects of regulation of private utilities lacks substantial support. The Canadian railroad work found no significant differences in total factor productivity between public and private. A study of US water utilities found costs were lower in private firms after allowing for differences in input prices but the larger public projects were not embraced in the sample. In summary there seems no general ground for believing managerial efficiency is less in public firms.
- The setting, by government, either explicitly or implicitly, of goals other than cost-minimisation would mean that costs could well be higher in public firms in such areas and whilst such a public/private comparison has not yet to my knowledge been documented it would be surprising if costs were not found to be lower in private firms—for example in the British steel industry. To isolate the role of managerial efficiency in such a context would not be an easy task. Moreover, government policy may or may not be misguided and *public enterprise* thereby inefficient by some different criterion of efficiency.
- Similarly, low profitability is not inconsistent with an efficient management. The price controls on nationalised industries in the last decade are only one manifestation of 'interventionist' UK government policies. But public enterprise might be inefficient for those who wish to judge efficiency in terms of profitability. Indeed the studies of tariff-setting in US electricity strongly suggest that such tariffs, in their discrimination between customer and cost

groups, are more profit-orientated in the private sector than the public sector. Urban bus transit systems in the USA seem to be put in public ownership and run at lower profit margins in cities where income levels and car ownership are lower than average. These results may be telling us something about vote-getting in the USA or about public enterprises as a tool of other policies. It is not yet clear that they are reflecting an inefficient management.

- Many of the public firms in the cost samples are municipal rather than nationalised. It is not impossible that this puts more pressure on public enterprise managers. However, refuse collection is also local and the evidence suggests that, subject to the absence of data on input prices, whilst public provision is less costly than an unfettered private user-charge system, private contract arrangements are even cheaper. It is not impossible that where public provision includes selling at a price, as in electricity, the associated financial controls are more effective in holding down costs than in areas financed from general tax revenue, but such a proposition needs further investigation.
- Similarly the comparable cost performance of the Canadian publicly owned railway *vis-à-vis* its privately owned rival, and the evidence that unit electricity costs are lower in US municipal firms facing competition than in those municipal firms which are not, is suggestive of the importance of market structure but the interrelationship between mode of ownership and market structure is not yet clear.

Part III

DEREGULATION AND EFFICIENCY

7

EXPRESS COACHING SINCE 1980: LIBERALISATION IN PRACTICE*

Evan Davis

I. Introduction

The rhetoric of privatisation proclaims the virtues of competitive forces. In practice, however, the major policy initiatives in this area have tended to focus on transferring the ownership of publicly owned enterprises to the private sector, rather than on the logically distinct problem of subjecting them to fiercer and more extensive competition. Asset sales have been presented as the prelude to genuine liberalisation. But there is one area in which an entirely different sequence of events has occurred: that of express coaching. In 1980 a substantive measure of deregulation was introduced into the industry, the intention being to expose both the dominant publicly owned incumbent, National Express, and British Rail to thoroughgoing competition from independent coach operators; no transfer of ownership has taken place, and privatisation of this sort is only now coming on to the policy agenda. The purpose of this paper is to evaluate the policy that has been adopted towards express coaching in recent years. This case is of importance not only in its own right, but also for the lessons it suggests in the broader context of the developing policy towards privatisation and competition.

* This article was first published in *Fiscal Studies*, 1984, 5, 1.

At the time of writing this article, Evan Davis was at St John's College, Oxford; he is now a Research Officer at the Institute for Fiscal Studies.

The author is grateful to Michael Keen for helpful comments and advice in the writing of this article. The work reported here is part of the Institute for Fiscal Studies's project on Regulation in the UK, financially supported by the Economic and Social Research Council.

II. Deregulation: The 1980 Act

In the half-century following the 1930 Road Traffic Act, public passenger road transport in the UK was subject to strict regulation. Before the 1980 Transport Act, tight restrictions were placed on both the introduction of any bus or coach service and the conditions under which it was subsequently operated. At the heart of the regulatory structure were (and are) the Traffic Commissioners, regional transport officers appointed as guardians of the public interest. Any operator wishing to establish any service was required to obtain a licence from the relevant Commissioners, who were required to grant one only if positively persuaded that the proposed service was in the public interest. The Commissioners exercised similar powers in respect of fares, frequency, time of service, and so on. Change required lengthy and bureaucratic procedures, often involving not only the applying operator but also defensive competitors, British Rail and local authorities; and with the presumption of public interest against those seeking to introduce change, innovation can only have been further discouraged.

The 1980 Transport Act marks a sharp reversal of policy in this area. Much of the regulatory apparatus has been dismantled. The Act has reduced the Commissioners' powers to control fares. It has established a presumption in favour of new services. But the most important provisions of the Act are those relating to express coach services (which it defines as those on which all passengers travel at least thirty miles). All restrictions on express services have been removed, other than those relating to competence and safety: any firm possessing an operators' licence can offer any express service, the only additional requirement being that the Commissioners be informed of new or altered services.

At the time of the 1980 Act express coaching was dominated by the publicly owned operators: National Express (a marketing subdivision of the National Bus Company, NBC) and its Scottish counterpart, the Scottish Bus Group. Few routes were served by more than one operator, and there was no major network of services run by independent firms.

III. Express coaching since 1980

It was generally anticipated that deregulation would have powerful effects on both the performance and the structure of the express coaching industry: performance was expected to conform to some competitive outcome, which in turn was believed to meet some criterion of social desirability (a point to which I shall return briefly below), and the dominance of National Express—the central feature of the pre-existing structure—was expected to dissolve. Expectations have been borne out much more fully in respect of performance than they have in respect of structure.

The performance of the express coaching industry has, without any doubt, changed dramatically since the 1980 Act. The most spectacular developments have been in the areas of output and fares. Whilst it is difficult to quantify these developments with any precision, the orders of magnitude involved are clearly substantial. Since the period prior to deregulation, the total number of passengers carried seems to have increased by at least 60 per cent.[1] This is in stark contrast to a decline in traffic carried by National Express during the latter half of the 1970s. Growth on a number of individual trunk routes has been especially dramatic: White (1983) estimates, for instance, that traffic on the London–Manchester and London–Birmingham routes increased by 200 per cent in the three months immediately after deregulation. The general level of fares has fallen substantially since 1980: in some cases they are still lower even in nominal terms than they were in 1980. This largely reflects the particularly marked price reductions made between 1980 and 1981; since then, the impression is one of constant or gently rising prices.

The period since deregulation has also seen substantial changes in the quality and range of express services available. Frequency of service has typically risen on inter-city routes

[1] The annual reports of the NBC put passenger journeys on National Express at 9.2 million in 1980 and 14 million in 1982. The first of these figures includes traffic carried in the first three months after deregulation, and may be taken as an upper limit. White (1983) estimates carryings by private operators at 1 to 2 million per annum; allowing 0.5 million such journeys prior to 1980 and 1.5 million since, these figures suggest that 60 per cent is a rather cautious estimate of the expansion of output.

between the major centres, particularly on those emanating from London. On the other hand many smaller towns have lost express services which previously stopped there. A number of innovative services have been introduced, the most notable examples being the expansion of airport-linked services and the introduction of luxury services (offering videos, refreshments, toilets, hostesses, and the like) of a kind previously unknown in this country.

In contrast, the structure of the industry has not altered fundamentally since 1980: National Express has retained its dominant position essentially unscathed, and has increased its profits in doing so (raising them from £3.1 million to £5.4 million between 1980 and 1982). With a few exceptions, the competitive initiatives of independent operators have led either to ultimate failure or to joint ventures with National. The major failure has been that of British Coachways (BC), a consortium of leading independent operators. From the day of enactment of the 1980 Act, BC offered a fairly comprehensive network of inter-city services run in direct competition with National; aiming itself at the lower end of the market, BC in many cases set its fares at about half the pre-existing level. Survey evidence reported by White (1983) indicates that in the comparatively heady days of 1981 the independent operators—primarily the members of BC—carried more than 10 per cent of the express traffic from London. But BC was soon in trouble, a principal founding member withdrawing as early as mid-1981 (apparently as a result of management disputes); the enterprise finally disintegrated in January 1983. There has been no other attempt to challenge National's dominance on such a wholesale basis.

Nor has there been any piecemeal erosion of National's hold over the bulk of express business. Rather, the few successful private initiatives have involved the identification of a particular niche in the market that National had failed to fill: independent operators pioneered luxury services, and have expanded both airport-linked and commuter operations. In all these areas, however, National has been recovering in position, both by direct competition and (particularly in the provision of up-market 'Rapide' services) by entering into joint ventures with independent operators.[2] As a result, the independents' share of the total market has slipped back from the level attained in 1981. Only on Anglo-Scottish routes, where their share is around 30 per cent, have entirely independent operations continued to make a particularly noticeable dent in the position of the publicly owned operators.

IV. The continued dominance of National Express

The mere fact that National Express has been able to maintain its dominant market share substantially intact since de-regulation does not of itself imply that public policy towards express coaching has failed to generate a satisfactory out-come. It could be that National, by virtue of the extent and scope of the activities that it had established under the pre-existing regulatory regime, has been able to provide services at a lower cost than could any collection of more specialised operators; by exposing each of National's operations to the possibility of competition from a fringe of operators ready and able to switch resources in response to apparent profit prospects, deregulation may have ensured that the inherent advantages of single-firm production are fully reflected in the market-place, resulting in a socially efficient allocation of resources within the industry. Express coaching may be a natural monopoly, and National may have been able to sur-vive only by turning its inherent advantages to the public interest.[3] The story is superficially a rather plausible one, be-ing consistent with the combination of substantially altered performance and unchanged structure that has characterised express coaching since 1980. In particular, there continues to exist a large number of smaller independent operators whose assets and skills are employed in areas close to those of

[2] For instance, in the early months after deregulation four operators were active in the corridor between London and the south-west, and the three in-dependents—especially those operating luxury services—were able to obtain sub-stantial market shares. National subsequently entered a joint venture with Trathens in the provision of an up-market service, and the other operators have now withdrawn.

[3] On the general issue involved here, see the discussion in Chapter 8 of Baumol, Panzar, and Willig (1982).

National, and who have proved themselves capable of occasional forays to exploit opportunities unrealised by National. But the elements of this argument need to be examined more closely, since there are other and less wholesome possible explanations of National's success.

There is in fact little evidence that the essential technology of express coaching places a large firm producing a range of services at an inherent advantage relative to less extensive operators. The production of express coach services on a small scale is comparatively easy, as the very existence of a periphery of independent operators indicates. Doubtless increases in the scale of operations enable some additional economies to be realised: laws of large numbers, for instance, should enable more efficient utilisation of maintenance and other specialised facilities (just as, in another context, they enable larger firms to carry lower inventory/sales ratios). There may also be cost advantages in providing express services as part of a broad range of bus and coach operations: unlike National, for instance, independent commuter operators have had difficulty finding profitable uses for their coaches during the day-time. But it is difficult to believe that any such cost savings to National Express are substantial. Nor is it likely that National achieves significant cost advantages by exploiting any monopsony power in the purchase of its inputs. National may be able to obtain particularly favourable terms in purchasing coaches, but has restricted itself to a comparatively expensive policy of buying British; the position in respect of the labour market is still more unclear. Overall, National Express may enjoy some cost advantages over its potential competitors; but it is difficult to believe that technical efficiency alone required that express coaching be dominated by any single firm to the extent that it has been by National.

In one important respect, however, the very dominance of the position established by National Express prior to deregulation has placed it in a particularly strong position in the subsequent period. Both the name of National and the nature of its operations would have been well-known to most potential coach travellers; the independents, in contrast, were typically little known outside their home territories, and have found it especially difficult to establish awareness of their presence within the crucial London market. Given an initial familiarity with National and the comparatively small money sums involved, the marginal return to seeking information on alternative services available is likely to have been low for many customers; and the very perception that the general level of fares had fallen may itself have tended to discourage search, exacerbating the difficulties faced by the independents.

This general issue of consumer information is important in two rather different respects. First, it is clear that large-scale operations offer real advantages in terms of consumer awareness. In other transport contexts, for instance, it is repeatedly found that operators offering larger shares of the total capacity on any route enjoy a disproportionately large share of the total custom. Indeed in the absence of effects of this sort it is difficult to see why NBC should choose to use 'National Express' as a generic trade name at all, when it could instead operate services under the names of the local subsidiaries (which provide both coach and driver). Second, many of the costs that operators must incur in order to establish their presence in the market are not costs that can be recovered in the event of a subsequent decision to leave the market; as such, they are particularly liable to deter entrants. To the extent that it is necessary to realise marketing benefits that are of genuine value to consumers, the domination of the market by a single supplier can be socially efficient. So long as entry is free, one would then expect National to be able to realise monopoly profits only to the extent that entry is deterred by precisely the marketing advantages associated with single-firm production. It may indeed be that National's continued dominance reflects the value consumers place on a familiar and unified marketing structure covering the totality of services.

But there have been two other important factors at work. First, National's response to the pricing initiatives of independent operators has been extremely aggressive. It matched the fares offered by BC within a week, and has responded forcefully to localised challenges (dropping fares by 40 per cent for instance to match those offered by Bartons on the

London—Nottingham route). There can be no doubt that National's dominance could not have been maintained without this competitive and flexible policy. Discussion of whether or not National's behaviour has been predatory would take us into deep and murky waters, but two points are clear. First, it may well have been rational for National to incur short-term losses in order to dismiss the opposition that emerged immediately after deregulation, since by doing so it might hope to establish a reputation for ruthlessness serving to discourage subsequent challenges. Second, UK competition policy attempts no clear statement of proscribed practices and so gives National little cause to worry whether or not its behaviour might reasonably be judged predatory; the difficulties of devising satisfactory anti-predation legislation are well-known, but dangers of the sort just described emphasise the potential benefits from measures that at least encourage second thoughts.

There is another and very tangible factor behind National's continued dominance. It enjoys uniquely privileged access to Victoria Coach Station and many of the other major terminals throughout the country, which are owned by NBC. These terminals were widely known amongst the public at the time of deregulation, and commonly occupy prime city sites. There are clear indications that National's effective control of access has exacerbated the difficulties inevitably faced by the independents in establishing their presence in markets historically dominated by National, and placed it in a particularly strong position to meet competitors. Since deregulation, NBC has adopted a firm policy of denying access to its stations to operators attempting to compete with National Express; indeed independent operators using these terminals have been required to leave when subsequently launching services in competition with National (even, in at least one case, when the service did not use the terminal concerned). The consequent difficulties faced by independent carriers have been especially acute in London, at the heart of the national network. Denied access to Victoria, the independent services have been run from a coach park at Gloucester Road (not even fully surfaced) and from hotel car parks in the Kings Cross area; public awareness of these arrangements is extremely limited. National, meanwhile, has been able to exploit to the full the potential advantages offered by the extent and range of its activities: with 24 per cent of passengers arriving at Victoria changing coach there, the restrictions on access have doubtless made it easier for National to preserve for itself the bulk of interchanging traffic. In many of the joint ventures between National and independents it is clear that the essential advantage offered to the independent is precisely access to Victoria.

National's privileged access to the major coach terminals has been a powerful factor preventing a genuine free-for-all in express coaching. It is difficult for the independents to make serious inroads into National's position without a substantial, risky and perhaps socially undesirable investment in the establishment of coach stations capable of attracting custom away from the traditional terminals. This does not reflect any immutable characteristic of the technology, but simply established organisational structures; as such, the problem may be susceptible to further measures of liberalisation.

V. Evaluating deregulation

The purpose in deregulating express coaching was, of course, to generate some benefit to society; and the expectation of such a benefit reflected an underlying belief that free competition is the most appropriate mode of organisation for the industry. These two propositions are logically distinct. The first is an essentially empirical (and political) judgement, to which I shall turn in a moment. Before doing so, however, it should be noted that formal economic theory is not entirely reassuring on the latter point. In city-pair transport markets, for instance, the value placed by consumers on the frequency of services may be such that it is desirable for services to be run even at a loss.[4] Nor is it clear that competition can be

---

[4] Intuitively, the problem is that an increase in frequency conveys an external benefit on travellers by making the overall service more convenient. With economies of scale in capacity provision (per seat, coaches are cheaper than taxis) it may be excessively costly to carry frequency to the point at which, at the margin, this effect

relied on to produce appropriate route structures. Moreover, there is in principle some possibility that stable outcomes may not emerge,[5] raising the spectre of destructive competition of the sort that initially prompted regulatory intervention in the industry.[6] But competitive outcomes, even if less than entirely socially efficient, may be better than those that can be hoped for even from benevolent but imperfectly informed regulation. In particular, competition may offer valuable dynamic advantages in terms of enhanced innovativeness. Thus some fundamental questions remain open; but this does not deny that deregulation may in practice have produced a generally favourable effect.

The performance of the express coach service industry since 1980 has doubtless been affected by factors other than deregulation. But it is difficult to detect genuinely exogenous influences powerful enough to account in any substantial degree for the marked developments described above. Coaching may have benefited from the rail strikes of 1982 and, to the extent that it is perceived as an inferior mode of travel, from the recession. But White (1983) concludes that the strikes gave the industry (at best) only a temporary boost, and the effects of recession are not unambiguous, since much traffic is leisure-motivated and for that reason presumably sensitive to reduced expenditures. Nor are there any signs of substantial movements in the real prices of the inputs used by the industry. It is impossible to know whether in the absence of deregulation National Express might have adopted a more aggressive marketing policy as a result of the marketing analysis project commissioned in the 1970s and applied to express services, in the event, less than three weeks before the enactment of the 1980 Act.

It does seem, though, that exogenous factors cannot account for all the change that has occurred in the performance of the industry. We must thus look to mechanisms in-

vanishes. If fares are set optimally (and so reflect the cost that each passenger imposes on all others by his or her presence in the market) an increase in frequency is therefore always desirable if the additional service does not make a loss. Formal analyses of this issue are given in Panzar (1979) and Forsyth (1983a).

[5] See, for instance, the example given in Sharkey (1982), pp. 141–3.

[6] A vivid description of some early excesses is given in Chapter 12 of Dyos and Aldcroft (1974).

duced by deregulation to account for changes. Although the structure of the industry has not altered greatly, competition has been stimulated, and it is competitive effects which provide the most plausible account of recent events. Undeniably, small coach operators have inaugurated consumer benefits, but perhaps most importantly, deregulation has opened the way for increased competition between coach and rail.

Of especial importance is the adoption by British Rail (BR) of a much more aggressive pricing policy, particularly with the proliferation of various 'Saver' fares. Although this was certainly prompted to some extent by the recession there is no doubt that it has also been spurred by—and in turn has spurred —invigorated competition from express coaching; it is notable, for instance, that many of BR's initiatives have been aimed at customers (students, the aged) who have traditionally been regarded as the mainstay of coach business. National itself has welcomed the elimination of the Traffic Commissioners' powers to control coach fares precisely on the grounds that this enables it to compete much more effectively with BR. The combination of an unchanged structure and altered performance since deregulation may reflect a tendency for regulated fares to have been set at levels requiring National to forgo profits in order to protect the position of BR.

Developments since 1980 have generated clearly identified groups of winners and losers. The major beneficiaries have been coach travellers on the major trunk routes, who have unambiguously gained from the emergence of a cheaper, more frequent, and in other respects improved service; other consumers have benefited from the variety of new services pioneered by independents. Another winner has been National Express itself, which has not only survived deregulation but increased its profit in doing so. Many BR travellers can be presumed to have benefited from the changes in its fare structure.

British Rail, on the other hand, has been a loser, suffering a revenue loss of the order of £10–15 million. The main group of consumers who may have lost from deregulation are those in smaller towns which have lost express services previously stopping there. (Even here, however, it is conceivable that gains have been made: if an adequate service to a major town is available then improvements on the trunk routes may be enough to outweigh the costs of a less convenient pattern of service).

This raises the general issue of cross-subsidisation, much discussed at the time of deregulation. One would indeed expect one of the most powerful effects of enhanced competition to be the elimination of inherently unprofitable routes, particularly when it comes in the wake of a regulatory regime resistant to change. In the event, however, effects of this sort have not been dramatic. This may indicate either that widespread cross-subsidisation had not been occurring or that regulated fares were so far above profit-maximising levels that National has been able to reduce them substantially without a major cutback of costly services. Stronger competition from independents would reduce still further any remaining ability to cross-subsidise. In terms of the general principles involved, the issue of cross-subsidisation is a complex one. To the extent, however, that competitive markets can sustain price structures sufficiently differentiated to turn the value consumers place on services into cash paid for them, there is some presumption that competition will result in an appropriate range of services being offered.

Not everybody has benefited from deregulation; and the losers have not been compensated. But in the absence of any particular reason to attach an especially heavy weight to the losses resulting from the withdrawal of unprofitable services it is difficult to avoid the conclusion that developments since deregulation have been broadly beneficial.

VI. More liberalisation? Freeing access to terminals

Whatever benefits deregulation has already brought, there is one area in which a further measure of liberalisation would seem almost certain to prove beneficial. As described above, National has been placed at a considerable advantage over the independent operators as a result of its privileged access to the established major terminals of the coach network (particularly Victoria but also, for instance, those at Birmingham, Manchester, Sheffield, and Exeter); it is as if British Airways had been allowed to control access to both Heathrow and

Gatwick (and, for good measure, a few other airports dotted around the world). Few intrinsic social benefits seem to arise from the provision by a single firm of both coach services and terminal facilities. Yet the market cannot lightly be relied on to challenge the power that National has been able to exercise, and—despite persistent rumblings—it has not done so; establishing comprehensive terminal facilities is an expensive and risky business. Moreover the duplication that this would involve may be unnecessary; the obvious solution is to separate the control of access to existing terminals from the operation of coach services, enabling the adoption of procedures more favourable to the efficient allocation of scarce capacity at coach stations.

It is not difficult to suggest ways in which this could be done.[7] Slots at coach stations might be allocated by auctioning procedures, being awarded to operators willing to pay most for them; the ability of rival operators to switch operations between services in response to apparent profit opportunities would then be expected to limit the extent to which effective monopoly power could be exercised on any one. Safeguards may be needed to prevent the emergence of collusion between operators granted access and to facilitate the entry of new operators, and perhaps also to ensure that the prices paid by the operators reflect the full social costs of their activities (in terms, for instance, of congestion caused). No special problems arise in the provision of other terminal facilities—refreshments, office space, and the like—which could be left in the hands of NBC or franchised.

Schemes of this sort could substantially increase the ability of independent operators to compete effectively with National. But they do not seem to figure in the Government's current plans for the bus and coach industry. Here the most prominent ideas seem to be either the hiving-off of National Express from NBC or the privatisation of NBC as a whole.[a] Neither of these offers very substantial benefits. The first would eliminate any genuine cost advantages arising from joint operation, advantages that might more usefully be turned to the public benefit by stimulating competition in the other

[7] There is a close parallel here with the issues discussed by Forsyth (1984) in connection with the privatisation of the British Airports Authority.

areas of NBC's activities. The second might result in some gains in productive efficiency and innovativeness, though it is not clear that the transfer of ownership would provide substantially stronger incentives in this direction than would enhanced competition. The liberalisation of access to terminals currently controlled by the NBC is a much more promising area for policy initiatives.

VII. Conclusions

With some qualification, the consequences of deregulating express coach services have been broadly beneficial. At the same time, and contrary to expectations, National Express has maintained its dominant position in the industry almost unscathed. In the absence of technical imperatives favouring single-firm production, National's success seems to reflect marketing and other advantages stemming from its pre-eminence during the period of regulation and, more tangibly, from its privileged access to established coach stations; the latter, which has underpinned the former, is susceptible to further liberalisation. Given the difficulty of mounting an effective attack on National the pattern of developments since deregulation may reflect not so much the disciplinary effect of potential competition from independent operators as it does National's increased ability to compete with British Rail, regulated coach fares having previously been set at levels effectively protecting the position of BR.

Within the broader context of policy towards privatisation and liberalisation—and there is an obvious parallel, for instance, with Telecoms—this experience with express coaching illustrates two important points. First, liberalising markets dominated by a publicly owned incumbent can generate substantial benefits even without a transference of ownership; in comparison, the social benefits of asset sales alone seem slight. Second, the very fact of their historical dominance may place such incumbents in a strong position to meet newcomers, and they can have a powerful incentive to exploit these advantages to the full in attempting to dismiss the early competition emerging after deregulation. As with the terminal access problem, some of the incumbent's advantages may be difficult to foresee and subsequent action to eliminate unanticipated impediments to thorough liberalisation may prove politically difficult if they have been capitalised in the prices at which assets were sold.

EDITORS' NOTE

a. Current government proposals include legislation for the deregulation of local bus services and the privatisation of NBC.

8

BRITISH AIRWAYS: PRIVATISATION AND AIRLINE REGULATORY POLICY*

Mark Ashworth and Peter Forsyth

I. The regulatory scene

British Airways (BA) operates within a regulatory framework which is only partly under the control of the British Government; the Government is unable to alter unilaterally the terms of the air service agreements with other countries. Privatisation of BA will not, of itself, change this regulatory framework. If the Government wants to increase competition to foster efficient performance in the industry, it is feasible to do this; though policy is constrained by overseas partners. There are several options for increasing competition such as dual designation (nominating two airlines to provide the UK's share of a service), domestic deregulation (allowing free entry to domestic routes), and route transfers (transferring routes between UK airlines). We discuss the most desirable pattern of changes at the end of this article. These changes would be desirable whether or not BA were privatised.

* This article summarises the main findings from M. H. Ashworth and P. J. Forsyth, *Civil Aviation Policy and the Privatisation of British Airways*, 1984, IFS Report Series 12.

Mark Ashworth is a Research Associate of the Institute for Fiscal Studies and is training as a barrister.

Peter Forsyth is a Visiting Senior Research Fellow at the Australian National University at Canberra and is a Research Associate of the Institute for Fiscal Studies.

The authors are grateful to Nicola Spencer for assistance with the empirical part of the study, and to Christopher Beauman, Andrew Dilnot, Christopher Findlay, John Kay, Michael Keen, Andrew Likierman, Stephen Littlechild, Tom Sharpe, Stephen Shaw, David Starkie, David Thompson, and Martin Wolf for advice and comments on earlier drafts of the Report. The research on which this article is based was financially supported by the Economic and Social Research Council.

The general case for privatisation of BA lies with its potential effect on productive efficiency (i.e. producing a given output at the lowest possible cost). At present it is not a very efficient airline, and there is considerable scope for improvement. A privately owned airline, oriented towards profit, has a more direct incentive to improve efficiency than a government airline. Privatisation may therefore yield advantages even in the absence of changes in the regulatory framework. The extent to which privatisation actually achieves this objective depends however on how effective the new management is, and the extent to which it actively seeks profit. If the airline is insulated against take-over, then a private management's performance may be no better than that of the public management.

The gainers from the expected improvement in efficiency will be the Government, and ultimately the taxpayer. Few of the benefits of improved efficiency will be passed directly on to the customer in the form of lower fares or better services, at least in the immediate future. This is a result of regulatory agreements made with overseas governments which reduce both the ability and the incentive for airlines to reduce prices for many types of travellers. Improvements in efficiency will be largely reflected in increased profits and the UK Government will receive a price for the airline which is based on possible and expected improvements in productivity and profit performance. If the market is unduly pessimistic about this on flotation, then the new owners will gain as actual performance outstrips expectations.

Regulation, because it excludes or reduces competition, is valuable to the airline. To maximise the overall benefits from operation of the industry, it is desirable that competition also be maximised. This will reduce profits and reduce the proceeds from the asset sale. To the extent that the Government has the option of increasing competition, it will be reducing the receipts it receives. From Britain's overall viewpoint, it is desirable that competition be encouraged, even though this means lower asset receipts received.

To this end, it is of crucial importance that regulation be liberalised before rather than after BA is sold. If this happens, the Government takes the loss. Since selling BA involves selling an airline and rights to regulated routes, it will be very difficult for the Government to remove regulation and thereby effectively reduce the profits of the owners to whom it has sold the airline. This is especially true if the regulatory changes are not expected, but it is still true if liberalisation is foreshadowed at point of sale. The new owners will always have an incentive to oppose deregulation. Unexpected deregulation after sale could be regarded as a breach of contract which imposes a loss on the buyer. It may, however, be feasible for the Government to introduce some competitive incentives short of complete deregulation, without reducing the financial benefits of privatisation, by introducing a system of franchising or leasing routes; we discuss this possibility further below.

The regulatory framework may change over the foreseeable future. It may become possible for regulation of air routes from Britain to continental Europe and elsewhere to be liberalised as other countries change their attitudes and objectives. Britain may take advantage of this and agree to liberalise. It has not always done so in the past. A statement of intent cannot commit the Government to liberalisation, but the more clearly it is understood the better. It may weaken the bargaining power of an airline in seeking to maintain regulation.

If the Government wishes to encourage competition in the airline industry, now is the time. It may be too difficult after privatisation of BA. It ought also to state its intentions on regulation for when its partner countries alter their policies. If competition is to be encouraged, and the benefits that it brings are to be secured, liberalisation must come before privatisation. If complete deregulation is considered infeasible on the current timetable for privatisation then competition *for* the market should be encouraged by making routes transferable, ideally through franchising or leasing routes; BA should be sold on this basis. We discuss at the end of this article the proposals made in the Government's White Paper (Department of Transport, 1984).

II. The performance of British Airways

BA is not one of the more efficient international airlines. This has been true for some time, and it has been indicated by a number of studies.[1] BA has improved relative to other airlines over the past few years, though it remains a weak performer. Its improvement over the past three years has been good, though hardly spectacular. Overall productivity has increased much less rapidly than one partial aspect of productivity—labour productivity. The much publicised view of a dramatic improvement in efficiency is not borne out by the evidence. What this implies is that there remains considerable scope to increase productivity; privatisation may result in this opportunity being taken up.

A major factor in the recovery in BA's profits has been the exchange rate. When sterling rose, the airline was badly hit—hence the poor profit performance around 1980–1. The subsequent fall in sterling relative to the US dollar helped BA significantly. This is what could be expected of an export industry, but it is something that tends to be neglected in favour of more specific factors which influence performance. This highlights how vulnerable to exchange rate movements an international airline is.

Privatisation may affect the airline's wage and employment policy. The objectives of employees may not change, but the objectives of management will. They may be less inclined to accede to demands which increase costs. This of itself is not necessarily a good or a bad thing. There is some evidence, though, that when airline wages are higher than for comparable work in other industries, inefficient practices develop when potential employees seek well-paid, but scarce, airline jobs.

Cross-subsidisation has existed, and probably still exists, within BA's operations. Regulation creates potential profits (although because costs are inefficiently high this may not be reflected in actual profits). Some routes are potentially quite profitable, yet the airline itself has been barely so. The explanation is that some routes have been loss-makers. It is very difficult to judge from outside just how profits and losses are distributed. Routes are not always independent, and there may be routes which currently incur losses but which may

---

[1] In particular see Taussig Report (1977), the Anglo-American study (reported in British Airways, 1977), Pearson (1976), Morrell and Taneja (1979), Mackay (1979), and Findlay and Forsyth (1984).

earn profits. Notwithstanding this, it is possible that BA is still serving routes on which it is never likely to make a profit. On some routes, it may be operating with too great a level of capacity and market share. Already the airline has been cut back, and this has improved profitability. There may be a case for further cuts, and these may become essential if some airline markets, such as the European routes, are liberalised.

BA's current profitability is quite high, and there are some reasons to expect it to continue so over the immediate future. In the longer term, the position of British airlines looks good, whether or not there is liberalisation in Europe. If BA is able to improve its productivity substantially, to match or exceed that of other international airlines, its future looks good under most conditions. If it is not able to improve efficiency by much, it may find it difficult to survive with its present size and routes in a deregulated environment. Whatever the environment it faces, it is likely to have a fluctuating profit performance because of its sensitivity to general economic conditions and the exchange rate.

As an enterprise BA looks quite valuable. Its assets are probably accurately measured in the current cost accounts (CCA)—these give a more optimistic picture than the (misleading) historic cost accounts. Its main assets—aircraft—have a ready market. This might not be so if there were an immediate sale of all assets, but that is unlikely. If the airline were to reduce size over a couple of years, it would not find it difficult to dispose of aircraft at prices close to replacement cost less depreciation. (Even in the recession, prices of second-hand aircraft did not tumble. Excess aircraft were stored instead.) With its aircraft and its routes (less easily negotiated, but still valuable), BA would at least be attractive to a patient asset-stripper, if not as a going concern. With its current asset and debt structure, the balance-sheet is not very much affected by exchange rate changes though profits, and thus the value of the firm, are.

As a package, BA is quite attractive. It does have scope, however, to improve its overall performance. There are questions about performance which are difficult to answer from outside. The most important of these concerns the existence of loss-making routes. It may be that BA is still too large, and that it should reduce or cease operations in some markets. It is likely to remain a volatile profit performer, and its long-term profit performance is highly conditional on the regulation it faces, as well as on exchange rates.

III. Preparing British Airways for sale

There are several re-arrangements which can be made to the structure of BA before sale. These include injecting capital and writing off debt, allowing or disallowing past losses as offsets against taxation, changes to the superannuation scheme, breaking it into separate airlines, and transferring routes. In general, there is no economic case for doing things one way or another. Appropriately done, the expected net price received for the package of assets and liabilities will be the same.

Because of information gaps or transaction costs, there may be a case for structuring British Airways in a particular form. It may be easier to sell if it has a debt/asset structure similar to that of other private international airlines (and therefore the new owners do not need to restructure debt and assets after purchase). There may be a case for selling BA in parts, or transferring routes (by selling them). This should be possible without affecting the Government's net receipts (that is, the proceeds from the sale less any expenditure on financial reconstruction). If done badly, however, receipts could be affected. For example, if routes which are best operated together are separated, there may be an efficiency loss which will be reflected in the price. The timing of the net receipts from the sale will be affected as well. For example, if losses are allowed as offsets against taxation, the Government will sell the airline for a larger sum, but it will receive less in taxation revenues later.

IV. Civil aviation policy

There are several options the Government has open to it, within current international constraints, to increase competition. It can allow competition in domestic markets, and indeed the recent White Paper (Department of Transport,

1984) foreshadows the deregulation of domestic services. It can relax regulation in those markets for which Britain is the more restrictive partner. It can encourage indirect competition between different airlines on slightly different routes. Where its partners allow, it can permit dual designation. When capacity is controlled this involves allocating some of BA's capacity to another airline. In such a case, this will achieve little increase in competition. Where capacity is not controlled, there may be an increase in competition (as there has been on the Hong Kong route). However, while there are a lot of changes possible, there are many routes for which Britain must acquiesce in tight regulation.

Most, though not all, of BA's routes form part of a consistent network stretching from a hub—London Heathrow. It would be possible to divide BA into component parts. If this were done on a route (or regional) basis, the result would be non-competitive airlines. They would lose economies of integration achieved, for instance, through being able to offer passengers a through service between two points other than London. They can remedy this by forming interlining agreements. This would mean that a horizontally integrated firm was being replaced by firms linked by contracts. There would be no gain in competition, and possibly some loss in operational efficiency. Other ways of dividing up BA could result in more than one British airline on certain routes—but this would lead to operational inefficiency, and it would achieve no more than dual designation could accomplish. It would be subject to the same international constraints. It might be argued that it is desirable to have several airlines 'strong enough' to take on a particular route. However, it is probably the case that there are already sufficient independent airlines willing and able to take up any opportunities.

The possibility of predatory pricing is always present if there are one or two airlines much larger than the rest. It would be difficult to remove the risk by restructuring BA—it will remain big, and will continue to have access to advantages, such as profitable, non-competitive routes. Current Civil Aviation Authority (CAA) regulations are very unlikely to be able to control it. There may be a case for tighter restrictions on predatory pricing, which would substantially increase the risk of penalties if caught (though not necessarily proven). If the smaller airlines are regarded as financially weak, the best solution would be for them to form links with stronger, non-airline companies (which some have). Predatory behaviour is unlikely to be controlled effectively by weakening the dominant firm in the industry. It is probably best handled directly if, by the nature of the problem, crudely.

When competition in the market is not possible, competition for the market may be the next best alternative. Thus it would be desirable to induce airlines to compete for routes, or groups of routes. The obvious way would be to auction franchises to operate routes for specific periods. This is rather different from the current practice, but the proposal should not be dismissed merely for this reason. In fact, many of the supposed difficulties are imaginary. For example, if it is not too difficult to define distinct routes in order to transfer them, as the Government proposes in its White Paper (Department of Transport, 1984), it should not be too difficult to sell or auction them. Naturally most airlines will object to paying for rights to earn profits which currently they obtain free.

The objectives of such a system should be:

- to achieve transferability of routes so that the airlines best suited to serving them have the chance to do so
- to increase competitive incentives toward greater efficiency
- to achieve such an increase in competitive incentives without reducing the Government's overall receipts from privatisation (any reduction in the price received for BA should be matched by the flow of receipts from the franchises)
- to minimise the stake which airlines (in particular BA) have in maintaining the present regulatory structure.

It may not be necessary to sell or auction routes to achieve efficient transferability. If BA has a route it is unsuited to serve, it will do better by selling it to another airline. If it does not seek to maximise profit, it may not do so—it may hang on to loss-making routes. In times when it is financially stretched, it may be forced to sell routes—as US airlines have done. Transferability of routes may not always achieve actual transfer when that is efficient. BA will still have a stake in maintaining the status quo. Transferability is, however, a desirable step along the way. It is a simple and straight-forward step towards a more efficient airline industry. Route licences may not be property now, but they ought to be.

Arbitrary route transfers, as proposed by the CAA, are undesirable for a number of reasons. They may be efficient transfers to the airline best suited to serving them, or they may be inefficient transfers. The CAA does not have the information to determine which transfers are desirable. The method of allocation, through hearings, is a socially wasteful method. Allocating monopoly routes to additional airlines gives them all a stake in a continued restriction of competi-tion. It is difficult to see how transfer of monopoly routes will increase competition. A gift of a valuable profit-earning opportunity will add to the financial strength of independent airlines.

BA does have an unfair advantage in competing with other British airlines. This arises from its having privileged access to London Heathrow, at lower than market prices. This enables it to attract traffic through easier access and better connections. Its advantage is considerable—it may be equiv-alent to an implicit subsidy of the order of £50 million per annum. If other British airlines are to be able to compete with BA, either directly or indirectly, this imbalance must be cor-rected. This can be done by giving equal potential access to London Heathrow to all.

This is not feasible with the current pricing policy at London Heathrow. It is desirable that the prices for using Heathrow reflect the scarcity of capacity, and that capacity be allocated to the airlines which value it most. There are several ways of achieving this. The theoretically most appeal-ing, but perhaps least practical, would be to divide capacity into slots and auction these. Alternatively, present arrange-ments could be continued, but the margin in prices between Heathrow and Gatwick could be raised to such an extent that Heathrow capacity was no longer scarce, and any airline pre-pared to pay the price could use Heathrow. This can be achieved partly through lowering Gatwick's prices as well as by raising Heathrow's. Some airlines would have to pay more, but others would pay less. It would be desirable to eliminate the current discrimination against large aircraft. In general, long-haul flights (including US flights) may pay less or more, though short-haul flights would pay more. The current structure, as well as level, of charges at Heathrow worsens the allocation problem.

Both these solutions may result in certain airlines paying more to use Heathrow. This may be considered undesirable, especially if there is a possibility of some retaliation. Another alternative which requires minimal change, and which does not disadvantage existing users, is to define clear property rights, for a specified period, and make them fully transferable. Any airline then using Heathrow will take account of the price it could obtain for a Heathrow slot if it shifted to Gatwick. Airlines which wish to use Heathrow will be able to do so at a price. This policy may be seen as a gift to current users; but this is what the current policy amounts to. An efficient gift is preferable to an inefficient gift. In selling BA with its airport slots, the Government would recoup the value of its gift. This approach has one weakness in comparison with the options proposed in the previous paragraph: giving BA defined property rights for its access to slots strengthens the existing incentive to oppose any change to the allocation of capacity at Heathrow.

In fact, most of Britain's independent airlines would not wish to use Heathrow at levels of charges which reflected the market clearing price. They are likely to opt for the lower price of Gatwick. They would not be as able as BA is to take advantage of the connecting advantages of Heathrow. However, if airline competition is to be effective, one of the competitors must not be given preferential access to a valuable resource. Efficient allocation of Heathrow's scarce capacity is a precondition for this. Only when this capacity is allocated efficiently can competition amongst airlines be equal.

Perhaps one of the most serious problems which becomes apparent is that of information. There is not sufficient information available to the public to enable anything like an accurate assessment of the value of the firm which the Government proposes to sell. There are some assets about which little is known. BA's rights to fly certain routes are valuable, but it is not possible to determine just how valuable. To do so requires information about route profitability; much of this should not be regarded as commercially confidential. Our study (Ashworth and Forsyth, 1984) illustrates the principles, but it is based on inadequate data. If a firm is to be sold, its assets should be specified and then their earning potential measured. With a substantial proportion of BA's assets, this is not the case.

Another aspect of the importance of information concerns future regulation and the precise conditions under which BA can operate its services. There are very many options, concerned with airport pricing, rights to routes, and overall regulatory policy, which will affect the value of BA. Some of these, such as the question of route transfers, are being considered. Many are not, however, and it is possible that the Government will privatise BA without being specific about many of them. At present, it is even difficult to determine the Government's overall regulatory policy. It appears to favour more competition, but how much competition is it going to allow? Ideally, the Government should be as specific as possible about the various policies over which it has discretion which will affect the value of BA.

In summary, to encourage efficiency in the airline industry, it is desirable to allow competition and free access to markets. Where airport capacity is limited or British capacity on routes is restricted, this is not possible. To put all airlines on an equal basis, and encourage a situation where those most efficient in using a right or resource in fact do so, it is necessary to make access to these rights or resources as unrestricted as possible. This can be done, by the various methods we have suggested, if rights to use airports or fly routes are defined and made transferable (at a negotiated price). This is a straightforward step, which does not worsen the position of airlines, their passengers or the taxpayer, but which would allow maximum competition within these constraints.

The White Paper (Department of Transport, 1984) goes a limited way towards achieving this aim. It is, however, rather unspecific, and it proposes a structure within which there will be a fair degree of scope for *ad hoc* regulation, and this scope will tend to be used notwithstanding overall policy. Agreed one-off route swaps are better than arbitrary transfers, though they fall short of transferability. The controls over predatory pricing are likely to be ineffective should the problem arise. There are further important limitations to the White Paper. It does not provide any specific proposals in relation to the rights which a privatised BA may, or may not, continue to hold over the provision of services on regulated routes.

Part IV

THE NATURAL MONOPOLIES: PROMOTING COMPETITION AND REGULATORY ISSUES

9

BRITISH RAILWAYS: OPPORTUNITIES FOR A CONTESTABLE MARKET*

David Starkie

I. Introduction

The public sector can be privatised in a number of ways but with British Railways (BR), attention has focused on the sale to the private sector of assets in non-rail subsidiaries. Hotels have been disposed of and other non-rail activities have been grouped under a holding company—British Rail Investments Ltd—with a view to selling equity in them to private sector shareholders. Suggestions have recently been made for treating similarly the wholly-owned subsidiary, British Rail Engineering Ltd (BREL), which carries out extensive repair work for BR and builds much of its rolling-stock.

On the operational side there have been proposals for the private sector to take over railway lines. The two most publicised schemes are from Victoria to Gatwick Airport, and Fenchurch Street to Southend. The Fenchurch Street line runs for about forty miles through southern Essex and operates very much as a separate part of the rail network. A business consortium has expressed an interest in its purchase.

It is arguable whether such transfers would promote the objective most strongly canvassed by the privatisers—increased efficiency in the supply of services and therefore more benefits to consumers. Efficiency is associated with competition, but it

* This article was first published as 'BR—privatisation without tears' in *Economic Affairs*, 1984, October–December; it appears here by permission of the Longman Group Limited.

At the time of writing this article, David Starkie was South Australian Government Professorial Fellow in the Department of Economics at the University of Adelaide; he is now with TM Economics and a Research Associate of the Institute for Fiscal Studies.

is not necessarily true (even if it seems likely) that a simple transfer of assets to the private sector has the effect of sharpening competitive forces.

Professors Michael Beesley and Stephen Littlechild (1983) have argued that privatisation without increased competition will, nonetheless, procure benefits. Private firms are able to respond more easily to demand by having better access to capital, and they will have a stronger incentive to produce goods and services in the quantity and variety that consumers prefer, especially where monopoly power is limited by the existence (even when only potential) of close substitutes. But privatisation which enhances competition is more likely to secure a wider range of benefits. The issue thus is what form of privatisation will increase competitive forces within the railway industry.

II. Are railways a natural monopoly?

A major barrier to competition in the railway industry is its large, unavoidable fixed costs of production, which arise because many inputs into the industry are 'lumpy'. To run one train service between two cities, for example, requires a minimum outlay on track formation, motive power, rolling-stock, and administration. As these inputs are used more intensively, i.e. as more services are run, their cost is spread over more units of output so that average costs fall until the point when the railway is used so intensively that the track becomes congested and management over-stretched. But railways normally operate on the falling segment of their cost curves. Either market demand will have decreased, leaving spare capacity in the system, or new technologies such as centralised traffic control (CTC) will have enabled higher capacities to be achieved from existing plant. Railways therefore are referred to as 'natural' monopolies in the sense that a single, vertically integrated firm can fulfil market demand more cheaply than two.

Although railways are natural monopolies in this sense, their true monopoly power as means of *transport* has now been all but eliminated by competition from aviation and road transport. But despite this competition BR is not as efficient as it might be. A cost analysis by Stewart Joy (later to become BR's chief economist) during the 1960s (Joy, 1964) suggested that BR was capable of reducing its permanent way costs to a substantial degree. More recently, the Select Committee on Nationalised Industries (1977) and the Report of the Serpell Committee (1983) have pointed to inefficiencies in the use of both equipment and personnel.

When inefficiency is substantial, falling average costs are not enough to maintain the railway monopolist's inherent advantage. The opportunity exists for a more efficient firm to set up in competition but producing at a lower cost. What prevents this happening is a second important characteristic of many railway assets. Embankments and cuttings, the rail formation and the platforms etc. are fixed *in situ*—they are sunk, committed irreversibly to a specified market. Consequently potential competitors are faced with substantial risks to enter a particular market in this way. They face BR with equivalent infrastructure written down or written off and with the potential to eliminate its inefficiencies that provide the opportunity for a private enterprise company. Once entry is accomplished the inefficiencies of BR might quickly disappear leaving competitors with unamortised assets they are unable to transfer.

It is thus not feasible for the private sector to build new permanent way and terminals in competition with BR. There may be special cases which provide exceptions; for instance, where existing track and terminal capacity is saturated and the particular market still has considerable growth potential (the Victoria–Gatwick Airport service may be in this category). But even in these circumstances, it is most likely that BR will be able to add to its existing infrastructure at a lower cost than a potential rival could build new rights-of-way or terminus facilities.

If competition from new rail infrastructure is out of the question, private enterprise could take over existing permanent way (at book value) in competition with BR (or other private companies). But BR has eliminated some of the obvious spare capacity in the system established by competing rail companies in the nineteenth century to achieve precisely these economies of use. Consequently, the opportunities for competing rail services using alternative, existing infrastructure between common centres are few (London–Southend services are an exception).

Similar, but again limited, opportunities for increased competition exist where the permanent way carries multiple tracks so that track ownership can be divided. Although modern CTC makes it feasible to divide double tracks into lengths of single track with two-way operations,[1] more flexibility can be achieved where there are four running tracks with competing companies handling two each (and each having restricted running rights over competitors' lines). However, there is a limited length of quadruple track and the train control, rail formation, and stations would have to remain in single ownership. Although worthy of further investigation (especially where there is not too much mixing of freight, slow passenger, and fast passenger traffic), it is probable that in many instances the additional complexities of operation would negate the increased efficiency achieved by competition.

III. Track and trains: divided ownership

A more logical way to proceed would be to work with and not against the constraints to competition inherent in the technology of railway systems. This approach would recognise that most large scale-effects are inherent in the permanent way, train control, and stations—precisely the assets irretrievably committed to a particular rail market once installed. In contrast the rail vehicles—locomotives, wagons, carriages—are mobile between markets, and economies in their use are well encompassed by the market opportunities available. This distinction begs for wider recognition within the institutional framework.

By distinguishing the ownership of the permanent way from the ownership of the vehicles an opportunity presents itself for having competing trains running on shared track. In other words one would emulate a practice which is common

---

[1] Some of the world's busiest lines in terms of tonnages handled are single track (but highly specialised) railways.

in road and air transport; public sector buses (National Bus Company) compete against private coach companies on the state-owned motorway system and rival airlines (some in the private sector) utilise airports in separate and often state ownership. The last analogy is the more useful because of the scheduling and safety implications. Airlines arrange for access times to the terminal and runways and immediate air space; in effect, they rent this access. Translated into rail terms, access to lines and terminals would be rented by competing train companies who would then sell services directly to the public.

Such a policy may sound distinctly different from that which we associate with railways in modern Britain but its strength lies in the fact that it represents a further development of what is now happening and what used to happen on a large scale until 1948.

Before nationalisation in 1948, railways in Britain had developed quite complex structures reflecting in some cases a distinction between ownership of track and ownership of rolling-stock.

One example of this was the Cheshire Lines Railway which controlled lines between Manchester and Liverpool and between Chester and Stockport.[2] It was a statutory railway company under its own management but with parent companies (originally three and then two) represented on the Board. Its singular feature was that each year it handled millions of passengers without owning a single locomotive and millions of tons of freight without owning a single wagon. Locomotives were hired from another rail company and wagons came from a variety of sources including non-railway companies. (In the early 1930s there were something like 700,000 private rail wagons.)

The Cheshire Lines Railway disappeared as a separate entity in 1948, at the same time as much of the huge private wagon fleet was incorporated within the nationalised railway. For the private wagon fleets this at least was but a temporary demise: private wagons never disappeared entirely from the network (some specialist wagons were retained by private

---

[2] For further details, see Griffiths (1947).

companies in 1948) and in recent years their role has grown very rapidly.

They now form a substantial component within the rail freight system.[3] In terms of tonne miles, private wagons carried 40 per cent of BR's freight traffic in 1982. If coal and coke tonnage, carried mostly in 'merry-go-round' fleets running between collieries and power stations, was excluded, the private wagon proportion accounted for as much as two-thirds of tonne-miles. Within this total, individual companies generate large flows of ore, cement, aggregates, and oil as well as general freight, and their investment in private wagons is substantial: oil and chemical industries alone have around £300 million invested.

Thus there already exists in the operational railway system a large private sector component and one that is based on a distinction between mobile and sunk assets. The next logical step would be for the private sector to extend into the motive power sector, purchase locomotives, employ or lease crews, and offer train services directly in competition with each other and with British Railways. Some of the large companies generating large volumes of traffic might consider it worthwhile to operate their own freight trains, just as many now operate 'own-account' lorries carrying road freight. But this would depend on their ability to utilise the locomotives adequately. The majority would probably prefer to hire the locomotive and train services (just as in effect they now do) but with the option of buying services from private 'hire and reward' train companies.

Wagon hirers already exist and a number have combined to form the British Wagon Hirers Association. Included is the multinational transport conglomerate, VTG, with a European fleet of 26,000 hire wagons, many of which operate over the BR network. VTG also operates in Europe large petroleum tank terminals and about a hundred river-going vessels, and an extension into railway locomotives would appear to complement its specialist transport activities. The provision of complete train services on a 'hire and reward' basis might be particularly attractive to transport distribution companies like National Carriers or the new-to-Britain,

---

[3] For further information see Private Wagon Federation (1983).

aggressive, rapidly growing Thomas Nationwide Transport (with experience of chartering company trains in Australia).

The Venice-Simplon Orient-Express Company Ltd operating private coach stock between Victoria and the Channel Ports is an example, albeit rather special, of the principle extended into the rail passenger market. The company agrees with BR the 'train path' in the busy south-east network and hires the locomotive and crew. With a more flexible approach the locomotives and crew could be hired from a private sector company quoting a rate for the job in competition with the state sector.

This extension of the private sector in the operational railway would be facilitated if the assets of BR were divided into two groups. The permanent way, train control, maintenance depots, and termini could be vested in one company (the name British Railways remains appropriate), which would also handle overhead functions like general administration.[4] Rolling-stock could be vested in a separate, public sector company or companies (which I shall refer to collectively as British Trains—BT). BR's charges to BT and private sector competitors would be based on direct train control cost, track wear and tear, and directly attributable terminus costs, supplemented by additional charges, broadly reflecting judgements of what the market will bear, to assist with covering joint costs. At times when passenger and freight demand is high the train companies would bid against each other for available train paths. The resulting 'rents' accruing to the permanent way company would help to cover the joint and common costs of the network (see Figure 1).

IV. Passenger services and the 'social' railway

The approach assumes that train services, if they operate at all, cover the marginal costs of operation. But there is a large 'social' railway—services considered necessary for social reasons—which fails to cover its direct costs. These services would exist alongside competitive services. But there is the danger that the Public Service Obligation (PSO) grant, paid

---

[4] There would be some divestment of administration and marketing to train companies.

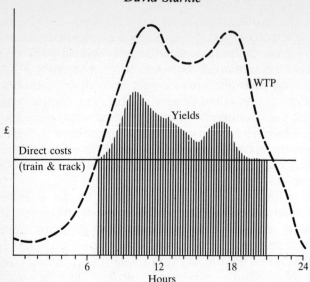

The dashed line in the chart illustrates the aggregate willingness to pay (WTP) for a journey between two towns (at a specified quality of service) at different times of the day. Train operators are not able to expropriate the whole of this because of an inability to discriminate perfectly when charging. The yield to the train company from each service operated is shown by the vertical lines. The amount exceeding direct costs (the latter shown as constant per service) represents the maximum that the permanent way company can expect to extract as a contribution towards the joint and common costs of the right-of-way.

Figure 1. Bidding for the Use of the Rail Right-of-Way

to maintain social services, might be used to cross-subsidise BT's competitive bids for use of BR's system. This could happen, for example, where social and competitive services offered by BT used common rolling-stock. To eliminate this possibility, one approach would be to fence in the competitive market to prevent misuse of the PSO grant.

This fencing-in is already taking place in BR's adoption of sector management. BR is now divided into five operating sectors: freight, parcels, London and south-east passenger services, other provincial passenger services, and inter-city passenger services. Freight and inter-city have been set a commercial quasi-target and it is here that the privatisation proposals outlined would apply more easily. Data in the Serpell Report suggest, for example, that only a small proportion of inter-city train miles (about 10 per cent) were failing to cover direct costs (see Figure 2). With competition resulting in higher efficiency, it is likely that the total number of inter-city train miles covering these costs could be increased.

A substantial proportion of train miles in the London and south-east network also cover their direct costs, some by a large margin. But there is a minor, but not insignificant, proportion making large operating losses. It is difficult to judge from the information available whether the spur of competition would radically alter this picture without a reduction of services. The size of the positive externalities attached to some of these services (reduced road congestion in London is one example) and the political implications advise caution. For the time being at least, this sector is better considered, along with services in the provincial sector, as lying outside the potential for developing commercially competing services.

For this large proportion of the present railway not susceptible to provision by direct competition, competitive franchising would provide a means of improving efficiency. The essence of the franchising idea is that services would be open for tender to be operated in a specified manner for a particular period. A distinction between 'track' and 'trains' is appropriate also when franchising the social railway. The expertise required to operate train services *per se* is different from that required for maintaining the permanent way—recognised in BR's existing corporate structure which distinguishes between operations and engineering.

With an extended role for the private sector, it will be important to ensure that the economies of an integrated railway system are maintained. These economies are realised through new technologies like British Railways' computerised wagon information system—TOPS—whereby the progress of each wagon (privately owned as well as BR stock) is monitored as it passes through the rail network. Private train companies, too, will need to have access to the TOPS information system. An integrated passenger timetable is another example; the present one includes more than a score of private, seasonal

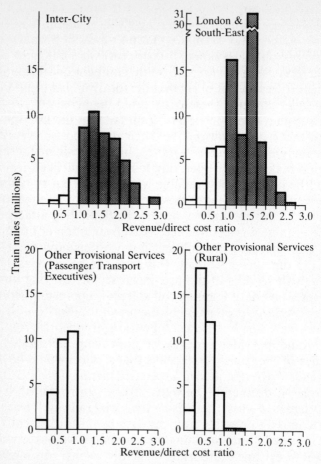

Figure 2. Revenue/Cost Ratios for Different Sectors

railways aimed at the tourist market (and for the most part run by volunteers). Professional, private sector services as they develop will need to be incorporated in the system-wide time-table.

V. Conclusions

The suggested approach begs the question of the extent to which a more efficient railway system would be achieved. The report of the Serpell enquiry contains estimates which suggest that, by 1986, the financial performance of inter-city rail and rail freight could be improved by £84 million by the adoption of various cost-cutting measures. This figure is based upon improvements to services currently provided by these two sectors and reflects opportunities for reducing train costs by purchasing cheaper equipment (buying low-cost locomotives overseas was mentioned specifically); by the better utilisation of both equipment and labour; and by savings in locomotive and rolling-stock maintenance. One would expect private sector train companies to avail themselves of these opportunities and to force the pace of adoption by the state sector railway.

The benefits of competition extend beyond the savings pinpointed in the Serpell Report. Competition in services would have the effect of optimising the price and quality of services offered. For the passenger railway, BR displays a tendency to market a standard service with increasing emphasis on quality —speed, on-board catering, air-conditioning—manifest in the High Speed Train Services. It may have judged the market accurately. But it is possible also that the market could support a wider variety of price/quality packages.[5] For example, the private sector may wish to test-market a lower standard of inter-city service based on the new rail-bus technology. Crew savings, lower fuel consumption, reduced vehicle depreciation, and less wear and tear on the track could produce a lower ticket price acceptable, despite the slower, less comfortable ride,[6] to a number sufficient to support the service—the young, pensioners, and so on.

A further benefit of the suggested competitive model would be the provision of better guidance for investment in rail infrastructure and a reduction, if not the elimination, of the present arbitrary allocation of overhead and joint costs to the inter-city sector. Inter-city rail is expected to earn a surplus on direct and 'indirect costs' equivalent to a 5 per cent discounted cash flow on certain defined capital assets. As Mr Alfred Goldstein, a member of the Serpell Committee,

---

[5] More freedom of entry into airline markets has produced this effect. See Forsyth (1983b) and Starkie and Starrs (1984).

[6] There might be a beneficial effect of smaller trains operating at more frequent intervals. See Walters (1982) for a discussion of trade-offs between vehicle size and service frequency.

remarked in his Minority Report, the rationale of this test has not been satisfactorily explained. Under the proposed framework for competitive services, the contribution towards costs not attributable to the direct provision of a train service would come from track 'rents'. If these rents fail to cover renewal of infrastructure specific to a competitive sector, the market will have signalled an eventual withdrawal of these services. Conversely, where competitive bidding for train paths pushes up rents, expansion of track and terminus capacity will be called for.

Finally, one can speculate on the long-term structure of a competitive railway industry. We might expect an initial increase in the overall size of the freight and inter-city sectors. A wider variety of services and/or lower fares and charges should produce an increase in demand for rail travel. In the longer term, the character of the industry will depend also on the Government's view on the size of the social railway and thus on the amount of infrastructure that the Government is willing to support.

It is difficult to judge whether the public sector's involvement in freight and inter-city services would continue as at present. This depends upon whether there are economies or diseconomies of scale and scope in the provision of train services.[7] Large companies may be able to balance and match rolling-stock to different market demands rather better but at the expense of managerial diseconomies.[8] The most plausible outcome is that the state sector will maintain a substantial presence alongside a range of private sector firms—as it does in today's airline and bus industries.

---

[7] Economies of scale are to be distinguished from economies of utilisation (sometimes referred to as economies of traffic density). Economies of scope refers to the advantages of jointly producing multiple outputs, i.e. different types of services.

[8] Recent studies of US railroads have suggested only limited economies of scale. Spady (1979), for example, concludes that there are managerial diseconomies of scale in rail transport.

10

REGULATION AND COMPETITION IN THE ELECTRICITY SUPPLY INDUSTRY*

George Yarrow

I. Introduction

Electricity supply is the largest of the UK's nationalised industries in terms of turnover and capital employed: sales revenue in 1985 will be of the order of £11 billion on a capital stock of close to £40 billion (valued on a current cost accounting (CCA) basis). Generation and distribution of electricity also exhibit a number of economic characteristics normally associated with market failures, including environmental side-effects and natural monopoly conditions in the transmission system. The combination of large scale and market failures makes the industry an obvious target for extensive regulation, and an examination of recent and current policy options with respect to pricing, coal stocks, the coal/nuclear balance, atmospheric emissions of waste gases, etc. immediately reveals the importance of the issues at stake.

This short paper does not aim to provide a full discussion of all the major, regulatory problems resulting from the economic characteristics of the electricity supply industry (ESI), and the following discussion will be restricted principally to pricing policy. Even so, the range of issues encompassed by this heading is wide. There are questions about the application and monitoring of marginal cost pricing policies; the effects of tariffs on income distribution; the second-best difficulties associated with coal and gas pricing, and with the fact that the outputs of the industry are both intermediate and final goods; and the scope for predatory pricing aimed at

* This article is based on a paper prepared for an Institute for Fiscal Studies conference on Competition and Regulation held in London in May 1985.

George Yarrow is a Fellow and Tutor in Economics at Hertford College Oxford.

blocking new entry. The coverage of some of these topics will therefore necessarily be rather cursory.

The paper is organised as follows. Sections II and III outline the salient economic features of the industry, its organisational structure, and the current regulatory framework. Sections IV and V examine and evaluate the way in which policy towards the industry has developed. Sections VI and VII take up the questions of new entry and potential competition, and include a brief evaluation of some of the provisions of the Energy Act 1983. Finally, Section VIII offers a few remarks on the privatisation issue.

II. Salient features of the industry

The major activities of the electricity supply industry can be broken down into generation and distribution (transmission). Natural monopoly conditions pertain on the transmission side—at the regional level at least—but the static efficiency case for a single generating firm is much less clear. From an economic perspective the industry supplies a spectrum of differentiated goods, the major distinguishing features of different outputs being time, location, and voltage level. There are, for example, systematic seasonal and time-of-day variations in demand for electricity, so that, adopting the industry's own basic unit of duration (the half-hour), time differentiation alone implies 17,520 different outputs in each year. Since electricity is, to a first approximation, non-storable (though limited, economically viable techniques exist in the form of pumped storage hydro stations, night storage heaters, etc.) tariff design involves some quite complex peak-load pricing problems. Moreover, technological features of integrated transmission systems imply that supply failures at one point cannot be completely localised, and demand/supply imbalances can therefore give rise to substantial external effects. Hence, the selection and pricing of alternative levels of security of supply is also a key issue.

The industry is capital-intensive, its assets tend to have long economic lives, there are long lead times on the construction of new generating plant, and capital costs are generally non-recoverable. Thus a decision to build a power station today typically implies a lagged input availability for about a thirty-year period. The two main generating technologies (coal-fired steam plant and nuclear plant) both produce significant environmental externalities. The major input to the industry is coal (accounting for nearly 50 per cent of generating costs in a normal year), mostly obtained from the nationalised NCB at prices which bear little relation to marginal costs. Finally, the ESI's outputs compete with gas and other fuels in both intermediate and final goods markets.

In England and Wales the industry is divided into a public corporation responsible for generation (the Central Electricity Generating Board—CEGB) and twelve public corporations responsible for the distribution and retailing of electricity (the Area Boards). In Scotland the arrangements are somewhat different: the South of Scotland Electricity Board and the North of Scotland Hydro Electric Board each engage in both generation and distribution/retailing activities, though they operate a pooling scheme on the production side to facilitate efficient use of the latter's hydro capacity.

Virtually all of the CEGB's output (around 99 per cent) is sold to the Area Boards, and they in turn obtain nearly all of their supplies from the CEGB. The prices at which these transfers of electricity are made are set out in the CEGB's Bulk Supply Tariff (BST), which is the key pricing instrument of the industry.

Although the CEGB and Area Boards are separate statutory bodies, there is a good deal of 'informal' vertical integration in England and Wales. The general policy of the ESI (including the BST) is discussed in the Electricity Council, a statutory body whose membership is dominated by the Chairmen of the thirteen Boards. In 1976, the Plowden Committee recommended unification of the industry in England and Wales, but legislation to this effect did not come on to the statute book and the proposal has subsequently been abandoned.

III. The framework of regulation

The regulatory framework for the ESI has been set out in various Acts of Parliament and in successive White Papers

(HM Treasury, 1961, 1967, and 1978). The Electricity Acts, 1947 and 1957, lay down the functions and working procedures of the ESI, and of the supervising Minister. Thus, for example, the principal statutory duty of the CEGB is to:

develop and maintain an efficient, co-ordinated and economical system of supply of electricity in bulk for all parts of England and Wales, and for that purpose:
a) to generate or acquire supplies of electricity; and
b) to provide bulk supplies of electricity for the Area Boards for distribution by those Boards.

In respect of pricing policy, other relevant statutory provisions for the CEGB include duties to:

- break even, taking one year with another
- properly charge outgoings to revenue account
- avoid undue preference in the provision of supplies
- consult with the Electricity Council before fixing prices
- frame tariffs so as to show the methods by which and principles on which charges are made
- publish tariffs in a manner that will secure adequate publicity.

The most recent of the White Papers (HM Treasury, 1978) adds to these statutory duties a number of further requirements, the most important of which are:

- a financial target, defined in terms of operating profit expressed as a percentage return on average capital employed (calculated on a CCA basis)
- a required real, pre-tax return of 5 per cent on new investment as a whole
- that prices should generally reflect long-run marginal costs, using, where appropriate, the 5 per cent required rate of return to reflect the capital element
- the achievement of further performance goals to be set by the Minister (which, for the ESI, have recently taken the form of targets for reductions in real controllable costs).

Finally, since 1976 a system of cash limits has been adopted for the public sector. Thus the ESI is set an external financing limit (EFL) which constrains its annual change in net in-debtedness to central government.

The ESI therefore operates under a rather extensive set of constraints imposed by central government. Much has been made of possible inconsistencies and redundancies in these constraints, and the Treasury published a consultative docu-ment in 1984 which discussed the updating of various aspects of nationalised industry statutes (HM Treasury, 1984a). On the whole, however, these arguments have tended to be over-stated and have directed attention from some of the more important regulatory issues at stake. For example, phrases such as 'break even, taking one year with another' are suscept-ible to a variety of interpretations and are not necessarily inconsistent with the sorts of levels currently being set for financial targets. Similarly, while it is easy to construct models in which the guidelines of the 1978 White Paper are inconsistent (particularly the EFL and required rate of return requirements), this sometimes occurs because of the restricted number of industry decision variables embodied in the models. With richer and more realistic choice sets, the prob-lem tends to be less severe. Thus if cost levels are endogenous an industry may be able to obtain additional finance for profitable projects from improvements in internal efficiency.

The forms of the constraints imposed upon the industry (and particularly the financial target) invite comparison with US regulatory structures. Indeed, the system can be viewed as a variant of rate-of-return regulation, and it is tempting to follow an Averch–Johnson (1962) approach in analysing the effects of regulation. There are, however, at least four major distinguishing features of the ESI's regulatory system that would modify the analysis and results:

- the equivalent of the US allowable rate of return (the financial target, currently 2.75 per cent) is *less* than the implicit cost of capital, and represents a minimum, rather than a maximum, performance level
- the UK industry does not have access to the private capital market and faces an additional capital budgeting con-straint in the form of the external financing limit
- the objectives of the regulated firms are rather different in the two cases

- there are few obstacles to direct ministerial interventions in decision-making.

The last of these is the most difficult to incorporate into formal economic models. Regulation is not confined to the establishment of a few, stable rules and procedures, and government can impose its own priorities on the firm at any stage. Unfortunately, governmental objectives are likely to shift over time, reflecting the short-run political preoccupations of the day.

Taking account of these points, and of empirical work in the US, it seems unlikely that general approaches of the Averch–Johnson type will take us very far towards understanding the effects of regulation in the ESI. The underlying models are rarely sufficiently rich to capture all the important aspects of the regulatory situation. The options available to management are typically much wider than those assumed, and constraint levels are usually set after some bargaining process between interested parties, rather than being imposed by the regulatory agency and subsequently accepted by the firms. Putting the second point a different way, simple Stackelberg models are unlikely to be a good way of representing the interaction between regulators and firms. Finally, nothing is said about the behaviour of a regulated firm that faces frequent interventions by ministers whose priorities may well exhibit considerable variation from period to period.

Thus, while it would be useful to have analytical models that are capable of predicting the effects of regulatory changes on the ESI, the existing approaches are inadequate. Simple models abstract from too many relevant, important factors and more comprehensive, tractable analyses have yet to be produced. Assessment of the consequences of alternative policies must therefore be based upon less formal approaches to the problem.

IV. Regulation in practice

Leaving aside issues connected with the 1984/5 miners' strike, the current Government's approach to the ESI has been strongly influenced by the PSBR targets of the Medium

Term Financial Strategy. Thus the industry has been required to meet increasingly stringent financial constraints over the past few years, and the trend is likely to continue. The figures in Table 1 summarise the position with respect to financial targets and EFLs.

In the absence of EFLs, over-achievement of the financial target in, say, 1985/6 could be expected to lead to a lower operating target in the following years. EFLs tend to prevent this happening: over-performance in one year does not lead

Table 1. Financial Targets and External Financing Limits for the Electricity Industry

Financial target (per cent)

Year	Target	Outturn
1980/1 1981/2 1982/3	1.7	2.3
1983/4 1984/5	1.4	2.6 (1983/4 only)
1985/6 1986/7 1987/8	2.75	

Note: the asset base for 1980/1 to 1982/3 excluded capital work in progress (CWIP). Since then CWIP has been included, so the earlier and later figures are not directly comparable. Allowing for this factor, there was little change in the financial target between 1980/1–1982/3 and 1983/4–1984/5.

External financing (£ million)

Year	Target	Outturn
1978/9	−75	−100
1979/80	232	190
1980/1	187	140
1981/2	−165	−221
1982/3	−148	−153
1983/4	−418	−483
1984/5	−746	—
1985/6	−1,128	—

to an equivalent reduction in the EFL for the next. Thus, on the assumption that the industry takes the EFL to be a minimum (rather than an average) cash flow requirement, even if the EFL is consistent with the financial target in each individual year its impact is, in practice, to raise the effective value of the financial target.

In addition to this effect, the EFLs have also placed upward pressure on prices by virtue of being set at levels in excess of those which would be consistent with the financial target. Following ministerial intervention to increase prices, the Select Committee on Energy (1984) estimated that this deviation amounted to about £380 million in 1984/5. It is apparent, therefore, that the annual external financing limits have become the operative financial constraint on the industry in the most recent period.

Some indication of the likely trend in cash transfers from the industry to central government can be gleaned from the projections in Table 2, drawn from the ESI's Medium Term Development Plan, 1984–91.

Table 2. Projected Revenue and Operating Surplus for the Electricity Supply Industry

(£ million)

Year	ESI revenue	ESI surplus over operating costs	Government receipts
1984/5	9,878	2,279	1,171
1985/6	10,321	2,360	1,395
1986/7	10,805	2,487	1,850

Government receipts are defined as interest payments plus corporation tax less the EFL. The plan was drawn up before the miners' strike and before the upward revisions in financial targets and EFLs (i.e. they are based upon a financial target of 1.4 per cent). Thus while the 1984/5 figure is a gross over-estimate of the payments to government, the later figures are likely to understate the flow considerably.

It is ironic that the driving force towards higher prices has come from changes in government constraints imposed upon the industry. Price regulation is usually viewed as a means of preventing detriments to the consumer arising from the exploitation of market power. In practice, government appears increasingly willing to use that same market power to extract larger revenue contributions from the industry by forcing up prices to levels that appear, on best available evidence, to be significantly in excess of marginal costs.

Revenue from the ESI is not, of course, the only variable of interest to central government, and there is clearly some sensitivity to the political effects of sharp increases in prices. Lobbying by industrial consumers, for example, has had a limited amount of success in obtaining EFL concessions to allow for the further development of load management schemes.[a] Nevertheless, priorities have shifted, with the emphasis now being placed on tightening the financial constraints on the industry.

In defence of current policy, it has sometimes been argued that the higher financial targets and more stringent EFLs do not conflict with the economic efficiency objectives encapsulated in the marginal cost pricing guidelines. The argument runs as follows. Along with the other nationalised industries, the ESI is required to achieve a 5 per cent real rate of return on new investment and, in the long run, achievement of such a target should lead, given appropriate pricing, to a real return on assets as a whole of approximately 5 per cent. Hence, a financial target of around 5 per cent should be consistent with long-run marginal cost pricing.

This line of reasoning begs the question of whether or not existing CCA asset valuations are reasonably accurate measures of the economic value of plant in the conditions of suboptimal capacity levels that now face the industry. Evidence on long-run marginal costs from sources such as the Sizewell B Inquiry and the Coopers and Lybrand Report (1982) on the Bulk Supply Tariff Review suggests that they are not, and that prices do indeed exceed such costs.

One interesting aspect of the efficiency argument for an increased financial target is the timing of its appearance, which illustrates an important point about the way in which regulation operates in the UK. Detailed attention to pricing policy tends to occur sporadically, and in response to a specific political pressure (in this case the desire to bolster up the case for a higher financial target, motivated chiefly by PSBR targets). On the whole, governments have been content simply to enunciate general pricing principles and then let the public corporations get on with it. Monitoring and enforcement of the application of those principles have been patchy, with reliance being placed upon occasional reports of the Monopolies and Mergers Commission and of outside consultants (e.g. the Coopers and Lybrand Report, 1982). Moreover, in recent years, where the conclusions of such reports have pointed towards the relaxation of financial constraints, the recommendations have been quietly ignored.

The ESI has taken marginal cost pricing guidelines much more seriously than most other nationalised industries, but the fact that many public corporations have paid so little attention to them makes the general monitoring and enforcement point very clearly. Thus rather different pricing strategies are followed in the related industries of gas and coal (which raise some difficult second-best problems regarding electricity pricing policy) and, overall, there are insufficient incentives for compliance with the guidelines.

Establishment and enforcement of performance targets appear to occur in the same, unrigorous way. The ESI's target, to reduce real controllable costs by a designated percentage over a given period, exists in recognition of the dangers of cost inefficiencies emerging as a result of lack of competition. But it is difficult to know whether or not the constraint is being set in a way that adequately takes into account the available opportunities for cost reduction. Here a major problem is the lack of information available to regulators. Given the structure of the industry, the key information source on the generating side is the CEGB itself, which has incentives to present its performance in the best possible light. The only domestic bench-marks for evaluations are the Scottish Boards, but they have rather different structures and operating conditions (a greater proportion of hydro capacity, for example) and comparisons therefore have to be made with some degree of care. This is, of course, a classic difficulty with the regulation of monopoly, but the structure of the UK industry exacerbates the problem compared, say, with the US where the existence of regional utilities offers a potentially richer set of data for studies of comparative performance.

V. The implementation of pricing policy

Many of the weaknesses of past and current regulation of the ESI arise from the overall framework of control for the nationalised industries established in the 1967 and 1978 White Papers. The latter have been extensively discussed elsewhere (see, for example, Heald, 1980, and Vickers and Yarrow, 1985) and no attempt will be made here to summarise the various, general points of criticism that have been raised. Instead the discussion will be limited to an evaluation of the Bulk Supply Tariff, using this as an illustration of the effects of regulatory deficiencies.

The Bulk Supply Tariff has three main components:

- a range of time-of-day and seasonal prices (energy charges)
- charges levied at times of peak demand and at various other times during the winter demand plateau (demand charges)
- a levy based upon an Area Board's maximum demand in the previous tariff period (the system service charge).

The rationale for this tariff structure is (roughly) that energy charges correspond to marginal operating costs, the demand charges to marginal capacity costs, and the system service charge (newly introduced in 1984/5) to overhead costs not recovered by the other components.

Although there have been criticisms of the methods by which marginal operating costs are measured, it has been the demand charges that, over the years, have attracted the most comment. One anomaly was that increases in system peak load were subject to lower demand charges than off-peak increments in load during the winter plateau. This outcome is clearly incompatible with marginal cost pricing and appears to have arisen from the use of differing time horizons in different parts of the capital cost calculations—a point noted by the Monopolies and Mergers Commission in its report on the CEGB (1981a). Yet, despite the Commission's findings, the error remained uncorrected in the three subsequent tariff periods.

With respect to pricing policy in general, it can be conjectured that the flexibility afforded by the absence of close, external monitoring of tariffs leads to a rather creative use of marginal cost principles in which conflicts between the revenue-raising and efficiency objectives of the BST are obscured. Since there are several ways of increasing capacity (deferring plant retirements, new gas turbine plant, new coal-fired plant, new nuclear plant) capital costs depend heavily upon assumptions about the availability of each option (i.e. about which capital inputs are fixed and which are variable), which in turn depends upon the length of the time horizon adopted in the tariff calculations. Discretion regarding the choice of time horizon therefore gives price-setters a range of possible 'marginal cost' tariff structures, from which they can select the one most favourable to their own objectives. Needless to say, the resulting structure may not be the one that achieves the greatest allocative efficiency.

In fact, on the basis of the CEGB's own background information, there is evidence to suggest that the BST's demand charges have, over a period of years, been significantly in excess of marginal capacity costs for both *'short'* (less than fifteen years) and *long* time horizons (Coopers and Lybrand, 1982, Slater and Yarrow, 1983). Given that marginal operating costs are an increasing function of output (by virtue of the availability of plants with differing technical characteristics) and that they are reasonably accurately reflected in energy charges, the implication of this evidence is that BST prices exceed both marginal and average (avoidable) costs (defined in terms of the chosen time horizon).

Partial recognition of the marginal capacity cost problem is implicit in the 1984/5 BST, which reduced demand charges and introduced a new system service charge to replace the revenue lost by the adjustment. Nevertheless, the bias remains and the restructuring of the tariff does nothing to close the gap between average charges and avoidable costs, since the former will include a system service element. Perhaps the most interesting aspect of the 1984/5 reform is the motivation for the change of heart. It has not occurred through regulatory interventions based upon the work of the Monopolies Commission, outside consultants or academics. Rather, the driving force appears to have been the desire to alter the tariff structure in a way that will hinder new entry now that the Energy Act 1983 has removed some of the other obstacles to potential competition (see Section VII).

If it is accepted that the ESI's financial constraints have forced prices up above the levels of marginal and average opportunity costs, we are left with the question of how second-best policies are to be applied. As in the case of the choice of time horizon, we find an absence of guidelines for and monitoring of the resulting adjustments: the industry is, by and large, simply left to its own devices. One problem here is that the industry makes no systematic distinction between intermediate and final consumers of electricity, indicating consequent distortions to allocative efficiency. Thus VAT extension is likely to be a more efficient way of raising government revenue from the ESI than increasing the financial target, and equity objections to the former are not very convincing given the availability of other tax or benefit instruments for income redistribution.

A second problem is that, by falling most heavily upon demand and service charges, the 'second-best' price adjustments made by the CEGB distort the cost messages contained in the BST in a damaging way. To illustrate, consider the case of consumers evaluating one of the available load management options. The incentives for load management are closely linked to the level of demand charges, and, if the latter are excessive, firms will be encouraged to install their own 'peak' generating capacity to take advantage of the options when their requirements could have been supplied at lower cost by the public corporations.

To summarise, given its implicit efficiency objectives, the Bulk Supply Tariff contains a number of anomalies and the existing system of regulation has shown itself to be ineffective in obtaining the (often simple) corrections needed to improve its cost messages. Regulators have been primarily concerned with financial performance and the average level of prices, rather than with the tariff structure. Yet misalignments in the latter are likely to lead to non-trivial allocative inefficiencies by virtue of the responsiveness of demand to changes in the relative levels of the tariff components. Efficiency performance could therefore be improved by more open and more systematic monitoring and enforcement of pricing policies.

VI. Competition and entry

The role of competition in electricity supply is, given the present structure of the industry, relatively limited. Rivalry with gas, for example, although it undoubtedly exists, does not provide sufficiently strong incentives to warrant abandonment of price regulation.[b] Even if the ESI were reorganised into competing, regional corporations, the extent of local monopoly power resulting from high 'transport' costs would still justify some central control of pricing decisions. Interest in improving performance by increasing competition has, therefore, focused mainly upon the possible beneficial effects of reducing entry barriers into the industry.

Until 1983, public policy adopted the familiar line of protecting the established firms from entry threats. Thus the Electric Lighting Act 1909 prohibited persons other than the Electricity Boards from commencing to supply or distribute electricity, while the Electricity (Supply) Act 1919 restricted the establishment and extension of generating stations. Both sets of provisions were, however, repealed by the Energy Act 1983.

In assessing both the recent liberalisation and possible further measures with the same intent, it will be useful to focus upon two broad arguments that question the benefits likely to be derived from the removal of statutory entry barriers. The first is that, since the industry is a natural monopoly, new entry would be undesirable; the second is that eliminating statutory barriers would either be ineffective or lead to the (costly) erection of alternative strategic entry barriers.

In the case of the ESI, the first of these arguments carries little force. Even if the industry *were* a natural monopoly, it is not necessarily the case that single-firm production would be optimal. Analyses which are based upon comparisons between the welfare properties of, say, a free entry Cournot–Nash equilibrium and an idealised public corporation typically abstract from informational and incentive problems. When the latter are brought into the play the conclusions can be quite different. Thus the existence of more than one firm provides greater information for the monitoring of the industry (whether by private shareholders, government Ministers or regulatory agencies), enabling those aspects of performance which can be ascribed to managerial actions to be distinguished from those which are non-controllable. By linking rewards to performance *relative* to other firms in the industry, it may be possible to improve the incentives for cost efficiency significantly.

Electricity generation, however, may not be a (strict) natural monopoly in current economic conditions. One reason for this emerges from the economics of co-generation (the generation of electricity in conjunction with the production of steam or heat for industrial or domestic purposes). Benefits from the vertical integration of steam production with manufacturing processes mean that the costs of co-generated electricity could sometimes be lower than those of the comparable outputs of a cost-efficient CEGB.

The argument that removal of statutory entry barriers is likely to prove ineffective in promoting competition is a more substantial point. The exclusionary use of control over monopoly bottle-necks in transmission, coupled with the CEGB's dominant market position, could in themselves constitute major obstacles to new entry. There is also the point that the existence of substantial sunk costs in generation gives rise to entry barriers which confer additional market power on the CEGB.

To illustrate these points, consider the possible response of the CEGB to a company seeking to enter the market to supply industrial users of electricity. Transmission losses facilitate the localisation of the entry threat: any cost advantage of the new competitor will be greatest for customers close to the generating plant(s). The CEGB can therefore meet the competition by cutting prices in only a fraction of its market, and can drop prices to short-run marginal costs without violating the underlying principles set out by the regulatory regime. Such price cuts can be achieved via the load management provisions of the BST, which allow considerable discretion to the Board in its treatment of industrial purchases. Moreover, the national dominance of the CEGB implies that there will be strong incentives for aggressive behaviour in the face of local entry: a reputation for toughness serves to discourage later entry elsewhere. Finally, in the absence of close monitoring of tariffs, there is the danger that predatory pricing (i.e. prices set at less than short-run marginal costs) could be used to drive out any existing competitor and deter potential competitors.

One conclusion to be drawn from this argument is that effective liberalisation requires that the removal of statutory barriers be accompanied by supporting regulatory measures, designed to counter anti-competitive behaviour on the part of the dominant supplier (since the current provisions and institutions of UK competition policy are clearly less than adequate for the task).

Some of the immediate goals of regulatory reform are clear: we would ideally like to see a cost-efficient production pattern, for example. Thus if a private company can generate electricity at a lower marginal cost than the CEGB, policy should attempt to ensure that it is not discouraged from expanding output by the latter's actions. The question is: what measures are necessary to bring this about?

In the US the Public Utility Regulatory Policies Act of 1978 requires the electric utilities to interconnect with private generators, to provide those operators with back-up power supplies on non-discriminatory terms, and to purchase electricity from them at rates equal to the avoidable costs of the utilities. In the UK the Energy Act 1983 contains similar provisions. Both Acts are intensely regulatory in nature and represent steps to facilitate competitive entry. Ultimately, however, their degree of success will depend upon the rigour with which they are enforced and, in particular, upon the way in which the avoidable cost clauses are interpreted and applied. For the UK at least, there are strong grounds for concern in respect of this last point, as will now be argued.

VII. The Energy Act 1983

The Energy Act 1983 removed the statutory barriers to entry contained in the 1909 and 1919 Electricity Acts. It also laid down conditions under which the various Electricity Boards are required to purchase power from, and make their transmission facilities available to, private generators of electricity.

In respect of purchases of power the relevant clause states:

The principles on which tariffs are fixed and prices proposed by an Electricity Board . . . shall include the principle that a purchase by the Board . . . should be on terms which

a) will not increase the prices payable by customers of the Board for electricity supplied to them by the Board, and

b) will reflect the costs that would have been incurred by the Board but for the purchase.

In respect of the transmission system the relevant clause states:

The principles on which tariffs are fixed and prices proposed by an Electricity Board . . . shall include the principle that charges should be no more than sufficient to provide a return on the relevant assets comparable to any return that the Board expects to receive on comparable assets.

The most interesting point about these provisions is that the CEGB is excluded from the first. Thus it is the avoidable costs of the *Area Boards* that form the basis of Energy Act tariffs. Since Area Board avoidable costs are effectively the prices of the Bulk Supply Tariff, we would expect to see prices paid to private generators which were closely in line with BST rates.

This would be a satisfactory outcome if the BST charges properly reflected the CEGB's cost structure. But if, as argued earlier, BST prices are constrained to be above both marginal and average avoidable costs by the public corporation's financial target and external financing limit, the consequence of Area Boards paying the same prices to private generators as to the CEGB will be inefficiency: the incentives for private production will be too great. The underlying aim is equalisation of marginal *generating* costs (adjusted for transmission losses) between the two sectors and, in the absence of regulatory reform, this will not necessarily be achieved, even approximately, by the current legislation. In this context it is worth noting that the problem does not arise in the case of the Scottish Boards, which can legitimately argue that their avoided costs *are* marginal generating costs;

it is the separation of generation and transmission/retailing that causes the difficulty in England and Wales.

In practice, the ESI has been able to get around the problem by changing the structure of the BST and, on the Area Board side, adopting a one-year time horizon for the purposes of measuring avoidable costs. The CEGB introduced a new system service charge in 1984/5 which incorporated cost elements that were previously treated as capacity-related (and therefore included in long-run marginal costs). The charge is based upon an Area Board's maximum demand *in the previous year*. Hence, an Area Board can argue that, within any one year, the charge is unavoidable and should therefore not be used in the calculation of Energy Act tariffs. The net result is that, over a period of several years, the prices paid to private generators could be significantly lower than those paid to the CEGB. For the future, the CEGB clearly has incentives to increase the relative level of the system service charge and, to the extent that the CEGB continues to receive support from the Area Boards, it can be expected that further moves in this direction will occur.

The outcome illustrates a number of unsatisfactory features of current regulatory procedures. In particular, it demonstrates quite clearly the discretionary powers of the public corporations with respect to the framing of tariff structures, and the ability of those corporations to adopt discriminatory practices designed to retard entry. The actual result may not be too bad in present circumstances—the discrimination compensates for the excessive financial target and retards entry in a period of excess capacity—but there are no guarantees that it will always be so beneficial. Indeed, those who believe that BST prices (inclusive of the system service charge) are now close to (or below) long-run marginal costs must also believe that the intentions of the Energy Act have been subverted.

The preferred solution would be to leave the Energy Act provisions intact, enforce them more stringently (i.e. prevent discrimination between public and private producers), establish a regulatory agency with a mandate to enforce marginal cost pricing policies, and make good any government revenue shortfalls by extension of the VAT base or other fiscal adjustments. Alternative approaches include legislation requiring that tariffs for purchases from private generators be based on avoidable generating costs, or a restructuring of the industry to integrate generation and transmission activities (as in Scotland).

VIII. Privatisation

It is not likely that privatisation of the ESI could be effected in a way that would render regulation of the industry undesirable. Natural monopoly conditions in transmission point in the other direction and, even on the generating side, cost conditions suggest an industrial structure featuring dominant firms—if only at the regional level—and possibly surrounded by a fringe of smaller producers (see Joskow and Schmalensee, 1983, for a discussion of minimum efficient scale in electricity generation). Questions of regulatory policy would therefore continue to be of central importance for the future performance of the industry.

Nevertheless, it can be argued that privatisation might introduce incentives that would facilitate improvements in performance. Take the case of Area Board privatisation. A privately owned company would have fewer incentives to interpret the Energy Act in a way favourable to the CEGB. It would be more willing to shop around for sources of supply and to switch to private generators if they offered prices lower than those of the BST. But, while this would increase competitive pressure on the CEGB, the outcome might not be entirely satisfactory. To the extent that the CEGB continues to be constrained by a financial target which implies that it must set prices above economic opportunity costs, there will be a policy-induced distortion in competition favouring the private sector. Thus the impact of privatisation of the Area Boards depends heavily upon the regulatory regime facing the CEGB, and the negative effects of weaknesses in the latter will not be eliminated—and could possibly be made even more severe—by the transfer of ownership.

Consider next the option of privatising the CEGB in its present form. Again much depends upon the associated regulatory system, since such a company would retain market dominance for the foreseeable future. Moreover the regulatory problems would be much the same as those arising in the case of a dominant public corporation. Considerable reliance would have to be placed upon entry threats to increase the pressures for cost reduction, and again a prime requirement of policy would be the prevention of strategies aimed at raising entry barriers.

Other, feasible privatisation options are, of course, available. One would be based upon the establishment of privately owned, regional generating companies. In such cases, however, the major benefits likely to ensue are linked more to the organisational changes than to the transfer of ownership. The danger associated with the privatisation options is that the ownership question may distract attention from the more fundamental issues surrounding regulation and competition, leading to solutions featuring weak and/or illiberal regulatory systems. The British Telecom example serves as a warning on this point.[c]

IX. Conclusions

Policy towards the electricity supply industry in Britain can be criticised on a number of grounds. In principle, the framework for the control of the nationalised industries set out in the relevant White Papers could serve as a reasonable basis for regulation of the industry. In practice, the preoccupation of governments with macro-economic issues, and the lack of attention given to micro-economic questions, have led to a poor track record in the regulatory field. Governments have typically been content to set out general principles of policy and, with the exception of the financial constraints, have not been much concerned with monitoring performance and enforcing compliance. Regulation would be much improved by more specific guidelines and a more rigorous approach to enforcement. Establishment of an independent regulatory commission would be one way forward, and issues concerning the structure of the industry also merit re-examination.

The liberalising provisions of the Energy Act are to be welcomed, offering, as they do, some prospects for increased competitive pressures on the CEGB. The Act, however, suffers from some deficiencies which have been outlined in this paper. Revision and/or stricter regulation of pricing policies are called for if its effectiveness is to be improved.

Finally, privatisation cannot be regarded as a substitute for improvements in regulation, and should not be allowed to delay measures to increase competitive pressures. To the extent that it is allowed to distract attention from the more fundamental questions of regulation, liberalisation, and organisational reform it is, on balance, undesirable. If, on the other hand, ownership transfer were seen as a means of facilitating the desired policy changes in these areas, the balance of advantage would shift more in its favour.

EDITORS' NOTES

a. Under a load management scheme, a customer is offered a reduced tariff if he undertakes to reduce his demand for power during peak periods if requested to do so.
b. Some evidence on elasticities is reproduced in the article by Hammond, Helm, and Thompson in Part IV.
c. This issue is further discussed by Vickers and Yarrow in Part IV.

11

LONDON'S AIRPORTS: THE PRIVATISATION OPTIONS*

David Starkie and David Thompson

I. Introduction

The present pattern of ownership of civil airfields in Britain is a complex mixture reflecting in part the ebb and flow of post-war policies towards public ownership. The 1983 Conservative Manifesto pledged that 'as many as possible of Britain's airports shall become private sector companies'. Airports are at present owned by several different public sector bodies—the British Airports Authority (BAA), local authorities, and the Civil Aviation Authority—and there is one significant privately owned airport (Southampton). However, BAA's London airports (Heathrow, Gatwick, and Stansted) handle nearly two-thirds of UK passenger traffic and issues regarding the effective use of capacity and investment are most sharply identified in the south-east.

The activities of the London airports can be divided into two broad categories: first, and most obviously, the airports provide for the landing and handling of aircraft and passengers; second, they provide a range of commercial services for passengers (such as banking, car hire facilities, and duty-free shops) and for airlines (e.g. refuelling). These two groups of activities are of equal importance in the total turnover of

* This article summarises the findings in D. N. M. Starkie and D. J. Thompson, *Privatising London's Airports: Options for Competition*, 1985, IFS Report Series 16.

David Starkie is with TM Economics and a Research Associate of the Institute for Fiscal Studies.

David Thompson is a Programme Director at the Institute for Fiscal Studies.

The authors are grateful to Tim Burfoot, Alex Gibbs, and Sue Jaffer for help in the preparation of the Report, and to Mark Ashworth, Peter Forsyth, and John Kay for providing many useful comments on earlier drafts of the Report. The research on which this article is based was financially supported by the Economic and Social Research Council.

London's airports. However, BAA does not itself provide many commercial services. Instead it franchises these operations to specialist firms in the private sector (for example Trusthouse Forte); BAA's income from these services includes fees for the franchises and payments for services such as heating, electricity, water, etc. Thus the total turnover (or customers' expenditure) on the commercial services at major airports is many times greater (seven times greater at Heathrow) than the turnover earned from landing fees and from handling aircraft and passengers.

Because many activities are not carried out directly by BAA but are subcontracted to specialist companies, BAA is different in character from other nationalised industries. Only 10 per cent of the workforce at BAA's airports are direct employees of BAA; the remaining 90 per cent work for the airlines, for franchisees, and for companies providing contracted services. The main tasks undertaken by BAA's direct workforce relate to airport security, portering services, and the provision of emergency services. Many franchised activities are subcontracted to a particular company for a limited duration on the basis of competitive tenders; at the end of the period the 'franchise' is re-opened to tender. In other cases (for example aircraft refuelling at Heathrow), services are provided by a range of specialist companies acting in competition with one another. Both approaches might be expected to keep unit costs to a minimum and it can be concluded that, at least in relation to its commercial services, BAA is achieving productive efficiency (although these incentives do not apply to the infrastructure which BAA provides for its franchisees).

Its achievement of allocative efficiency is more questionable. BAA's policy for air traffic services is to set charges on the basis of long-run marginal costs. Because Heathrow in particular is operating at capacity for long periods, a more efficient solution would be to set prices to ration scarce capacity. However, analysis shows that BAA's stated policy of charging at long-run marginal cost does not appear to have been applied consistently or thoroughly. In 1980 BAA carried out a detailed study of the incremental costs incurred at both Heathrow and Gatwick Airports in preparation for legal proceedings brought against BAA by a number of airlines who argued that BAA's charges were discriminatory. The results from this analysis can be used to make a comparison between BAA's actual charges and the level of charges required to cover long-run marginal costs. Table 1 shows the revenues which it is estimated would be generated by setting charges equal to long-run marginal costs and compares these with the revenues which would be generated by the actual charges prevailing during 1983/4. The calculations indicate that charges in 1983/4 at Heathrow and Gatwick were substantially below BAA's own estimate of its long-run marginal costs in 1983/4.

BAA's objective in the case of its commercial services is to maximise profits (qualified by its public enterprise obligations and the long-term credibility of its pricing policies). We have noted already that BAA promotes productive efficiency in the operation of these services by franchising them to specialist companies in the private sector on the basis of competitive tenders. However, to achieve its aim of maximising the profits earned from these services BAA does have an incentive to reduce or minimise the degree of competition that the franchisee faces. With reduced competition, fran-

Table 1. Traffic Revenues Implied by Cost Analysis compared with 1983/4 Charges (1982 Traffic Pattern) for Heathrow and Gatwick Airports   (*£ million*)

Cost/Charge category	HEATHROW		GATWICK	
	April 1983 charges	Cost-based charges	April 1983 charges	Cost-based charges
Aircraft weight and movement	20	10	6	6
Passenger charge (incl. security)	52	86	17	29
Parking	20	34	4	15
Total charges	92	130	27	50

Source: BAA, 1983b, Table 10.1; BAA, 1983a, Table 8.1.

chisees will be able to charge higher prices than they would otherwise be able to do and, consequently, they are able to increase their bids for the right to operate franchises. In practice the degree to which BAA restricts competition varies. The services provided to airlines at London's airports (such as refuelling) are moderately competitive. In contrast, most services to passengers (such as retailing) are subject to little competition within a terminal, and face only limited competition from off-airport or in-flight facilities.

To summarise, BAA appears to have chosen to set charges for air-traffic services well below marginal costs. In the case of many commercial services, competition has been restricted to ensure that prices are raised well above costs. Both policies are inefficient in allocative terms and have the effect that scarce capacity is not allocated to the most beneficial uses. Also, under-charging is exaggerating the requirement for costly new investment.

II. Competition and privatisation

There are a number of factors which might have contributed to this state of affairs. First, as a public enterprise BAA is not expected to maximise profits and is sheltered from take-over by organisations identifying opportunities for increased returns on capital. The Government does set a financial target (the agreed target for the London airports for the current period is a minimum rate of return on average net assets of 3 per cent plus a growth-related increment), but it is difficult for the Government to judge how efficient the Authority could be. Although the Authority will aim to achieve the agreed targets, it has no real incentive to maximise its return and therefore cover costs across all its outputs.

Second, the Authority is subject to pressures from a range of organisations which seek to modify its practices in their favour and the statutory consultation requirements placed on the Authority provide a convenient avenue for such pressures. The airlines in particular are adept at putting pressure on the Authority. They gain substantially from the Authority failing to charge economic prices for the use of traffic facilities and consequently they are prepared to expend substantial resources on keeping down traffic charges. Because the Authority, unlike many airlines, does not itself seek to maximise profits and is not subject to pressures from commercial investors, its ability and its resolve to resist pressures to act inefficiently are heavily compromised.

Third, and related to the preceding factors, because the Authority is not required, or motivated, to maximise the return on its invested capital, it could have an incentive to pursue the alternative goals of maximising output or maximising the scale of its capital assets. Its under-charging of traffic services (cross-subsidised from retailing activities) and its powerful advocacy of an enormous investment in Stansted in the absence of clear signals by the market that such an expansion is justified financially are features consistent with such goals.

Privatising BAA in its present form would not, however, be an adequate solution: The London airport system has significant market power and privatisation as a system would suggest a need for regulation on a substantial scale. But experience in the US shows that tightly regulated private monopolies display many of the weaknesses which we have identified in BAA. In addition, the threat of take-over to such a large and specialised organisation is unlikely to be strong. There is a danger that a privatised BAA would retrench on the policy of franchising commercial services (although a strictly profit-maximising management is likely to retain large-scale franchising). For these reasons the efficiency incentives resulting from *en bloc* privatisation are likely to be weak.

A more promising option is to privatise in a manner which promotes competition. There is considerable scope for increasing competition in the south-east provided that the ownership of BAA's airports is divided. Separate ownership of BAA's London airports would introduce more competition into the large market associated with travel to and from London and the south-east region. Stansted and Gatwick have the potential to compete strongly with each other (and with Luton) in the large and 'footloose' inclusive-tour and intercontinental discount fare markets where cross-elasticities are high. In addition, Gatwick is shaping up as a promising competitor to Heathrow for scheduled traffic; it now serves more UK regional centres and more cities in the US than does Heathrow. (And if the proposed services from the Docklands STOL(short take-off and landing)-port obtain approval this will add a further, albeit small, competitive element.)

Separate ownership will not eliminate monopoly power at the south-eastern airports. Heathrow especially will retain such power to a considerable degree in specific segments of the market. But, with divided ownership, these segments will be fewer and, overall, the demand curve for any one airport will be much more elastic than if Heathrow, Stansted, and Gatwick are maintained in unified ownership.

BAA has argued that breaking up the Authority's airports will introduce a number of disadvantages, but these seem to be more apparent than real. There do not appear to be any marked economies to be gained by keeping the airports as one management unit. Nor do we foresee, from an investment perspective, problems arising. It is possible to expand many airport facilities by small increments and we would expect this to become a more common approach under a competitive regime. On the whole, the investment problems alluded to are not, in either content or scale, really different from those faced by a number of other economic sectors in which large sunk costs and competition are the norm, e.g. large-scale retailing, and chemical industries.

However, competition between airports is most unlikely to reduce the monopoly rents currently earned from commercial services. At Heathrow and at Gatwick, where there are multiple terminals, it has been suggested that these assets might be set up on a competing basis. If passenger services within these terminals continue to be awarded to franchisees on an exclusive basis this is unlikely to be effective. A better option would be to introduce or extend competition in the actual provision of these services within the terminal building, although in some cases there are physical constraints which make this difficult to achieve.

At the present time a small degree of competition is introduced by off-site facilities (e.g. in-flight duty-free sales by airlines and car-hire firms operating from perimeter hotels). A more radical departure along these lines would be to permit the sale of duty-free items at selected retail outlets in city

centres. This is done on a large scale in Australia where it has
had the effect of reducing prices across a wide range of tax-
free goods.

There is a strong case, however, for regarding the duty-free
concession as a tax distortion. The rationale for this tax concession is unclear; it is unlikely that it was intended as an implicit subsidy for the airport industry. The offer price for the
airports could be expected to reflect these potential rents thus
redirecting them to the Exchequer. But it is preferable that
the Government awards (directly or indirectly through an
appointed agent) the trading concessions for duty/tax-free
goods so that fees from the concession flow directly to the
Exchequer.

Overall, we see the introduction of more competition between airports and within airport services as an essential element in the case for privatisation. Privatisation without
establishing a more competitive structure will require a degree
of regulation and intervention that must place a question-
mark over the basic case for privatisation. Thus, if dividing
the ownership of the London airports is ruled out, to retain
BAA's airports in the public sector and use the various
powers the Government has to encourage a more efficient
outcome is an option which must be given serious consideration. Such intervention would be unpopular, it would be
contrary to the present Government's predilection to intervene less, and it would place the Government increasingly in
the role of second-guessing the market. But if it is not possible to establish a competitive market this might be the best
way to proceed.

III. Regulation and privatisation

Dividing the ownership of London's airports would introduce more competition but individual airports would still
retain a degree of market power; there remains a case for adding to existing regulation. For example, it has been suggested
that there should be rate-of-return regulation exercised by a
specialist body similar to the Office of Telecommunications.
The basic idea of rate-of-return regulation (a common practice in the US for regulating public utilities) is that the

regulated firm is allowed a 'fair' rate of return on its 'rate base'—a measure of the firm's capital assets. A major limitation of this approach is the well-known overcapitalisation or Averch—Johnson (1962) effect. The firm can increase total profits by expanding the assets (rate base) on which a proportionate return is allowed (provided that the allowed rate of return exceeds the cost of capital to the firm). Consequently, there is a tendency towards over-investment.

Sherman and Visscher (1982) have shown that rate-of-return regulation also has an effect on the structure of prices —it encourages the use of multipart tariffs, price discrimination and, in some circumstances, the setting of marginal price below marginal cost for those activities which require marginally more capital. Therefore, rate base regulation results in inefficiencies of the type that appear to be associated with the current system of specifying for BAA a target rate of return on assets. Indeed, if there are pressures not to exceed the target or penalties in doing so (e.g. the threat of litigation from disgruntled airlines), then the target rate of return will produce exactly the same undesirable effects as rate-base regulation.

The alternative to rate-base regulation that has been suggested is to regulate monopoly power by specifying an acceptable rate of growth in charges and tariffs (Littlechild, 1983). This approach has been adopted in the case of British Telecom and articulated in the form of 'RPI minus X' (i.e. increases are permitted only up to a level set at X percentage points below the change in the retail price index). The absolute or proportional size of the return on capital is not limited by this method and thus the problem of overcapitalisation is avoided. There remains an incentive to efficiency.

Applying this approach to BAA's airports suggests that prices charged by airport retailers could be subject to an $RPI - X$ formula; charges for traffic services (which are set below marginal costs) could be subject to a formula once prices had risen to cover marginal costs.

The regulatory question has an obvious implication for the monies that the Government will realise from the sale of BAA's assets. Restructuring BAA's assets prior to privatisation also raises questions as to whether and to what extent there will be an effect on the aggregate sale proceeds received by the Treasury.

Increasing competition in the market reduces the potential scope to generate monopoly rents. For this reason it may be argued that the options which enhance competitive forces in the airport industry will have an adverse effect on the sale price of the assets. A desire by the Government to maximise the proceeds from privatisation appears to be in conflict with the objective of increased efficiency; if the south-eastern airports are divided between different owners and this increases competition between, for example, Gatwick and Stansted, then privatisation proceeds will be reduced. This is to oversimplify the issue. If the profits generated by a privatised BAA are regulated (either directly or through the regulation of prices) then dividing ownership and enhancing competition will have only a limited impact on the sale price.

There also appears little substance to the notion that, because divided ownership reduces the opportunities for economies of scale or cross-subsidisation, it also reduces the sale proceeds. First, it is doubtful that there are significant economies of scale to be realised by multiple airport ownership. Management and administrative overheads, in which some savings from common ownership might appear feasible, account for only 10 per cent of total expenditure. In addition, our analysis indicated constant returns to airport numbers in this category of expenditure. Second, it makes little difference whether loss-making activities are wrapped up in a large asset portfolio or disposed of separately. Because losses can be offset against profits for tax purposes a broad portfolio will reduce the tax burden and thereby increase the sale price. A narrow portfolio (i.e. Heathrow, Gatwick, and Stansted separated) will increase the Treasury's tax receipts but will reduce the sale proceeds. The pluses and minuses will tend to balance out to produce a similar sum (provided that similar discount rates are adopted in the public and private sectors).

Existing capacity at Heathrow and Gatwick is limited relative to peak demands. Because of this, airside access to Heathrow and Gatwick is valuable and should be allocated by price to those who value access most. A market in access should be established. This can be done by allowing incumbent airlines to trade (via a broker to reduce the risk of predatory behaviour) their existing rights, although assigning resale rights to the airlines will affect the market value of the airport assets.

A final, and important, factor to take account of is the possibility of litigation—a repeat of the Pan Am Case. This can be expected to have a depressing effect on asset values. The previous dispute was 'set aside' and a future action could, it seems, invoke previous contentions. The dispute was set aside on the basis of a Memorandum of Understanding between the American and UK Governments. None of the preferred privatisation policies we have discussed appear to contradict, in principle, the elements of the Memorandum. This does not prevent a different interpretation by the airlines and, therefore, the threat of litigious action can be expected to remain in the background. There is no simple solution to this problem, although one way forward would be for the UK Government to adopt the risks involved. It could do this by assuming liability for past claims set aside and it could agree also to accept responsibility for a proportion of any settlements that might arise from new claims.

IV. Conclusions

Improving the efficiency with which resources are used in the airports sector depends critically upon increasing the degree of competition between individual airports and, in the case of commercial services, at each airport site. A privatised, competitively structured airport industry will be less inclined to develop facilities without proven demand and will be less inclined to cross-subsidise and view size as an end in itself.

One can speculate endlessly on what might have been, but we suspect that if London's airports had been privatised and their ownership divided two decades ago, the Stansted saga would never have occurred and certainly not in the form in which it has. Even now, it is unlikely that an independent, privatised Stansted will push to increase capacity to fifteen million units or even half that figure. It is not evident that existing forecasts of demand will be sustainable if Stansted's users have to cover the costs of expanding capacity. And it is not certain how quickly demand will grow if charges at Heathrow and Gatwick too are based 'on sound economic principles' (Memorandum of Understanding, 1983). At the moment these charges are far from being economic or soundly based.

12

TELECOMMUNICATIONS: LIBERALISATION AND THE PRIVATISATION OF BRITISH TELECOM*

John Vickers and George Yarrow

I. Introduction

Telecommunications is a prime example of an industry which contains elements of natural monopoly (for example local networks) and areas in which normal competition can be effective (for example terminal equipment). In this paper, we begin with a brief outline of the telecommunications industry. We then describe and assess the development of the current regime of competition and regulation in the industry. Finally we consider future policy towards the industry.

Recent government policy towards the telecommunications industry has had two strands. First, there has been partial *liberalisation* of the industry: statutory barriers to certain forms of competition have been removed. Secondly, the majority of the shares of British Telecommunications (BT) have been transferred from public to *private ownership*, with accompanying regulatory measures. The liberalisation of the industry is most welcome, so far as it goes, and in a few areas it promises substantial benefits to the consumer in the form

* This article was first published as part of a report prepared for the Public Policy Centre by J. Vickers and G. Yarrow, *Privatization and the Natural Monopolies*, 1985, Public Policy Centre, 37 Golden Square, London W1, price £3.40 including postage.

John Vickers is a Fellow at Nuffield College, Oxford.

George Yarrow is a Fellow and Tutor in Economics at Hertford College, Oxford.

The authors are most grateful to Jonathan Aylen, Chris Beauman, Ron Dore, Ken George, Dieter Helm, John Kay, Bruce Laidlaw, Roger Liddle, Robin Matthews, Colin Mayer, Peter McGregor, Peter Oppenheimer, David Sawyers, Tom Sharpe, Aubrey Silberston, Dick Taverne, and Ralph Turvey for very helpful advice and comments received in preparing the book.

of lower prices and technological advance. But in view of the potential gains to be had from liberalisation, it is regrettable that the Government did not go further. In several important respects, the regime in which BT and Mercury are to operate is by no means liberal—for example the refusal to license more public networks, and the prohibition of 'resale'. These are major restrictions on competition. Indeed, there is reason to think that the urgency with which the Government sold BT shares to the private sector had the effect of *limiting* the extent of liberalisation (consequently increasing the likely proceeds of the sale). For example, there was no attempt to restructure BT to promote competition, as happened recently in the United States with American Telephone and Telegraph (AT&T). In any event, further steps towards liberalisation may be more difficult now that BT has been privatised than if it had remained in the public sector somewhat longer. Nevertheless they should be taken.

II. The telecommunications industry[1]

The telecommunications industry has three basic elements: (i) the supply of equipment (including switches, transmission media, and terminals); (ii) the running of networks; and (iii) the supply of services (whether basic or value added). Communications technology is constantly advancing. A wide range of terminal apparatus can now be attached to telecommunications networks, including word-processing equipment, new types of telex machines, private branch exchanges (PBXs), facsimile machines, as well as an expanding variety of telephone handsets. Electronic technology is increasingly being used as the switching technology, instead of electromechanical methods. In transmission, optical fibres, cellular radio, and satellites are being used, along with conventional coaxial cable and microwave radio.

To each technology corresponds a different structure of costs. It follows that technological change may transform a natural monopoly into an industry whose cost conditions

[1] For an excellent introduction to the issues involved, see Kay (1984). For more detailed accounts of the economics of telecommunications, see Littlechild (1979), Brock (1981), and Sharkey, (1982, Chap. 9). Our description is greatly simplified and is intended as general background to broad issues.

permit effective competition (and vice versa). It is possible that new 'modes' of competition, based on alternative technologies (e.g. cellular radio or cable TV networks), will seriously threaten and even displace traditional telecommunications networks. But we must begin by asking which parts of the industry are naturally monopolistic at present.

We see no reason to expect *natural* monopoly in the provision of terminal apparatus (although BT in fact enjoys a dominant position in respect of the supply of most types of terminal equipment). Competition in the markets for terminal equipment should be as free as possible (subject to standards safeguarding the integrity of the system overall). Perhaps one of the main threats to competition in this area has to do with the terms on which terminal equipment can be attached to the rest of the system. Experience with AT&T in the United States shows how, in the absence of adequate safeguards, the dominant firm can employ numerous strategies concerning interconnection to restrict and distort competition for terminal equipment. When AT&T's anti-trust suit ended in January 1982, AT&T divested itself of its local operating companies (but retained its manufacturing subsidiary, Western Electric, its long-distance division, and Bell Labs.), and the local operating companies are required to supply apparatus through separate subsidiaries. Such restructuring of the dominant firm diminishes this threat to competition. The British Government chose not to restructure BT before privatisation, and the threat to competition therefore remains.

The evidence is that natural monopoly is more likely to exist in the telecommunication network facilities, i.e. switching and transmission (see Sharkey, 1982, Chapter 9). These must be considered jointly, because there is a trade-off between switching and transmission in the design of a network. Less switching equipment is required if there are more direct transmission links: if A and B are joined directly, communication between them need not be routed via an exchange.

The nature of demand for communications is a major reason why natural monopoly is likely to be present in the running of networks. A person's demand for the services of a

telecommunications network depends upon who else sub-
scribes to that network. If A wishes to call B (and/or hopes
that B will call him), he must subscribe to the same network
as B. This interdependence of demand means that supply of
telecommunications services by two or more firms may be inefficient, and also that a supplier with many subscribers will
tend to drive out suppliers with fewer subscribers if he can
deny them interconnection on fair terms. The duplication of
complete networks would obviously be inefficient, and so
natural monopoly is likely. This argument pertains especially
to local networks, where the prospects for competition are
bleak. In long-distance communications (including international) there is more hope that some competition will
emerge, especially if the running of networks can be separated
(by regulation) from the supply of services, so as to allow
several suppliers of services to compete on the same network.
But no major competition to the dominant firm's provision
of trunk services is to be expected in the near future, in part
because of the restrictions that have been placed upon competition.

Finally we come to 'value added network services' (VANS)
and the question of resale. A VANS is a service which is additional to the conveying of messages. (A precise definition of
VANS is hard to find.) For example, a VANS might process, as
well as transmit, data. In liberalising VANS the Government
has allowed competition in the supply of data services (the proposed joint venture between BT and IBM in this area was also
blocked). By contrast, competition in the supply of voice services has been restricted: the Government has not permitted
competition with BT and Mercury in telecommunications
transmission for the next five years, and it has prohibited the
buying and reselling of BT capacity by independent providers
of telecommunications services. We shall return to these issues
after a discussion of the recent development of the framework
of competition and regulation in the UK.

III. The framework of competition and regulation

The Post Office was the monopoly supplier of telephone services in Britain from 1912 to 1981. The British Telecommuni-

cations Act 1981 established BT as a public corporation with responsibility for telecommunications services; the Post Office retained responsibility for postal services. The Act retained BT's exclusive privilege to run public networks and to regulate the industry. The 1981 Act also introduced some competition to the industry, notably in the market for terminal equipment (although BT retained important privileges here). In a White Paper in 1982 (Department of Trade, 1982), the Government announced its intention to sell just over half of BT's shares. The Telecommunications Act, which establishes the current framework of competition, received Royal Assent in April 1984. The Act abolished BT's statutory involvement in regulation. BT plc took over the business of the public corporation in August of that year, and, after a massive publicity campaign, 3 billion shares in BT (i.e. just over half the company) were sold to the public at the end of November 1984 at 130p per share payable in three instalments. When trading in the shares began, their value was almost 50p per share higher than the offer price. This huge premium reflected the very favourable yield (7.14 per cent) and price/earnings ratio (9.35) forecast in the prospectus. The premium represents a transfer in wealth of well over £1 billion to those who obtained BT shares from those who did not. The shares have since risen much higher. At the time of the flotation, there was considerable uncertainty as to the ability of the stock-market to absorb the massive share issue. Nevertheless it is unfortunate for the general tax-payer (who had to pay for the massive advertising campaign) that the Government failed to enjoy a larger proportion of the benefits of the sale.

Before considering the 1984 Act, and related developments, in more detail, we shall consider two important reports to the Secretary of State for Industry on telecommunications in the UK:

- The Beesley Report on 'Liberalisation of the Use of British Telecommunications Network' (January 1981)
- The Littlechild Report on 'Regulation of British Telecommunications' Profitability' (February 1983).

IV. The Beesley Report

In July 1980 Sir Keith Joseph announced to Parliament that the Government intended to relax BT's monopoly, in particular by allowing firms to use BT's circuits to offer services not currently provided by BT. Consequently, Professor Michael Beesley of the London Business School was commissioned:

To examine the scope for, and means of realising, profitable leasing of the network to users who would have unrestricted use of the capacity to provide services, taking account of:
(a) the need for such arrangements to operate to the benefit of the consumer;
(b) the effect of such arrangements on BT's present pricing structure and profitability. (Beesley Report, p. vii).

Professor Beesley considered the question of the *unrestricted* reselling of BT's capacity. He argued that to confine the study to 'value added' network services would be question-begging.

BT contended that unrestricted resale should not be allowed, on the grounds that it would lose revenues (with adverse effects upon investment); that its ability to cross-subsidise would be reduced; that its costs would rise; and that problems concerning standardisation and compatibility would arise. However, Professor Beesley was impressed by the potential advantages to customers of unrestricted resale, especially arising from the possibility of sharing lines and independent switching.

This would enable competitors to make the most efficient and innovative use of capacity. For example, a competitor who saw an opportunity to supply services to business customers by leasing a trunk line between two cities would be able to seize that opportunity. At present, such a competitor is not free to supply whatever services he chooses in this way. He is confined to value added network services (VANS). But since voice transmission forms the bulk of tele-communications activity, the most important benefits of resale (and the major impact upon BT's business) are likely to be in the voice market. However, VANS do not extend to voice transmission. Therefore the issue of whether resale should be unrestricted really is the central question. The gains to be had from liberalisation of VANS are important, but they are far less important than the benefits of liberalising the voice market by permitting unrestricted resale.

Professor Beesley concluded that:

(i) In the home market there should be no restriction on the freedom to offer services to third parties.

(ii) Consumer benefits are likely to outweigh the projected loss of net revenue by BT . . .

(iii) Prices at which BT offers leased circuits at home should continue to be decided by BT independently and announced. Customers should be able to lease these at the appropriate price irrespective of the use to be made of them.

(iv) BT should be free to engage in competition in the non-voice market, subject to regulatory safeguards . . ., and the pro-competitive mechanisms of the UK and EEC.

We share Professor Beesley's view that unrestricted resale should be permitted. The fact that it would threaten some of BT's business is a powerful argument in favour of permitting resale. That is how competition works. Moreover, resale would encourage innovation and efficiency in the use made of BT's capacity. The question is really whether the dominant supplier of telecommunications capacity should be protected from competition in the retailing of that capacity. Even with unrestricted resale, BT would be dominant in the retailing of capacity. Nevertheless, the presence of some competition— or at any rate the threat of it—is highly desirable. Even if substantial entry into the market did not actually take place, the threat of entry would constrain the behaviour of the dominant firm at least to some extent (look what has happened since liberalisation of the market for terminal equipment).

Resale inevitably poses problems of regulation and competition policy. Professor Beesley proposed that BT should independently decide the prices for leased circuits. If a firm wished to lease BT circuits in order to offer a service (e.g. line sharing) in competition with BT, then BT would have a clear incentive to discourage such competition by charging the firm a high price. Without some check on its pricing behaviour, BT would be able to exclude such competition altogether. BT's behaviour would be subject to scrutiny by regulatory and competition authorities, but the difficulties of determining what constitute 'fair' prices are very great. These problems are by no means unique to the issue of resale. They arise whenever a firm wishes to offer a product or service in conjunction with BT's network but in competition with BT. In principle, 'fair' terms for sale of capacity, or for interconnection, are related to the associated costs. But how are these costs to be defined and measured? The practical difficulties here are immense, especially since there are joint products. It is questionable whether BT itself—let alone a regulatory body or competition authority—could easily ascertain the relevant costs. These dangers would exist if BT was still publicly owned, but they are greater now that it has been privatised, because BT has a direct commercial motive to restrict competition. We consider the efficacy of competition policy as a check on BT's behaviour further below.

Despite Professor Beesley's conclusions, and the powerful arguments supporting them, the Government chose not to liberalise by permitting resale. In July 1984 the Minister announced that as a general principle, simple resale would not be licensed before July 1989. The rationale was to protect Mercury from competition while it constructs its rival network. Only in certain limited circumstances is it permissible for premises to be connected by private circuits. Cable companies are allowed to offer voice telephony services (and data services in a number of business centres) only in association with BT or with Mercury.

BT would have enjoyed great market power even if the Government had adopted a liberal stance on resale. The Government's decision not to permit resale makes that power greater still.

V. The Littlechild Report

In July 1982 the Government formally announced its intention to privatise BT in the White Paper on 'The Future of Telecommunications in Britain' (Department of Trade, 1982). The Telecommunications Bill was duly ordered by the House of Commons to be printed in November 1982. The Bill fell at the General Election in June 1983, but a new Telecommunications Bill received Royal Assent in April 1984. The Telecommunications Act lays down the basic framework of competition and regulation for the industry. The 1984 Act, the Office of Telecommunications (OFTEL), and the licences granted to BT and Mercury under the Act will be considered in more detail below. It was evident that BT's dominant position in telecommunications would continue after its privatisation, and the question of the regulation of BT's profitability therefore arose. At the end of October 1982, Professor Littlechild was commissioned to study and evaluate proposals to regulate BT's profitability.

Professor Littlechild judged alternative schemes against five criteria:

(i) protection against monopolistic exploitation of consumers;
(ii) encouragement of efficiency and innovation;
(iii) minimisation of the burden (i.e. cost and complexity) of regulation;
(iv) promotion and maintenance of effective competition;
(v) maximisation of net proceeds from the sale of BT; facilitation of its successful operation after flotation.

Clearly there is some degree of conflict between these criteria—for example between (i) and (iv) on the one hand and (v) on the other.

The background to Professor Littlechild's study is as follows. A committee of officials had originally proposed that BT's profits be regulated by setting a maximum profit rate. Professor Walters, the Prime Minister's economic adviser, argued that such regulation would be akin to a 100 per cent (excess) profits tax and therefore far removed from the spirit behind privatisation. He proposed instead an output-related profits levy (ORPL), according to which BT's profits would be taxed at a lower rate the more that BT expanded its output over the year. This would discourage monopolistic restriction of output to raise prices.

Various options were then considered by an Inter-Departmental Working Group, who suggested a modified maximum rate of return (MRR) scheme, under which BT would be taxed (at less than 100 per cent) if its profits exceeded the specified return on capital. They also suggested that certain powers concerning profit regulation be given to the Director General of Telecommunications (DGT)—see below for a discussion of OFTEL and the DGT.

Professor Littlechild appraised these schemes—and also the possibility of having no regulation of BT's profitability—but he finally recommended the local tariff reduction (LTR) scheme, according to which the prices of local services would be reduced in real terms. It was eventually decided to implement a similar scheme (commonly called 'RPI − X') in which the price index for a basket of services (trunk as well as local) must fall in real terms. He summarised his ranking of the five schemes against the five criteria as in Table 1.

Table 1. Comparison of Five Schemes for the Regulation of British Telecom

	No explicit constraints	Working Group MRR	ORPL	Profit ceiling	LTR
Protection against monopoly	5	3	2	4	1
Efficiency and innovation	1 =	4 =	4 =	3	1 =
Burden of regulation	1	5·	4	3	2
Promotion of competition	1	5	4	2 =	2 =
Proceeds and prospects	1 =	4	5	3	1 =

The MRR, ORPL, and profit ceiling schemes are all forms of rate-of-return regulation. Such regulation does not encourage efficiency—indeed it may positively promote inefficiency—and it is not easy to administer. The greater the element of discretion in regulation, the more costly and complex it becomes, and the greater the danger of 'capture' by incumbent firms. And regulation of the overall rate of return does not discriminate between different parts of the business

—it cannot focus on the areas where public policy concerns are most acute. A regime of no constraints (beyond OFTEL and the competition authorities) was judged not to offer sufficient protection against monopolistic exploitation, although in Littlechild's view it scored well in every other respect.

The scheme that has been adopted simply constrains BT to reduce prices on certain services by X per cent per annum (hence the 'RPI $-X$' tag). Professor Littlechild recommended that there should be an overall index for a 'basket' of the relevant telecommunications services (rather than having separate indices for business rentals, residential rentals, and local call charges) on grounds of simplicity and flexibility. The scheme is to apply for five years. X was subject to negotiation between BT and the Government, and was eventually fixed at 3 per cent. The 'tariff basket' scheme allows BT pricing flexibility within the basket of services, and protection against anti-competitive pricing will be necessary, although there is unlikely to be much competition in this area anyway.

Although consumers are guaranteed price reduction in real terms in respect of these services, we do not believe that the RPI -3 scheme places a particularly rigorous constraint upon BT, in view of the pace of technological advance in telecommunications and related areas (witness the price-performance improvements of data processing equipment). Note that Professor Littlechild judged that the proceeds of the sale of shares, and BT's prospects, were as good under the RPI $-X$ scheme as if there were no explicit constraints on BT. If correct, this view implies that the regulation of BT's profitability does not significantly constrain BT's behaviour. In any event, it is undesirable for X to be negotiated with BT. It should be decided by independent authority, and preferably by comparison with productivity improvements in the industry internationally.

Professor Littlechild contended that 'competition is by far the most effective means of protection against monopoly', and that 'profit regulation is merely a "stop-gap" until sufficient competition develops' (p. 1). We agree with the first of these points: it is precisely why the Government was wrong not to liberalise the telecommunications industry more than it did. However, we do not share Professor Littlechild's optimism that sufficient competition will develop to dispense with the need to regulate BT's profitability. In our view it is practically certain that regulation will have to continue after 1989 at the very least, even if further extensive liberalisation occurs then. The need for continued regulation means that the RPI $-X$ scheme might in effect be closer to rate-of-return regulation than appears at first. Suppose that in 1989 it was decided that the RPI $-X$ formula should apply for a further period of years. How would X be determined? In principle, X should be related to the rate of cost reduction that BT would ideally achieve. The record of cost improvement achieved by telecommunications suppliers abroad would contain useful information in this regard, but BT's actual cost performance would no doubt form the main basis for the determination of X. (Note that if BT had been restructured before privatisation, then it would have been possible to make comparisons between the parts of the company as a guide to tariff regulation.) However, if X is determined by reference to BT's actual costs, we are back to rate-of-return regulation, with all its attendant problems. In particular, if the permissible tariffs depend on the level of costs, then the incentive to cost efficiency is blunted. The point is not that Professor Littlechild's scheme is at fault. It is that his scheme may end up being roughly equivalent to the schemes he criticised. Thus the problems of rate-of-return regulation would appear to be hard to avoid in regulated private monopoly.

VI. The 1984 Act

The 1984 Act requires all operators of telecommunications systems to be licensed. BT's exclusive privilege to run telecommunications systems was abolished. The Act also empowered the Secretary of State to appoint the Director General of Telecommunications (DGT) who is in charge of the Office of Telecommunications (OFTEL). OFTEL is in some respects a model of the Office of Fair Trading but with particular responsibility for telecommunications. Professor Bryan Carsberg of the London School of Economics, an accountant, is the first DGT. He has a staff of about eighty.

The Secretary of State is responsible for granting licences, after consultation with the DGT. He may delegate the power to grant licences to the DGT. The DGT is responsible for enforcing licence conditions and for monitoring competition in the market. Under certain conditions he may modify licence conditions by consent of the licensee or by referral to the Monopolies and Mergers Commission (MMC). In the latter case, the MMC may propose a licence variation which the Secretary of State accepts or rejects but cannot amend.

Under the Act, licences for public networks have been granted to BT, Mercury, and the Kingston-upon-Hull City Council. (We do not consider the last any further here.) The Government has announced its intention *not to license any other operators* to provide the basic telecommunications service of conveying messages over their own fixed links, whether cable, radio, or satellite, either domestically or internationally, *until November 1990*. Other operators—such as cellular radio networks—are obliged to lease fixed links from BT or Mercury.

That is a remarkable restriction of competition. It shows that privatisation and competition do not necessarily go hand in hand. We discuss this question further after describing some of the terms of the licences granted to BT and Mercury under the Act.

(i) *BT's licence*

The most important of BT's licences under the 1984 Act is its licence to operate its public network. The licence requires BT to provide telecommunications services, including rural and international services, throughout the UK, and to supply, for example, emergency services, directory enquiries, and certain facilities for the disabled. The licence gives effect to the $RPI - X$ constraint on BT's pricing, discussed above. It also contains provisions to prevent some forms of price discrimination: BT must publish standard terms for providing some of its services, and must make uniform charges for maintenance and installation. BT is required not to show unfair favour to itself, or disfavour to others, in its pricing; 'tie-in' sales are restricted; and BT cannot impose exclusive dealing arrangements on suppliers. BT must permit the interconnection of other licensed systems on terms that ensure fair competition, and which also enable BT to recover costs and earn sufficient profits to cover its public service obligations. BT has to connect, on standard terms and conditions, any licensed apparatus that meets independent approval standards.

Although these provisions against anti-competitive behaviour, and the threat of MMC investigation, guard against blatant abuse of BT's monopoly power, it is likely that BT will have an opportunity to restrict and distort competition in various ways. Its very predominance in the market-place will give it considerable competitive advantages. Consider for example the position of BT Enterprises. As a supplier of terminal apparatus it competes with other suppliers, but it gains considerable competitive advantage from the market position of the rest of BT, which enables it to gain the bulk of the terminal equipment market. Consider also the question of the interconnection of Mercury's and BT's networks. Whatever the licence may say, this has been the subject of a long-running dispute between BT and Mercury, which OFTEL has seemed unable or unwilling to resolve. Consider finally the issue of pricing. The basket of services to which the $RPI - X$ formula applies is not all-embracing. The charges for some services outside the reach of $RPI - X$ have increased rapidly since BT was privatised.

No matter how vigilant Professor Carsberg and his staff at OFTEL may be, they cannot be expected to reduce the risk of anti-competitive practices by BT and its employees to a negligible level. These remarks are not just conjecture; American experience with AT&T, regulated by the huge Federal Communications Commission, provides ample warnings. These problems are magnified by the Government's illiberal policies on the licensing of public networks and resale.

(ii) *Mercury*

In February 1982 Mercury was granted its licence to run a telecommunications network. Mercury was then a consortium of Cable and Wireless, BP, and Barclays Bank, but it is now a wholly-owned subsidiary of Cable and Wireless, a company with international experience in telecommunications. The new licence granted to Mercury under the 1984 Act is similar to BT's licence, but it does not contain price regulation or the public service obligations. However, Mercury is required to provide certain services in some major conurbations. Mercury is in operation, and expects to invest some £200 million in the development of its basic network. Mercury's system is supposed to be interconnected with that of BT, on non-discriminatory terms, under the terms of BT's licence. This requirement means that there need be no wasteful duplication of local networks.

BT and Mercury will be the only suppliers of basic telecommunications services for the next five years. What is going to be the nature of competition between them? It is immediately clear that BT will be the dominant firm. Whereas Mercury plans to spend £200 million on the development of its network in *total*, BT plans to spend £1800 million *annually* on capital equipment in the next three years. The market value of BT's total assets is more than £10,000 million. Therefore there will be a vast disparity in size between Mercury and BT. Of course Mercury can be more selective than BT in choosing which areas of business to compete for (since it does not have the same public service obligations), and in these areas the disparity will not be quite as enormous, but it will be massive all the same. Mercury is in operation in the market for point-to-point digital leased lines. This market is about 1 or 2 per cent of BT's gross revenues, and Mercury aims to take a 5 to 10 per cent share of it. Mercury will not provide a public voice service until 1987 at the earliest.

There is therefore a substantial risk that competition between BT and Mercury will not be very severe. The duopolists have been given complete protection from competition in the supply of basic telecommunications services for the next five years, and competition in such a protected duopoly may well be limited. Mercury is for the present too small to pose a major threat to BT. In the few areas where Mercury is a rival, BT may be wary of engaging in strong competition with Mercury for fear of falling foul of the regulatory and competition authorities, and thereby jeopardising its power throughout the rest of the industry. Whether or not Mercury and BT arrive at peaceful coexistence, which would be detrimental to consumers, the preconditions for such an understanding could hardly be more favourable. This danger would have been diminished if the Government had not restricted competition in the ways it has done.

Why has the Government chosen to prevent other firms from entering the market? (We shall not discuss the effect of these restrictions upon the size of the proceeds from flotation, the maximisation of which was one—but not the only—objective of the Government.) The rationale does not appear to be the prevention of 'destructive competition', or the wasteful duplication of facilities. That rationale would imply perpetual restrictions of competition, and would in some ways be at odds even with the licensing of Mercury. The Government's remarks about the eventual emergence of competition point to a different motivation—the 'infant industry' argument. The idea is that Mercury needs to be protected while it gets a foothold in the market-place.

In our view the 'infant industry' argument here is dubious. The protection of BT and Mercury from competition favours them and nobody else. A policy of free entry (subject to proper licence conditions) should have been pursued, and should be introduced at the earliest opportunity. Liberalisation would not by itself guarantee that BT would face effective competition, but it would at least add to the competitive forces in the market.

(iii) *Cellular radio*

Cellular radio is an example of competition based on an alternative technology: the provision of mobile telephone services based on the use of high frequency radio waves. Much has been made of the competitive threat likely to come from suppliers of radiophone networks. There may indeed be effective competition in this field, but it is a specialised telecommunications service, and the competition would not impinge substantially upon BT's power in respect of the more traditional services. The extent of competition in cellular radio depends largely upon the Government's licensing policy. Two national networks have already been licensed; they are to cover more than 90 per cent of the UK by 1990. One of the licensees is Cellnet, which is 51 per cent owned by BT. It is probable that, via Cellnet, BT will have a powerful market position in the radiophone market. A limit to the extent of competition in this market is set by the availability of frequency bands. When more bands become free, the Government is to consider granting further licences to radiophone operators. Cellular radio (and other means of exploiting new technologies, such as cable TV) might eventually pose a significant challenge to mainstream telecommunications networks. However, that prospect is not immediate.

VII. The option of restructuring BT

One option open to the Government before the privatisation of BT was to restructure the company in order to promote competition. That is what happened in the United States to AT&T upon the settlement of the long-running anti-trust suit brought by the Department of Justice. Under this settlement, AT&T divested itself of its local telephone companies. It is conceivable that BT might one day be restructured in similar fashion, but this possibility is more remote now that privatisation has gone ahead. In any industry the time to restructure is before privatisation.[a]

Restructuring can promote competition in three ways. First, if a dominant enterprise is divided into component parts, there may be scope for competition between those parts (e.g. the break-up of Standard Oil after the anti-trust case in 1911). However, in telecommunications the scope for competition between the parts is limited. Local network A does not compete with local network B. Nevertheless, restructuring would mean that experience and expertise were widely distributed, rather than concentrated in the hands of a single enterprise. This would enhance competition in other areas of the industry—for example, local networks A and B could compete with each other in the long-distance market. Secondly, comparisons could be made between the performance of separate local networks. These could provide information about the cost and efficiency of the several networks, which might be useful for regulation. Thirdly, restructuring diminishes the dangers of anti-competitive behaviour. It has been described above how a fully integrated firm, such as BT, can influence the conditions of competition in one part of its business by its pricing and interconnection policies in other parts of its business. For example, AT&T's restrictive policy on interconnection to its local networks reduced the competition it faced in the long-distance market. The framework within which BT operates does contain some safeguards against practices of this sort, but it would be foolhardy to suppose that they eliminate substantial risk of anti-competitive behaviour, or that the competition authorities can do so. Restructuring BT would have reduced both the incentive and the ability to adopt anti-competitive practices of this kind. If the dominant operator of local networks is a separate entity from the dominant firm in the long-distance market, he would have nothing to gain from a restrictive policy on interconnection; on the contrary, he would favour a liberal regime. Many similar examples could be constructed.

Under private ownership the problem is to develop a framework of incentives and constraints that directs pursuit of private gain towards the public good. The restructuring of a firm can be seen as a restructuring of incentives towards that goal. Since BT has been left intact as a fully integrated firm, dominant throughout the industry, the structure of incentives is not favourable to competition. This implies that ever more reliance must be placed upon the regulatory authorities. The restructuring of a private monopoly is not inconceivable, but it is a remote possibility, being without precedent in UK competition policy. The time to consider restructuring was therefore before privatisation. Restructuring BT would not have solved all the problems at hand (especially that of natural monopoly in local networks) but it would have diminished some of them. The practical difficulties would have been great, and the timetable for privatisation would have been delayed. Even so, it is unfortunate that the American lesson did not prompt more consideration to be given to the option of restructuring BT.

VIII. Concluding remarks

The cynic might say that the Government chose to give BT considerable protection from competition in order to obtain larger revenues from the sale of BT shares; however, it priced the shares at a level that was clearly too low, and so in fact failed to maximise the proceeds of the sale by a margin of many hundreds of millions of pounds. Be that as it may, the Government's evident desire to privatise BT speedily was very favourable to BT's management. The timetable set by the Government did not leave adequate time to liberalise the industry, let alone restructure BT. And, just as important, it gave enormous bargaining power to BT, at the expense of the Government's bargaining position. The full co-operation of BT's management was essential for a speedy flotation, and that co-operation was facilitated by according to BT some important privileges. The parallel with British Airways and the recent route allocations is clear enough. In both cases, the pressing desire to transfer a company into private ownership has stood in the way of ensuring a proper framework for competition in the industry. After privatisation has occurred, it becomes harder (though none the less imperative) to promote competition, but the best opportunity has been lost. In our view, the benefits of liberalisation are far greater than whatever gains stem from the change of ownership. Contrary to government policy in telecommunications, the *primary* goal should have been liberalisation rather than privatisation. Policy in future should be rapidly to open up as many channels of competition to BT as is practicable. The essential complement is a rigorous regime of regulation and competition policy to prevent the exploitation of BT's considerable monopoly power.

IX. Postscript

On 14 October 1985 OFTEL announced its long-awaited rulings concerning the interconnection of BT's and Mercury's networks. There is to be full interconnection between the networks both for domestic and international calls. This means that Mercury will be able to offer its services to customers throughout the country: BT will make the local connections while Mercury carries the long-distance part of a customer's call. Mercury is to receive substantial discounts on BT's normal charges for the use of its lines.

These rulings by OFTEL are a bold and positive step. Full interconnection is an essential precondition for competition between the duopolists. However, the vast disparity of size between the two firms is likely to persist for the foreseeable future, and further entry is barred for the time being. The framework of competition and regulation within which the industry and OFTEL operate remains unduly restrictive of competition, but the ruling by OFTEL on interconnection is an important advance within that framework.

EDITORS' NOTE

a. See also the article by Ashworth and Forsyth in Part III.

13

BRITISH GAS: OPTIONS FOR PRIVATISATION*

Elizabeth Hammond, Dieter Helm, and David Thompson

I. Introduction

The announced intention to privatise the British Gas Corporation (BGC) represents the largest transfer of ownership from the public to the private sector to date. It is not only the boldest attempt yet at asset transfer but also a major step in the development of UK energy policy.

Energy policy since 1979 has combined a number of liberalising Acts with ownership transfers, departing from the postwar consensus of planning and control. First, traditional energy policy, in the sense of planning capacity based on demand forecasts, was abandoned with the annunciation of what might be called the 'Lawson energy doctrine'. As Secretary of State for Energy in 1982, he set out the market philosophy for energy—prices and hence output were best set by the market. As he put it, the Government's task is *not* seen 'as being to try and plan the future shape of energy production and consumption. It is not even primarily to try and balance UK demand and supply for energy. Our task is rather to set a framework which will ensure that the market operates in the energy sector with a minimum of distortion and that energy is produced and consumed efficiently' (Lawson, 1982).

* This article was first published in *Fiscal Studies*, 1985, 6, 4.

Elizabeth Hammond is a Research Officer at the Institute for Fiscal Studies.

Dieter Helm is a Fellow of Lady Margaret Hall, Oxford and a Research Associate of the Institute for Fiscal Studies.

David Thompson is a Programme Director at the Institute for Fiscal Studies.

The authors received helpful suggestions on an earlier draft of this paper from David Heald, John Kay, Michael Keen, Colin Mayer, Catherine Price, and George Yarrow; the usual disclaimer applies. The research on which this article is based was financially supported by the Economic and Social Research Council.

Consistent with that view, the Government scaled down its North Sea oil activities, selling BNOC and BP shares, and BGC was forced to disengage from oil-related activities.

Disengagement and the abandonment of planning were accompanied by policies which aimed to open up the energy monopolies in the state sector to greater competition. The two central liberalisation Acts were the Oil and Gas (Enterprise) Act 1982 and the Energy Act 1983. These legislative instruments were designed to introduce competition into the production of electricity, and into the sale of both electricity and gas to customers. The statutory monopoly in the generation of electricity 'as a main business' was relaxed. Private enterprises were allowed to lease use of the gas and electricity distribution systems to supply power direct to consumers. The coal industry, however, was left alone and the CEGB continued with its obligation to purchase from the National Coal Board.

Nevertheless, the Secretary of State's powers remained considerable, and have been exercised in such cases as the Sliepner gas purchase and the French electricity connection. Furthermore, despite the liberalisation introduced in gas and electricity supply, competition has remained peripheral and the energy sector has continued to be dominated by the nationalised industries.

The comparative failure of the attempted liberalisation of the gas industry has effectively left the Government with two routes to meet its objective of ensuring that 'energy is produced and consumed efficiently' (Lawson, 1982). The first would be to make a more effective attempt to introduce a competitive environment. The second would be to follow the approach outlined by the Financial Secretary to the Treasury earlier this year: 'Where competition is impractical privatisation policies have now been developed to such an extent, that regulated private ownership of natural monopolies is preferable to nationalisation'. (Moore, 1985. Some of this is reprinted in Part I.)

The Government's proposals to privatise British Gas firmly follow the second route. Our purpose in this paper is to examine the options for following the first route—introducing a more competitive environment—and to consider whether this might prove a more effective approach to improving the gas industry's performance.

Case studies of privatisation options have been carried out for various industries and there are interesting parallels, and contrasts, to the case of gas. In particular the reader is referred to studies of electricity supply (the article by Yarrow in this Part; Vickers and Yarrow, 1985a), telecoms (Beesley and Gist, 1984; Vickers and Yarrow, 1985b), airports (Starkie and Thompson, 1985), railways (the article by Starkie in Part IV), airlines (Ashworth and Forsyth, 1984), and coal (Boyfield, 1985).

In Section II of this paper we examine the present structure of the gas industry. The concept of efficiency and its measurement are contentious and we devote Section III of the paper to reviewing the evidence. In Section IV we look at several different structures for a privatised gas industry. We consider whether certain options are likely to yield any significant disadvantages by comparison with the present structure, in particular in terms of forgone economies of scale or scope, and whether they are likely to enhance the performance of the industry. We identify the natural monopoly aspects of the gas industry and in Section V of the paper consider the requirements and issues for the regulation of a privatised gas industry. In Section VI we draw together our conclusions.

II. The structure of the gas industry

The gas industry in the UK essentially involves the production of natural gas, the purchase of gas by BGC, transmission of gas from beach-head landing-points to different parts of the country, the distribution of gas to customers' premises, the sale of gas to customers, and the sale and servicing of gas appliances.

Exploration and gas extraction are largely carried out by oil companies as a joint product. As a natural resource gas is in limited supply, and hence there are associated questions of optimal depletion policy. BGC purchases gas through long-term contracts with the oil companies. The most important feature of these contracts is that the supply price to BGC is, in some cases, substantially lower than the cost of supplying gas from the most recently developed fields. For example, the supply price of gas from the Frigg field was 24 pence a therm in 1984 whilst the average supply price to BGC was 13.3 pence (Select Committee on Energy, 1985, para. 26, and Table 6); the supply price for some individual contracts is significantly lower still. These different supply prices reflect both the higher extraction costs associated with more recently developed fields and the absence of escalation clauses linked to the price of oil in contracts drawn up in the late 1960s. The consequences of this situation are twofold. First, there exist significant intra-marginal rents which at present are largely passed on to consumers through BGC's policy of pricing to cover average costs (an issue we return to in Section III). The Government obtains some of the rents through the Gas Levy, a tax on gas fields which were producing before 1975. The second consequence is that there is little prospect that an oil or gas company will be able to utilise successfully the liberalisation provisions in the 1982 Oil and Gas Act in order to supply gas to final consumers in direct competition with BGC. The price at which it could extract gas from a newly developed source is likely to be substantially higher than BGC's average cost of supply.

BGC's National Transmission System (NTS) takes North Sea gas supplies from the beach-head to 'off-take' points supplying each of BGC's twelve regions. (The map of the network shown is reproduced from BGC's Annual Report and Accounts 1984/5.) The operation of the NTS also involves matching the supply of gas to daily variations in demand in order that system pressure, and hence safety, is maintained. The demand for gas is subject to significant seasonal peaks, while the supply of gas from the main gas-supplying fields is relatively constant throughout the year. Increasing supply above the daily planned rate attracts significant additional costs and supply contracts usually specify a maximum daily supply figure in addition to a figure for annual supply. Daily forecasts are prepared of the level of demand and, where a shortfall is identified between demand and supply, the production of synthetic gas is implemented and/or the retrieval of stored gas is organised to meet the shortfall. The supply of gas from the NTS to each of the regions is subject to an internal pricing system. This provides charges for the volume of gas supplied and also charges each region in relation to the demands which it makes upon system capacity and upon the gas storage facilities. This charging structure includes penalty provisions if a region takes up more (or less) than its day-to-day forecasts of demand requirements. These differential tariffs are not, however, passed on to consumers (as we discuss in the next section).

Each of BGC's twelve regions takes gas from the NTS and supplies it through local distribution networks to the final customers. The regions are responsible for the maintenance and safety of their local distribution network and for meeting within-day variations in demand in their region by using small-scale local storage facilities and 'line-packing' (making small changes to system pressure in the pipeline).

The sale of gas to consumers is carried out by each of the regions, which conduct metering and billing. However, pricing and marketing policies are largely determined centrally for BGC as a whole. In particular (as we discuss in the next section) there is a uniform tariff structure which is used throughout the country.

Gas is in direct competition with other energy sources. Evidence indicates that demand is only moderately price-elastic, however. The major published sources include a Department of Energy paper for the Sizewell B Inquiry (1983) and a recent study by Pepper (1985). This latter study uses a demand model for the whole energy sector. There are interesting difficulties in estimating the appropriate equations given the fuel mix used since elasticities depend on the shares of each fuel in total energy demand. Tables 1 and 2 summarise findings from the Department of Energy paper (1983) on own-price and cross-price elasticities for the four central fuels—electricity, coal, oil, and gas.

As can be seen from the tables, industrial users' demand in the short run has a low elasticity (-0.3) but it is slightly higher than that for electricity; it has an elasticity of -1.5 in the long run (less than those for coal and oil, but much greater than that for electricity). This has the intuitive explanation that of the four fuels, electricity is used in the main for special purposes for which there are few substitutes. The

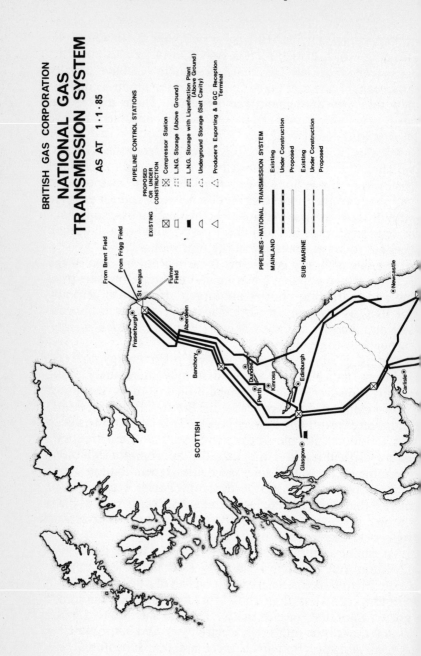

BRITISH GAS CORPORATION
NATIONAL GAS
TRANSMISSION SYSTEM
AS AT 1·1·85

PIPELINE CONTROL STATIONS

PROPOSED
OR UNDER
EXISTING   CONSTRUCTION

⊠   ⊠   Compressor Station

⊡   ⊡   L.N.G. Storage (Above Ground)

■   ⊡   L.N.G. Storage with Liquefaction Plant
              (Above Ground)

◁   ◁   Underground Storage (Salt Cavity)

△   △   Producer's Exporting & BGC Reception
              Terminal

PIPELINES - NATIONAL TRANSMISSION SYSTEM

MAINLAND   ▬▬▬▬   Existing
                 ▬ ▬ ▬   Under Construction
                              Proposed

SUB - MARINE   ▬▬▬▬   Existing
                      ▬ ▬ ▬   Under Construction
                                   Proposed

From Brent Field

From Frigg Field

Fulmer Field

St. Fergus

Fraserburgh

Aberdeen

Banchory

Dundee

Perth

Kinross

Edinburgh

Glasgow

SCOTTISH

Newcastle

Carlisle

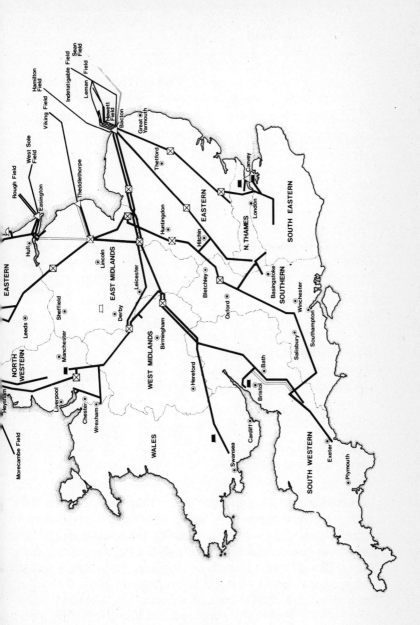

Table 1. Domestic Energy Demand: Price Elasticities

Short Run (same year)

	PERCENTAGE CHANGE IN DEMAND FOR:			
	Electricity	Coal	Oil	Gas
1% INCREASE IN PRICE OF:				
Electricity	−0.1	0	0	0
Coal	0	−0.2	0	0
Oil	0	0	−0.2	0
Gas	0	0	0	−0.2

Long Run

	PERCENTAGE CHANGE IN DEMAND FOR:			
	Electricity	Coal	Oil	Gas
1% INCREASE IN PRICE OF:				
Electricity	−0.6	0.4	0.3	0.2
Coal	0.1	−2.1	0.2	0.2
Oil	0	0.1	−2.6	0.1
Gas	0.5	2.4	1.7	−1.1

Source: Department of Energy, 1983.

domestic sector elasticities are lower than the industrial ones, indicating that industry is more flexible and responsive to price changes. Short-run elasticities are substantially lower than long-run elasticities because of the fixed capital requirements (for example in boilers, cookers, and central heating systems) associated with gas consumption. With a relatively high short-run capital cost of substitution, elasticity is correspondingly low in the short run but higher over the longer term as capital stock can be varied.

Table 2. Other Industry: Price Elasticities

Short Run (same year)

	PERCENTAGE CHANGE IN DEMAND FOR:			
	Electricity	Coal	Oil	Gas
1% INCREASE IN PRICE OF:				
Electricity	−0.2	0	0	0
Coal	0	−0.4	0.1	0.1
Oil	0.1	0.1	−0.2	0.1
Gas	0	0.2	0.1	−0.3

Long Run

	PERCENTAGE CHANGE IN DEMAND FOR:			
	Electricity	Coal	Oil	Gas
1% INCREASE IN PRICE OF:				
Electricity	−0.4	0.1	0.1	0.1
Coal	0.2	−2.4	2.9	1.4
Oil	0	1.2	−2.3	−0.1
Gas	0	0.8	−0.7	−1.5

Source: Department of Energy, 1983.
Note: The two negative cross-price elasticities are perverse and may arise because of correlations existing in the data—UK industrial gas prices fell in real terms during the 1970s when oil prices rose.

Finally, BGC's regions operate showrooms which sell gas appliances and carry out installation and servicing work on appliances.

III. Efficiency

In this section we review the evidence on BGC's current performance in terms of productive and allocative efficiency.

This provides criteria for appraising the different options for a privatised gas industry.

(i) *Productive efficiency*

Productive efficiency addresses the question of whether a firm produces a given level and quality of output at minimum cost. Two studies which provide evidence on the extent of BGC's productive efficiency are the British Gas Efficiency Study prepared by Deloitte, Haskins and Sells (DHS) in June 1983 and the MMC report (1980) on domestic gas appliances. The latter reported some evidence of productive inefficiency, but appliance sales are only a small, and peripheral, part of BGC's activities.

DHS's main conclusions on productive efficiency related to the varying performance records of BGC's twelve different regional organisations. DHS compared the unit costs incurred by different regions, finding substantial variation in unit expenditure. After making allowance for differences between regions relating to geography and the profile of market demand, DHS concluded that if the performance of the less efficient regions could be raised to that of the more efficient regions then expenditure savings of £100 million could be achieved. To put this figure in perspective, it is equivalent to broadly 4 per cent of BGC's operating costs (net of expenditure on gas).

There is therefore some evidence to suggest limited productive inefficiency on the part of BGC. The main focus of attention is, however, on allocative efficiency.

(ii) *Allocative efficiency*

Economic theory suggests that to achieve optimal resource allocation prices should be set at a level equal to marginal costs (given certain conditions which we discuss further below). Consumer choice between substitutes will direct the output paths of different products.

There are, however, two central problems which need to be addressed before using this approach as a criterion against which to judge the efficiency of BGC's pricing policy. The first problem is that marginal cost pricing is optimal only in circumstances where marginal cost prices are charged in closely related sectors. It is not at all clear, according to the second-best principle, that marginal cost pricing in a non-marginal cost pricing world is the preferred option. This result depends in practice crucially on the pricing of closely related products and their substitutability.

Evidence on elasticities (see Tables 1 and 2) suggests that, at least in the short run, the second-best consequences may be containable. Furthermore, the major substitute—electricity —is required to set prices on the basis of marginal costs (at least in principle), and oil has an active spot market. Coal may also be moving tentatively in the direction of marginal cost pricing.

The second major problem with marginal cost pricing lies in the implementation of the principle. Where the firm (or industry) has the optimal capital stock, short-run and long-run measures of marginal cost are equivalent but an estimate needs to be imputed of marginal costs in such circumstances. Calculating the long-run marginal cost (LRMC) for gas involves particular difficulties. These include, first, that each source of gas has its own associated unit costs and characteristics; second, that future discoveries of supplies are uncertain; third, that different types of customers have different associated costs of supply. The method of calculation that is typically employed is to estimate the cost of gas extraction from a recently developed field. The cost of supply from the Norwegian Frigg field has been used for this purpose.

The estimation of LRMC cannot therefore be precise; but this does not mean that the concept is inappropriate as a criterion. The efficiency of BGC's charging policies can be assessed against the criterion in two respects—in relation to the level of prices and in relation to the structure of prices charged in different markets.

The price level
DHS (1983) concluded that though prices were sufficient to cover the average costs of supply in all markets served, prices were generally below those necessary to meet costs of supply using the most recently contracted sources of gas (a measure of the level of LRMC). As noted earlier, the reason for the divergence between average costs and LRMC (measured in

this way) is a consequence of the nature of the early gas contracts. The early North Sea contracts in the late 1960s were priced at about 1.2 pence per therm. The continuing Southern Basin supplies remain much cheaper than the new Northern Basin gas supplies. For example, the large Frigg gas field (which straddles the UK and Norwegian sectors) has a price which reached 24 pence per therm in 1984.

The price structure

To achieve allocative efficiency in the structure of charges, prices in different markets should be related to any differences in the marginal costs of supply. Three aspects of potential differential prices can be identified: the prices charged to different types of customer, prices charged at different times of the year (peak demand pricing), and the prices charged to customers located in different geographical areas. We now summarise the evidence on each of these.

DHS looked at the prices charged by BGC to four categories of customers—domestic, non-domestic tariff, firm industrial, and interruptible.[1] They found that, in 1982/3, BGC was selling gas at less than the marginal cost of supply (as measured by the actual cost of imported gas from the Norwegian Frigg field) in all market sectors except the interruptible industrial market. A more recent study by Price (1984) confirmed that charges to domestic and firm industrial customers are still below estimated LRMC by a margin of between 12 and 17 per cent.

Price has also investigated peak demand costs. In her evidence to the Select Committee on Energy (1985), she estimated the potential price difference which would be required to reflect seasonal peak costs. By assuming a simple two-period tariff structure—six months in the winter and six months in the summer—with peak-related costs recovered in the winter, when two-thirds of the annual demand is taken, an estimate of domestic prices is made at 5 pence per therm more in the peak months and 10 pence per therm less in the

---

[1] An interruptible contract provides that the customer will reduce his demand on being given specified notice by BGC; the tariff charged is lower than for firm industrial contracts because BGC is effectively able to avoid some peak-related expenditure.

non-peak months. These are significantly different from current (uniform) rates: the average domestic tariff was 41.2 pence per therm in 1984/5.

On the third aspect of pricing structure—geographical cost differentials—the potential size of these is shown by the calculations summarised in Table 3 (based on Price, 1985). The estimates shown in the table indicate that the total marginal cost of transmitting gas to the parts of the country furthest away from the beach-head supplies are substantially higher than the costs of transmitting gas to customers located close to beach-head supplies. At present BGC has a uniform price structure, thus not reflecting this important source of differential costs.

Table 3. Marginal Distribution Costs of Gas Supply

		(Pence per therm)
	Eastern region	South-western region
Firm industrial	0.9	4.6
Interruptible industrial	difference of 1.2	
Domestic	1.1	5.9

Source: Price, 1985.

There is therefore considerable evidence to suggest that BGC's present charging structure is characterised by allocative inefficiency. The *level* of prices is considerably adrift from estimated LRMC, and the *structure* of pricing fails to represent adequately the separate costs of supply to different customers at different times of the year and in different parts of the country.

The potential for improving the allocative efficiency of BGC's charging structure by relating charges more systematically to marginal costs depends critically upon customers' response to changes in the charging structure. If demand is highly inelastic then changes in prices will have little impact upon consumption patterns or resource use. Evidence on elasticities suggests, however, that the demand for gas is not highly inelastic (see Tables 1 and 2).

This indicates that revising tariffs to reflect more closely the marginal costs of supply will have an impact upon consumption patterns and upon resource use. Raising the *level* of charges to nearer the level of marginal cost will slow the rate of depletion and conserve energy resources. Rebalancing the *structure* of charges between markets will, for example, enable expenditure undertaken to match seasonal peaks in demand to be reduced. The size of BGC's current investment in the Morecambe Gas Field and the Rough Field Storage indicates the level of resources being deployed to meet peaks in demand. The scope for improvements in allocative efficiency could therefore be substantial. We consider in the next section how effective different options for a privatised gas industry might prove to be in realising these potential benefits.

IV. Options for privatisation

Given the evidence in the previous section, the crucial question to address now is whether the incentives inherent in a privatised gas industry will improve on this situation. Will the new post-privatisation structure do any better? The answer to this question depends on the degree of competitive pressure which is introduced (in the product market or in the capital market) and on the type of regulation adopted. We have approached the issue by considering a number of different options for a privatised gas industry. The efficiency properties of the various solutions have been examined. We have considered possible sources of competition and the mechanism by which different incentive structures would work. Crucial variables of importance here are the effect of ownership structure on consumer prices and on cost levels.

We have also considered whether significant economies of scale or scope might be sacrificed by particular options for restructuring. Some activities, in particular the transmission and distribution networks, appear to be characterised by natural monopoly such that a single firm will be able to produce the industry's outputs more cheaply than a combination of several firms; the emergence of several competing suppliers in such an industry is therefore generally inefficient (see Sharkey, 1982, for a discussion of recent theory).

Restructuring of the gas industry can be considered in terms of both vertical and horizontal separation (see Webb, 1984, for a discussion). Horizontally, the distribution network in each part of the country can be separately owned, as can the NTS and the existing contracts for gas supply. Vertically, ownership of the distribution networks can be separated from the buying and selling of gas. These two propositions provide the classification shown in Table 4. This yields three basic options for a restructuring of BGC:

(i) an integrated private sector monopoly
(ii) regionalisation—twelve separate regional gas companies (responsible for both the pipe system and supplying gas to consumers), a separate company operating the NTS, and separate ownership of the existing contracts for gas supply;
(iii) vertical separation—restructuring of the distribution network as in option (ii) but with many separate companies supplying gas to consumers.

Table 4. Privatisation Options

	Horizontally integrated	*Horizontally separated*
Vertically integrated	Option (i): Private sector monopoly	Option (ii): Regionalisation 12 separate regional gas companies and 1 company owning NTS
Vertically separated	One company owns transmission and distribution pipelines, another company supplies gas	Option (iii): Many competing gas supply companies and company(ies) owning NTS pipelines and local distribution pipelines

(i) *Private sector monopoly*

A privatised gas corporation which retained BGC's near monopoly in the distribution and supply of gas would face competition only from other fuels. However, evidence on demand elasticities (see Tables 1 and 2) indicates that this competition would be very weak in the short run; and even over a longer-term horizon cross-price elasticities with other energy sources are not very high. The transfer of BGC to the private sector without any change to its current structure will therefore leave the privatised corporation with significant market power and will not increase the incentives to efficiency provided by the product market.

The change in ownership structure may provide different incentives in the capital market, however. In principle the most immediate effect will be to change BGC's objective function. The statutes governing the Corporation (and implemented by the Department of Energy) set multiple, and sometimes inconsistent, targets. After privatisation the Corporation will, in principle, face the more narrowly focused target of profit maximisation. It is important to note, however, that the degree to which profit maximisation is actually pursued after privatisation is far from clear. In practice BGC is likely to face little realistic threat of bankruptcy or take-over; BGC's size and specialist resources will make take-over especially difficult. Shareholders may be too loosely distributed to enforce their objectives and managers may have considerable freedom, in practice, in determining which policies to pursue. The impact of an adverse movement in share price is likely to be confined to the effect on the cost of raising capital and the scope for pursuing strategies of diversification.

To the extent that a privatised corporation does, however, pursue a policy of profit maximisation, this may be expected to have effects upon the level of prices, upon the structure of prices, upon the productive efficiency of the corporation, and upon social or distributive concerns.

Greater orientation toward profit maximisation may provide some incentive to restructure tariffs and to reduce uneconomic cross-subsidisation between markets. It may also provide incentives to improve productive efficiency. This may be manifested, for example, in the rationalisation of the extensive prime site showrooms across the UK and in a narrowing of the variation in regions' performance identified by DHS. Pursuit of profit maximisation may therefore yield improvements in both allocative and productive efficiency.

However, the economic theory of monopoly suggests that under this market structure there will be an incentive to set prices in excess of marginal costs. Indeed, one of the early rationales for nationalisation was to prevent monopoly pricing, with the gas legislation requiring that supply be provided at the lowest cost to consumers. Thus while public ownership attempts to provide safeguards by replacing overall targets— such as profit maximisation—with more precise pricing and allocation rules, a private sector profit-maximising monopoly can be expected a priori to raise prices against an inelastic demand to levels which exceed marginal cost.

However, the extent to which prices will be greater than marginal cost depends on the pricing strategy and time profile of profit maximisation. A long-run profit maximiser in a situation where market share shows a degree of long-run elasticity (as does gas) could in the short run either set a higher price, achieving higher profit and falling market share, or a lower short-run price, and thus lower short-run profit and rising market share (see Hicks, 1956, and Scherer, 1985). In the case of gas the market share strategy is important since consumers have to make substantial fixed capital expenditure on gas-consuming equipment (mainly boilers).

Raising prices to levels above marginal cost could be contained by regulatory control. But experience in other countries (in particular the US) indicates that regulated private monopolies may frequently be less productively efficient than corresponding public enterprises (see the article by Millward in Part II for a review of the evidence).

A private monopolist will have less incentive to provide consumer information (unless this is commercially worthwhile) and to retain less profitable 'high street' advisory functions. The incentives to consider safety issues may be changed to wholly commercial considerations and there will be incentives to pursue more rapidly the disconnection of indebted customers. However, these concerns, if considered material, appear readily susceptible to regulatory control (the specification of safety standards for electrical goods or motor vehicles provides one possible model).

Changes to the level and structure of prices will also have distributional consequences. It could be argued that a general government transfer to the poor is preferable to an artificially low particular price (because of substitution effects) although this argument has as a premise the assumption that such compensation takes place.

In summary, privatisation of BGC in its present form will at best provide only weak incentives to improved efficiency. There will be no change in the incentives provided by competition in the product market. Additional incentives will result from any re-orientation in objectives towards profit maximisation. However, the size and market power of a privatised BGC mean that this re-orientation is unlikely to be significant in effect.

(ii) *Regionalisation*

The regionalisation option enhances efficiency incentives in both the product market and the capital market by creating a market for the purchase and sale of gas. This option involves setting up twelve separate companies to take over the functions of BGC's regions plus an additional company to operate the NTS. Ownership of the existing gas supply contracts is also separated. This option is based on BGC's present regional structure, and the present arrangements and transactions between regions (and with the NTS) would become explicit contractual agreements between separate companies. Regionalisation retains the natural monopoly in each local distribution network, and in the NTS, and enables the associated scale economies to be exploited. Under this option the task of matching peak demand and supply, and the associated operation of storage facilities, could be co-ordinated centrally as part of the operation of the NTS (as happens at present). Therefore, to the extent that there exist economies of scale or scope in peak matching, these would not be forgone in this option. The peak costs associated with the demand profile in each region would be passed on via the internal charging system (as happens, in principle, at present). It seems unlikely that separate ownership would increase transactions costs between regions and the NTS. The present internal charging system already provides a structure for financial transactions and a system of incentives for the provision of accurate information.

The advantages of this system are twofold. First, there would be a greater incentive towards profit maximisation because the capital market would exert pressure on each of the thirteen new entities. There would be a more plausible threat of take-over and the very remote possibility of bankruptcy. Thus in addition to cost of capital effects, which this option shares with (i) above, there are additional pressures from the capital market. The incentives for the achievement of productive efficiency are therefore strengthened. The twelve regional companies are now explicit profit centres and hence provide information (both to their management and to shareholders and regulators) which enables their performance to be compared directly with eleven other similar enterprises.

The second advantage of this option is that the structure of charges is more likely to be related to marginal costs. This option removes the basis for uneconomic cross-subsidisation between regions, and charges in each region are likely to reflect more closely the marginal costs of supply in the particular region. It is also more likely that charges made to regions for the use of system capacity and storage facilities during periods of peak demand will be passed on to customers.

Whilst the regionalisation option holds significant advantages it does require that the ownership of the existing gas supply contracts is separated. Where a private monopoly exists the issues raised are essentially ones of monopoly rent. But when combined with the common-carrier NTS possibility, following the 1982 Oil and Gas Act, these may directly affect entry and the pricing structure. For if the private company operating the NTS also held the original contracts, at existing prices, competitors in supply (such as oil companies) would be at a disadvantage and little efficiency gain might be forthcoming. There are at least three possible methods by which ownership of the contracts can be separated. First, a wholesale agency could be set up to hold these contracts, with rents accruing to the State. Second, the contracts could be auctioned to the highest bidder and the returns remitted to the Government. Prices would then move toward marginal cost more immediately. The Treasury would gain its desired revenues and competition in the supply of gas would be facilitated. Third, all contracts could be cancelled and renegotiation initiated. Oil companies would then reap the economic rents, and this gain may be offset by a modified Gas Levy on oil and gas companies similar to Petroleum Revenue Tax.

The regionalisation option would go a substantial way toward establishing a market for gas, but the individual organisations would still retain varying degrees of market power. In particular the organisation owning the NTS would be able to exploit its monopoly position and some type of regulation would be required (we discuss what type below). Similarly each of the regional companies would continue to hold substantial market power in the supply of gas to domestic customers; supply to industrial customers may, however, become more competitive if the restructuring proposed enables the Oil and Gas Act 1982 provisions to be implemented more effectively.

(iii) *Vertical separation of gas sale and supply from ownership of the transmission and distribution network*

In principle it might be considered that market power in the supply of gas to domestic customers could be reduced by the complete separation of the sale of gas from ownership of the distribution system (that is the NTS, as in option (ii), and also the local distribution networks). Complete separation would involve individual households and firms in a particular area registering with different competing gas suppliers. Each household or firm would choose its supplier and be billed by that company. The owner of the distribution system would contract to provide a connection and the supplier of gas would lease 'line-space' from the owner of the distribution system.

Again this option would preserve the natural monopoly in each local distribution network and the NTS. The central drawback, however, is that there is likely to be a significant increase in transactions costs. Additional costs are likely to arise in contractual arrangements between the separate companies owning the distribution network and supplying gas which would not arise if these functions were to remain vertically integrated. In particular a contract between pipe owner and gas supply company needs to be able to identify and pass on to each gas supply company the peak costs imposed on the transmission and storage facilities by its customers' demands. In the absence of this capability there would be an incentive for each gas supply company to provide misleading information in its dealings with the owner(s) of the distribution network. To implement this option for supply to domestic customers requires more sophisticated metering equipment than at present in use. Furthermore, the risk of interruption and variation in supply is also likely to increase. Contractual arrangements would have to be three-way—between supplier, pipe owner and customer—and the assumption of legal liability would not be straightforward in the event of failure to supply.

Thus, although appealing in theoretical terms, the complete vertical separation of the sale of gas from ownership of the distribution system appears impractical at least as far as supply to domestic customers is concerned. However, as noted earlier, in the case of industrial consumers the scope for competitive entry under the provisions of the Oil and Gas Act 1982 should be enhanced under the proposed regionalisation option. Additional transaction costs are unlikely to be as significant because more sophisticated metering equipment will typically be in use and any additional costs will also be spread over a far larger volume of business.

V. Regulatory framework for a privatised gas industry

We conclude from the analysis in the preceding section that privatisation of the gas industry will only be effective in improving efficiency to the extent that it creates a market in the purchase and sale of gas; in other words only if the present public sector monopoly can be converted into a competitive private industry. We also conclude, however, that a fully competitive solution is not available due to the existence of natural monopoly elements in the transmission and distribution network. It seems clear that this natural monopoly would not be contestable (in any significant sense) and some type of regulatory control is likely to be desirable.

Regulation comes in many different forms, however, and in this section we set out three general criteria and suggest how these might be implemented. The criteria are the desirability of promoting competing sources of information, the general preference for price rather than rate-of-return regulation, and the separation of natural monopoly from competitive elements within the industry.

A regulatory authority is typically given general guidelines and rules to follow as well as specific licences to monitor. The gap between these rules and licences on the one hand, and the complexity of production and pricing policies on the other, is considerable. For this purpose the regulator needs information. The information is more likely to be accurate and reliable the more competitive is its method of production. In the absence of competing sources of information there is a greater danger of regulatory capture—that is, a situation where the regulatory authority forms a symbiotic relationship with the regulated industry in which the interests of the industry are promoted as well as, or instead of, the interests of the industry's customers (see Demsetz, 1968, and Bailey, 1973). The analysis in the previous section showed that the regionalisation option provides a range of competing sources of information for the regulatory authority. (See Yarrow, 1985b, for further elaboration on this point; Vickers and Yarrow, 1985a, discuss the possible application of this principle to telecoms.) In particular, the regionalisation option would yield information on the costs of distribution, rates of return and the effects of alternative pricing strategies. If regionalisation is not adopted then different cost and profit centres, replicating what would have happened had the option been pursued, should be set up to generate that information.

The second regulatory principle—of price rather than rate-of-return regulation—is the preferred route for two rather different sets of reasons. A major limitation of rate-of-return regulation is the well known overcapitalisation effect identified by Averch and Johnson (1962). Rate-of-return regulation may also distort the structure of prices set in markets with a different capital intensity in production (a material consideration for peak/off-peak price differentials: see Sherman and Visscher, 1982). Price regulation may also require less information than rate-of-return regulation and be more straightforward to monitor. Under price regulation a periodic assessment of the basis of the level of price control will be required (a five-year cycle is proposed in the case of British Telecom), but between each review comparatively little information and analysis are required. To the extent that this reduces the degree of discretion open to the regulatory authority, the risks of regulatory capture are also reduced (see Littlechild, 1983). There may, however, be practical difficulties in specifying a price regulatory formula which is much different in effect from rate-of-return regulation (Vickers and Yarrow, 1985a, discuss this point in relation to British Telecom).

The third regulatory principle is central to this paper. It is that natural monopoly elements should be isolated from competitive activities, so that regulatory rules applied to the control of the natural monopoly do not also interfere with the achievement of efficiency in activities where competition is feasible. This principle might be called the undesirability of 'cross-regulation'. The regionalisation option involves separation of the NTS and each of the local distribution networks from the purchase and sale of gas.

The problem of how to regulate residual natural monopoly elements effectively (given the problems identified above) remains. An old solution suggested in the literature is franchising—inducing competition, not directly in the production of the commodity, but for the right to exercise a monopoly (see Chadwick, 1859, and Demsetz, 1968). Thus, given the natural monopoly elements in the NTS and in the local distribution network, one possible option would be to auction the franchise rights regularly to competing managerial teams. In principle that team most able to distribute at lowest cost will put in the highest bid. Franchising has been used to allocate regional ITV contracts (Domberger and Middleton, 1985) and to allocate the operation of services at airports (Starkie and Thompson, 1985).

Franchising does, however, raise problems of its own. In an article in Part V of this volume, Domberger identifies two of the most serious of these as how to organise an efficient franchise bidding system and how to ensure a transfer of assets on termination consistent with appropriate incentives to invest, but not to over-invest, in necessary equipment. Experience with franchising ITV contracts (see Domberger and Middleton, 1985) indicates that incumbents may acquire advantages which deter competitive bids. The form of the tender might have to be quite complex since it would need to include provisions which relate to safety and security of supply. Franchising is thus an interesting theoretical option, but one where further exploration is required before its applicability to gas supply can be recommended.

VI. Conclusions

In this paper we have argued that there is prima-facie evidence to suggest that British Gas is characterised by allocative inefficiency in its charging policies. However, improvement depends less on privatisation *per se* than on the form of the privatised gas industry. This can best be illustrated by comparing two alternatives—one which is currently favoured by Government and management, and one which would involve creating a market in the supply of gas.

The first approach transfers an existing monopoly from the public to the private sector. It releases the industry from departmental regulation and allows a more clear-cut specification of objectives. In principle, privatisation might re-orientate objectives towards profit maximisation and this would provide incentives both to improved productive efficiency and to increased allocative efficiency by relating charges in different markets more closely to the different costs of supply. In practice these incentives are likely to prove extremely weak; the capital market pressures operating upon a privatised BGC are unlikely to be substantial and privatisation of BGC in its present form would not increase the competitive incentives provided in the product market; it may even reduce them. Transferring a public monopoly into the private sector is therefore unlikely in itself to provide any significant improvement in performance. It may, however, maximise the proceeds from the asset sale—a point where financial considerations conflict with greater liberalisation.

The second approach attempts to isolate out natural monopoly elements of the gas industry from competitive ones. The industry would be divided into twelve independent companies for area distribution, with a further company operating the NTS. Ownership of the existing contracts for the supply of gas to BGC would also be separated (we discussed possible options in Section IV). We have argued that this second approach will enhance incentives both in the product market and in the capital market. A market for the purchase and sale of gas would be established between the producers of gas (the oil and gas companies) and the companies which supply gas to consumers. Direct market entry by the producers into the supply of gas to industrial customers would no longer be forestalled (as it is at present) by BGC's ownership of both the gas supply contracts (with their associated advantageous supply price terms) and the NTS. The creation of twelve separate regional gas companies would increase the effectiveness of capital market incentives both by providing a sectoral bench-mark for each company's performance and by making take-over a more realistic proposition.

Nevertheless, even if the second approach is followed, the natural monopoly associated with the NTS and the regional distribution networks will provide the privatised companies with varying degrees of market power. Regulation is still likely to be required. But the second approach enables regulatory control to be focused on just those activities where monopoly power remains—that is the operation of the NTS and supply of gas to domestic customers. The potential adverse impact which regulation can have upon efficiency is therefore limited in scope. Furthermore, the second approach, by providing competing sources of information to the regulatory authority, is likely both to minimise the dangers of regulatory capture and to strengthen the capability of the regulatory authority to prevent overcapitalisation.

In summary, we conclude that privatisation of the gas industry is likely to meet the Government's objective of improving efficiency only to the extent that it enables competitive incentives (both in the product market and in the capital market) to be significantly enhanced. We have suggested how this might be achieved. But we find it difficult to see any significant benefits flowing from the Government's proposals to privatise BGC in its present structure.[2] The consequences may even be adverse. And privatisation on this basis is likely to make the task of introducing competitive incentives in the future more, rather than less, difficult to put into practice. In an uncertain situation, a policy which keeps the options for competition open is much preferable to one which closes them off.

[2] Kay and Thompson (1985) discuss why privatisation on this basis may have been adopted.

Part V

FRANCHISING AND COMPETITIVE TENDERING

14

ECONOMIC REGULATION THROUGH FRANCHISE CONTRACTS*

Simon Domberger

I. Introduction

A major theme of UK industrial policy at the present time is the rolling back of direct state and public involvement in economic activity. This policy, which is loosely referred to as privatisation and which is motivated by the desire to improve economic performance, has been most conspicuous by its attempts at systematic divestiture of public ownership from the nationalised industry sector.

However, the effects of the policy are likely to be influenced by the form in which it is implemented. Thus one possibility is denationalisation—the transfer of ownership of a statutory monopoly from the public to the private sector. Such a step is likely to improve the productive efficiency of the newly privatised enterprise which will now have incentives to be profitable, but it will do little for allocative efficiency unless steps are taken to reduce the degree of monopoly.

Another possibility is to retain public ownership but to encourage greater competition by removing artificial (in particular statutory) restrictions on entry into the industry. This is referred to as 'liberalisation' or 'deregulation' policy, a good example of which is the liberalisation of express coach services by the 1980 Transport Act (see the article by Davis in Part III).[1]

* This article is a version of a paper given at an Institute for Fiscal Studies conference on Competition and Regulation held in London in May 1985.

Simon Domberger is a Lecturer in Economics at the London Business School and a Research Associate of the Institute for Fiscal Studies.

The author wishes to acknowledge his debt to Dieter Helm, John Kay, and David Thompson for helpful comments and suggestions on a previous draft. Responsibility for errors and omissions is the author's alone.

[1] Although privatisation and liberalisation policies are not mutually exclusive there is a potentially serious conflict between them. It is easier to find investors will-

A third option is to grant franchise contracts to private sector firms for the supply of goods and services previously provided in the public sector. Franchising has been used extensively in the USA where it has fallen out of favour because of operational difficulties and suspicion of malpractice in the context of broadcasting franchises. By contrast, the UK experience with independent television franchising, although not immune from criticism, has been quite favourable (see Domberger and Middleton, 1985). More generally, franchising has attractive properties which suggest that if properly implemented it could go a considerable way towards meeting both objectives of productive and allocative efficiency. This paper addresses the issues which need to be considered if franchising is to become a significant instrument of policy.

II. Is regulation necessary?

At the risk of some over-simplification, the economic arguments for the regulation of industry may be classified under three headings. The first and traditional case for intervention arises from market failure caused by 'natural monopoly'. Briefly, a natural monopoly is defined as an industry in which least cost provision of a good (or service) requires that no more than one firm be in production. Electricity distribution is the classic example of natural monopoly because an extensive and costly distribution network is required to link all points of consumption with the point of supply or production. Clearly, duplication of such a network, which would be the consequence of a second operator entering the industry, would significantly increase the cost per unit of electricity supplied. (See Sharkey, 1982, for a full discussion.)

But while efficiency in production points to monopoly, it is well known that efficiency in the allocation of resources will not be achieved under monopoly because of the incentives to raise and maintain prices above costs. In these circumstances regulation, or nationalisation in the context of the UK economy, has been proposed as a means of securing optimal pricing and resource allocation.

ing to subscribe to an equity stake in a secure monopoly than in a firm which is about to be subjected to the bracing winds of competition.

Recently, Baumol and his associates (Baumol, Panzar, and Willig, 1982; Baumol and Willig, 1981) have seriously questioned this argument on the grounds that a 'sustainable' natural monopoly, whilst ruling out competition, is consistent with efficient pricing and thus resource allocation provided the market is 'perfectly contestable'. The essence of contestability is that socially desirable behaviour is enforced upon the incumbent monopolist not by actual but by potential competition—through the threat of new entry. Whenever the incumbent creates profitable opportunities for new entrants by raising prices above costs he becomes a target for 'hit and run' entry. Hence, equilibrium in a perfectly contestable market implies that the natural monopolist will be making no more than normal profits for otherwise he would become vulnerable to entry. The profound policy conclusion implied by Baumol's analysis is that removing artificial entry barriers is a more effective instrument for dealing with natural monopoly than regulation.

Unfortunately, it turns out that the assumptions required for perfect contestability are so stringent as to be rarely satisfied in practice. One crucial assumption is that entry must be costlessly reversible which means that the entrant must be able to exit from the market at no cost when it is no longer profitable to remain in it. It can be shown that for entry to be 'free' in this sense, there must be no 'sunk costs', that is costs which cannot be eliminated upon cessation of production. Sunk costs are likely to be considerable, however, whenever the fixed assets required for the operation are specialised and therefore have no alternative use (e.g. railway tracks), or when there are no secondary markets where they may be realised.[2] In the presence of sunk costs perfect contestability cannot be relied upon to ensure socially desirable pricing behaviour, and the case for regulation emerges once again.

A second case of market failure arises not because of natural monopoly *per se*, but because incumbents may nevertheless enjoy advantages which enable them to deter new entrants or force their eventual withdrawal from a newly liberalised market. This is referred to as the 'first-mover

---

[2] For a detailed discussion of the distinction between fixed costs and sunk costs, and the special significance of the latter, see Baumol, Panzar, and Willig (1982).

advantage'. Perhaps the best example of this phenomenon is seen in the impact of the 1980 Transport Act which effectively deregulated the express coach industry. Although the pace of new entry was vigorous for a time after introduction of the legislation, it was not sustained and the majority of entrants eventually left the industry. The incumbent National Express has retained its dominant position; its ownership of Victoria Coach Station provided a significant competitive advantage. (For details see the article by Davis in Part III). Moreover, the possibility of entrenched monopoly is extremely difficult to predict before deregulation and requires detailed knowledge of industry characteristics. Although deregulation might still be considered desirable in these circumstances, reliance will have to be placed on the instruments of competition policy for the identification and suppression of anticompetitive practices which may become apparent *ex post*. Where competition policy is ill-equipped to identify and deal with such cases within reasonable time, deregulation may fulfil little of its original promise.

The third case which merits intervention arises where there are 'externalities' or there is wider concern about the general effects or outcomes of certain types of economic activity. Broadcasting (television and radio) is a good example and is regulated in most countries not only because of potential problems with airband allocation, but because of strong public desire to control the nature of broadcast transmission. The need to monitor and enforce advertising standards is widely accepted in the UK and regulation to ensure that programme output complies with accepted norms of decency and fairness is seldom challenged. Thus regulation may be introduced to ensure the provision of public safeguards from undesirable effects of economic activity.

III. Problems with regulation

Notwithstanding its theoretical merits, the experience of regulation, particularly in the USA, has been less than encouraging. Criticisms of the activities of regulatory institutions charged with the protection of the public interest have been widely documented in recent years and it may be helpful to group them under four headings. First there is the problem of 'regulatory capture', originally promulgated by Stigler (1971), and which suggests that regulation ends up by serving the interests of the regulated companies instead of the public. Second, there is the problem of inefficient use of inputs leading to higher than minimum costs as a result of rate-of-return regulation. This is the well known Averch–Johnson (1962) effect which has been widely cited in the context of US public utility regulation. The third criticism arises from the biases and distortions which emerge when regulation is demanded and supplied to satisfy strong political and social interest groups. Finally, there is the criticism that regulation stifles innovation and slows down the adoption of best practice techniques thus keeping costs higher than they need be. Deregulation of air transport in the USA is often cited as an example which revealed the extent of inefficiency in the industry in terms of cost levels and route structure. For a discussion see Graham, Kaplan, and Silbey (1983), and Bailey (1985).

It should be noted, however, that the above criticisms are not about regulation *per se*, but largely about the way in which it has been implemented. The proper conclusion to draw from past experience is not that regulation must always be ineffective or inefficient but that reform of existing, or creation of alternative, modes of regulation is required.

In the UK, economic regulation of private enterprises has been confined to relatively few sectors such as express coaching and broadcasting. The UK solution to natural monopoly has been nationalisation. This amounts to regulation through ownership, and it has been applied to key sectors of the economy such as coal, steel, and rail transport. The current drive towards privatisation in the UK reflects a belief that public enterprise is prone to chronic productive inefficiency, to an extent which far outweighs any problems of allocative inefficiency. But as was indicated earlier, privatisation can take many forms and consideration needs to be given to alternative policy options. Franchising is one such option which according to Beesley and Littlechild (1983, p. 15) '. . . needs far more analytic attention before positive recommendations can be made'.

IV. The nature of franchising

Franchising involves conferring temporary monopoly rights of production and/or distribution of specified goods or services. It was essentially conceived as a method of introducing competition in circumstances where market failure was believed to be highly probable or where some measure of regulation was judged to be desirable. The principle was first enunciated by Chadwick (1859) who suggested that competition *for* the market can be a substitute for competition *in* the market. However, it was Demsetz (1968) who first argued for franchising as a serious alternative to regulation and nationalisation. Demsetz stressed that *ex post* monopoly in the supply of goods or services is consistent with *ex ante* competition for the right to be the sole supplier for a given period of time.

With franchising, competition is introduced prior to actual entry into the market through a contest or auction in which potential suppliers bid for the contract. In Demsetz's stylised example, the winner is awarded a contract to supply vehicle licence plates, the production of which is subject to continuously increasing returns, thus suggesting natural monopoly. The winner of the contest is the producer who bids the lowest supply price. Contract duration can be variable, but in Demsetz's example it is one year so that bidding is renewed at annual intervals.

The above has come to be known as the Chadwick/Demsetz auction in which the contract is awarded to the bidder offering the lowest consumer price or, alternatively, to the one offering the price/quality combination which is judged superior to all others. This bidding process is designed to bring prices down to levels which come close to expected unit costs of production.

An alternative bidding/auction process involves awarding the franchise contract to the bidder who offers to pay most for it. The value of the bid under this system is likely to reflect contestants' expectations of the discounted stream of monopoly rents which accrue to the operator over the life of the contract. The merit of this scheme lies in the fact that part if not all of future rents are appropriated by the franchiser

(the state); but it does nothing to alleviate the pricing inefficiencies associated with monopoly.

In parallel to the two types of bidding processes there
are essentially two forms of franchise contracts: owning or
operating. In the former case the contractor acquires ownership of the fixed assets which are needed for the production
and distribution of the good or service in question. In the case
of operating franchises, those assets remain in public ownership and become the responsibility of the regulatory authority.

Owning franchises require large capital investments by
operators who may be uncertain of their value upon franchise
termination. This immediately raises the possibility of significant sunk costs associated with the possibility of termination
which may deter potential franchisers from bidding. Whilst
overcoming these problems, operating franchises can lead to
inefficiencies in the deployment of assets which are not controlled by agents with incentives to minimise costs. They also
increase the burden of franchise regulation because of the
responsibility for maintenance and replacement which then lies
with the regulatory authority. Thus there is a trade-off involved in choosing between owning or operating franchises—
in the former case competition or contestability is likely to be
reduced whilst the latter is not incentive-compatible with
respect to deployment of fixed assets.

V. Towards an evaluation of franchising

Franchising can be viewed essentially as a mechanism for increasing market contestability. It does so by allowing firms to
bid for the rights to supply *before* they have committed
resources to the enterprise, i.e. by reducing the level of sunk
costs associated with entry. Of equal importance is the fact
that franchising is a mechanism for providing the regulator
with information about the competitiveness of potential suppliers. Such information generation is entirely absent under
traditional regulation and nationalisation and is a major advantage of the franchising method. Another advantage of
franchising over traditional forms of regulation is that it provides a sanction on poor performance, namely the threat of
franchise termination, which may in some circumstances be a

more credible sanction than the threat of take-over faced by a regulated enterprise. However, implementation of franchise contracts is not without its difficulties, which may be considered under four headings.

(i) *The bidding process*

For the franchising process to be effective, bidding must be competitive. This requires that the number of bidders be sufficiently large or that they be sufficiently dispersed to discourage collusion. However, this should not be taken to imply that the number of bidders must be as large as the number of suppliers in atomistic markets. For as Stiglitz (1984, p. 34) has argued, when imperfect information is present 'Markets with a limited number of firms may have much more effective competition than markets with a large number of firms'. Nevertheless, experience shows that collusive bidding can and does occur, and Schmalensee (1979) records several examples of collusive bidding for municipal services franchises.

Another factor likely to reduce the number of bidders is the presence of sunk costs. Sunk costs deter bidding because they increase the penalty of exit upon franchise termination and create an asymmetry, at the bidding stage, between the incumbent and the entrant. One way of reducing the element of sunk costs is to opt for operating franchises which do not impose an obligation upon the contractor to acquire costly assets. However, there are incentive problems associated with operating franchises which have already been discussed.

A third factor likely to discourage potential bids is the information advantage acquired by the incumbent franchisee during his contract tenure. This will increase the probability of the incumbent being re-awarded the contract and means that outsiders will not be bidding on equal terms. This may arise specifically from information regarding the preferences of the regulators which is likely to influence the criteria for selection of the winning bid. In order to avoid this potential information asymmetry reducing the degree of competition, the characteristics of the contract must be clearly specified so that outside bidders have as much information about what is required as the incumbent (see Domberger and Middleton,

1985, for a discussion of this problem in the context of ITV franchise contracts).

(ii) *Contract specification*

Generating effective competition, which is what makes franchising superior to traditional forms of regulation, creates a problem of contract specification and selection criteria which obviously does not arise under regulation. The first issue concerns the nature of the good or service to be supplied. This is relatively simple in the case, say, of vehicle licence plates, as in Demsetz's stylised example, but is more difficult in the case of television broadcasting where price setting is irrelevant and contestants are judged on the merits of their proposed programme schedules. Interestingly, contestants are not asked to indicate the expected costs of provision of the programmes offered. Posner (1972) suggested that contestants be invited to bid alternative price/quality combinations, but that leaves open the question of determining the optimal configuration of price and quality. Clearly franchising is likely to be most effective where the product or service to be supplied can be defined with relative precision.

A second issue concerns the problem of selection when the franchise involves supplying several jointly produced and well-defined outputs as, for example, trunk and local telephone services. One way to proceed is to base selection on the price of a single product or service leaving the price of the other(s) to be determined by negotiations with the franchise authority at a later stage. However, the case of the City of Oakland CATV franchise examined by Williamson (1976) shows that this method can lead to long-run pricing distortions.

A possible solution in the case of jointly supplied outputs is to link the bids to the price of a basket of products or services. In other words, the bids would be based on a weighted average of product prices, where the weights are specified in advance to all contestants. It may be more convenient to express the weighted average in index number form—where the base prices are those currently charged by the incumbent. The weights of the price index would be based on the shares of expenditure on the products/services in the basket in a manner analogous to the construction of the UK retail and producer price indexes. The expenditure share data could be obtained from publicly available sources such as the Family Expenditure Survey or from company data.

Apart from its simplicity, the advantage of compiling a price index of this type is that it gives an easily measured indicator of the potential gains, in terms of price reductions, of the franchising scheme. It is also worth noting that the weighting structure provides the contestants with an incentive to reduce price/cost margins on products with large expenditure shares and correspondingly increase them for products with low shares, *ceteris paribus*. It can be shown that this price index represents a good approximation to the theoretically appropriate measure of the welfare gains associated with lower bid prices.

It is evident from the above that creating competition for franchise contracts and obtaining information on contractors involves a cost, namely the specification of outputs and determination of unambiguous selection criteria. Moreover, the product or service specified in the contract remains unchanged during its lifetime. This may be undesirable in situations where rapid technological change is likely to influence supply and/or demand characteristics in the market. It also raises an important question regarding the appropriate contract length, to which we now turn.

(iii) *Contract duration*

Franchise bidding may be viewed as a surrogate process for the selection of efficient firms which is the important property of competitive markets. The crucial difference lies in the discrete nature of franchising—contracts are typically awarded for a period of years. However, by shortening the length of the contract period it is possible to make franchising more of a continuous process. Demsetz (1968) stipulated a contract period of one year for his vehicle licence plate franchise. In the case of ITV franchises a contract period of one year would severely reduce the number of bids. The reason can be found in the time stream of costs and revenues associated with the franchise and may be clarified with the help of the following highly simplified example.

Consider a franchise contract the duration of which is m years. Assume that the bidding costs are the only sunk costs associated with the franchise (operating contract) and are given by B_0 for all contestants. Suppose also that the 'representative' bidder's subjective assessment of the probability of winning the contract is given by α, $0 < \alpha < 1$. This is clearly a simplification since α is endogenous and depends *inter alia* on the number of contestants, but is convenient for analytical purposes. In general, a profit-maximising contestant will only bid for the contract if expected profits are positive and the following inequality is satisfied:

$$\alpha \sum_{t=1}^{m} \frac{R_t(Q)}{(1+r)^t} + (1-\alpha)R_0 > B_0 + \alpha \sum_{t=1}^{m} \frac{C_t(Q)}{(1+r)^t}$$
$$+ (1-\alpha)C_0 \qquad (1)$$

where $R(Q)$ and $C(Q)$ are the contestant's expected revenues and costs in each year in the life of the contract if the bid is successful, and r is the interest rate. R_0 and C_0 are the expected revenues and costs (other than bidding costs) if the bid is not successful; these can be assumed to be zero. For bidding to be profitable, expected revenues must exceed expected costs discounted over the contract period. But notice that B_0 enters with a probability of one, since bidding costs are sunk and are incurred whether the contract is awarded or not. Collecting terms we have:

$$\sum_{t=1}^{m} \frac{R_t(Q) - C_t(Q)}{(1+r)^t} > \frac{B_0}{\alpha} \qquad (2)$$

The above expression clarifies the significance of contract duration m in the bidding decision. Since we can expect production costs to exceed revenues in the early periods, inequality (2) is less likely to be satisfied with a short contract duration, that is with a low value of m. Note also that B_0 is scaled up by the reciprocal of the probability of success α. This indicates that large bidding costs and/or low probability of award will require high profitability and thus long contract duration to make bidding worthwhile.

In practice inequality (2) will vary for each and every contestant because their expectation of costs and revenues will differ. Thus in a population of potential bidders there will be a corresponding distribution of minimum contract duration below which no bidding takes place. Hence, as contract length is reduced the number of contestants who are willing to bid will shrink. In the limit that number reduces to zero.

The nature of the trade-off involved in determining contract length should now be clear. Shorter contracts increase the likelihood that the number of bidders will fall to levels which threaten the viability of the contest. Longer contracts make it more likely that incumbents will benefit from important informational and other advantages which impair competition at the bidding stage. This could also have the effect of reducing the perceived threat of franchise termination and thus weakening the ultimate sanction on poor performance. For the franchise authority the issue of optimal contract duration is, once again, a problem of information, without which it is difficult to identify the nature of the trade-off involved. The significance of this trade-off has been recognised in the recent White Paper (Home Office, 1983, p. 34) on the development of cable television.[3] Although this issue does not arise in the context of conventional forms of regulation it is one which in practice may not be difficult to resolve.

(iv) *Regulation and enforcement of contracts*

Regulation of franchise contracts is in principle much simpler than conventional forms of regulation. On the output side what is required is no more than periodic (e.g. annual) checks of realised versus specified performance standards. As regards prices, the quasi-competitive price structure generated by the bidding process should be maintained during the franchise term. The history of franchising is not short of cases of unrealistic bidding designed to get 'a foot in the door' in the knowledge that once the contract is secured, more favourable terms can then be negotiated and the base-period pricing structure adjusted towards monopoly levels. All the franchisee has to do in order to achieve this is to

---

[3] 'In the case of cable operations it is important that the franchise period should be sufficiently long to encourage investment and to enable programme and other services to establish themselves. However, the longer the period the greater would be the danger that monopolistic abuses might start to develop . . .'

persuade the authority that circumstances have changed significantly, namely that costs have risen. What is needed, therefore, is a contract which will make the initial price structure stick, in real terms. If known in advance this will discourage unrealistically low bids because contestants will be aware that subsequent renegotiation of prices is ruled out. Under this regime, bid prices are likely to reflect costs.

In the longer term costs are bound to rise and the franchise authority must have a mechanism for establishing warranted price increases. The UK Government has recently adopted a price regulation scheme put forward by Littlechild (1983) and known as the 'RPI $-X$' formula. The scheme was devised for regulating local telephone tariffs of the newly privatised British Telecom and allows the tariff index to rise, on an annual basis, by the same percentage as the UK retail price index, minus X per cent. The latter is the efficiency or productivity deduction which is there to ensure that the gains in operating efficiency are passed on to the consumer in terms of lower *relative* prices.

What this scheme effectively attempts to do is to regulate costs, rather than the difference between prices and costs which is the target of rate-of-return regulation. The scheme is singularly appropriate to franchise contracts and relatively easy to implement. However, a problem with the RPI is that it is likely to be a biased indicator of changes in costs relevant to the franchisee. An alternative and possibly better indicator, along the lines suggested by the Monopolies and Mergers Commission (1982), would essentially involve constructing an index of input prices (IPI) using information on the input structure appropriate to the industry. This would be feasible provided that the technology of production is known and that input prices are determined exogenously so that they are outside the control of the franchisee.

The important feature of this scheme is that unlike rate-of-return regulation it is incentive-compatible: it does not lead to distortions in the use of inputs which result in higher costs. Moreover, the franchisee has an incentive to increase efficiency beyond what is indicated by X and can do so by optimal substitution of inputs following relative price changes. Any such efficiency gains would be appropriated by the franchisee since the IPI would not capture the effect of input substitution. The operator therefore has strong incentives to keep costs down as this is the most direct method by which he can increase profitability.

VI. Conclusions: Franchising versus regulation

Section II of this paper suggested that some form of regulation is likely to be a necessary adjunct to a programme of privatisation. The privatisation of British Telecom and its aftermath demonstrate quite clearly that it is preferable to devise a combined policy in relation to privatisation and regulation at the outset than to adopt a piecemeal approach.

Our analysis of franchising indicates that it combines strong elements of competition with a regulatory framework which safeguards social welfare. Its key advantage over traditional forms of regulation lies in the information which it generates about the competitiveness of suppliers, the incentives which the operator has to achieve productive efficiency, and the existence of an effective sanction in the case of persistent underperformance, namely franchise termination.

It is clear from our evaluation of franchising, however, that its greatest scope lies in areas where technology of production is relatively simple and static, where the product or service can be specified with precision, and where significant demand fluctuations seem unlikely within the franchise term. Examples of activities which fulfil these conditions and which might, therefore, be suitable candidates for franchising are transport services (e.g. buses), electricity distribution, cleaning of hospitals and schools, and refuse disposal. It is interesting to note that some of these activities are already being franchised in the UK public sector, but as yet no substantive empirical evidence has emerged on their performance record.

Further research is still required to help shed light on issues which were raised in this paper. First, there is a need to examine the efficiency of franchising as a method of generating information for purposes of regulation. Second, there is a need to study alternative bidding processes and to establish, *inter alia*, the way in which optimal price/quality combinations offered by contractors might be identified.

Finally, in the context of owning franchises, there is a need to formulate an asset transfer rule which would facilitate smooth transition between franchisees and reduce the likelihood of sunk costs being incurred upon franchise termination.

15

CONTRACTING-OUT POLICY: THEORY AND EVIDENCE*

Keith Hartley and Meg Huby

I. Introduction

Contracting-out is one element of the current Government's privatisation policy. It is concerned with the central or local government *finance* of services which could be *supplied* by private contractors. In principle, contracting-out can be applied to a vast range of public sector services traditionally undertaken 'in-house'. Currently, it is the focus of major policy initiatives in local government, the National Health Service and defence (see Table 1). Not surprisingly, contracting-out has resulted in considerable controversy reflecting the views of the various groups likely to gain or lose from the policy. The topic is dominated by emotion, myths, claims and counter-claims, many of which need to be confronted with evidence. There is no shortage of hypotheses which need testing. This paper presents evidence on the major issues in the debate. Competitive tendering also offers a unique opportunity to compare the efficiency of the private and public sectors in a situation where both sectors are competing for a *given level of service*. Initially, some policy rules

* This material, which remains the copyright of *Public Money*, was extracted from the article 'Contracting-out in health and local authorities: prospects, progress and pitfalls' by Keith Hartley and Meg Huby, which appeared in the September 1985 issue of that journal. *Public Money* is available, on subscription, from the publishers: Chartered Institute of Public Finance & Accountancy, 3 Robert Street, London, WC2N 6BH.

Keith Hartley is Director of the Institute of Social and Economic Research at the University of York.

Meg Huby is a Research Fellow at the Institute of Social and Economic Research at the University of York.

The authors are most grateful to the Wincott Foundation for funding this project; the usual disclaimers apply.

for competitive tendering are outlined. These provide criteria for assessing current policy on contracting-out. Evidence from a recent survey shows what has actually been happening. The conclusion summarises the extent to which the criteria have been met and what still needs to be done.

Table 1. The Opportunities for Contracting-Out Services in the Public Sector

---

Local Authorities
- Current examples include refuse collection, catering and cleaning of offices, schools and streets.
- Since legislation in 1980, direct labour organisations are required to compete with private firms for most of their construction and maintenance work.
- The Government proposes to extend compulsory tendering to refuse collection, catering, cleaning streets and buildings, and the maintenance of grounds and vehicles (Department of Environment Consultation Paper, February 1985).
- Other possibilities for contracting-out include accountancy and architectural services, careers advice, computer and data processing services, housing valuation and sales, fire protection, and the management and operation of leisure facilities.

National Health Service
- Currently there is a major DHSS policy initiative to introduce competitive tendering for hospital catering, cleaning, and laundry services (i.e. domestic services).
- Other possibilities include ambulance and transport services, the contracting-out of major surgery and patient care to private hospitals, together with hospital management, and care for the elderly, disabled, and mentally handicapped.

Ministry of Defence
- Current examples include catering and cleaning at defence establishments, the re-fitting of warships (traditionally undertaken in the Royal Dockyards), some limited aircraft servicing and vehicle repair, air transport, and the management of stores.
- Other possibilities include air-traffic control, the maintenance and repair of all vehicles and weapons and the training activities of the Armed Forces such as the training of drivers, musicians, pilots, and technicians.

II. Rules for a competitive tendering policy

Right across the board, the Government has committed itself to contracting-out where possible. What does it have to do to ensure that its objectives are met? At the outset, it has to be recognised that if the Government wishes to improve efficiency, then contracting-out is not sufficient: genuine competition is required. This suggests some rules for a competitive tendering policy:

- Genuine rivalry requires opportunities for new firms to enter the market. Without the possibility of new entry, there is a danger that cartels and collusive arrangements will emerge resulting in private monopolies replacing public monopolies.

- Rivalry is needed for both a given and alternative levels of service. Genuine efficiency improvements require competitive tendering for different levels of service so that the public buyer can obtain accurate information on the costs of a little more or a little less. This enables the buyer to determine whether the existing level and quality of service is worthwhile, or whether a higher or lower level would be more beneficial.

- Contracts should be awarded to the lowest bidder in the competition. Successful bidders should be given a fixed price contract with penalty clauses for private firms and their equivalent for in-house units. Without fixed price contracts and budget constraints, private firms and in-house units have every incentive to 'buy into' a contract by offering optimistic estimates of price, quality, and delivery. To avoid optimistic estimates, the public procurement agents need competitively-determined, firm, fixed-price contracts and a willingness to enforce penalty clauses for poor quality and late delivery. In principle, in-house units which are successful in a competition need to be subject to the same penalties and incentives offered to private contractors.

- The results of competitions should be publicly available. Details of the winning and rival bids should be published: rate-payers and tax-payers have a right to know how their money is being spent. Moreover, publication reduces the danger of political patronage in the award of contracts and the information also contributes to the competitive process: winners and losers need to know how they compare.

III. The need for evidence

Evidence is needed to show what has actually been happening and how the implementation of policy compares with our criteria for competitive tendering. In addition, contracting-out has resulted in considerable controversy and many of the arguments for and against (see Table 2) can be resolved by empirical testing. Some of the arguments obviously represent special pleading by those interest groups most likely to gain or lose from the policy. Private industry which is likely to gain will stress the benefits of 'free enterprise and competition'. In reality, businessmen have a remarkable propensity for seeking monopoly, protection, and government subsidies leading to 'on-the-job' leisure and a quiet life. Similarly, contracting-out will be opposed by those trade unions and professional associations whose members are most likely to lose from the policy. They will readily report any examples of strikes, poor quality, and poor performance due to private contractors, referring to a perfect model of the public sector in which such problems are never encountered. Participants in the debate need to state whether they are comparing 'ideal' models of the economy, namely perfect competition and perfect socialism; or whether they are comparing one of these ideal states with actual institutions; or whether they are comparing two imperfect but real world organisational arrangements. Moreover, any assessment of contracting-out and in-house provision raises questions about the aims of public policy. For example, is the NHS concerned with the efficient provision of patient care, or with protecting jobs and solving Britain's unemployment and poverty problems? Evaluation cannot ignore the need for evidence. This need is reinforced by the fact that much of the available evidence, especially on the magnitude of cost savings, is limited, often based on US experience, is frequently flawed in that it fails to compare like with like, reflects political bias, and is usually based on casual empiricism. In other words, there is a general lack of reliable evidence on the results of the current policy initiative. We need to know which services are being contracted-out, whether tendering is competitive as defined by our criteria, the costs to the public sector of competitive tendering, and whether the policy is leading to cost savings.

To answer some of these questions, we undertook a questionnaire survey of local authorities, the NHS, and firms. For local authorities and the NHS, the aim was to obtain information on their actual experience of contracting out at least one specific service since January 1982. The respondent was allowed to choose the contract for which data would be provided. Authorities without actual experience of contracting-out were asked whether they planned to contract out any services within the next two years, together with their beliefs about likely cost savings from competitive tendering. Firms were also included in the survey to provide information on their views about the size and source of any cost savings.

Questionnaires were distributed during late 1984 and early 1985. All local authorities in England were sent a questionnaire. Out of 410 questionnaires distributed, we received 213 replies (52 per cent of total), comprising 75 completed questionnaires (18 per cent), 112 (27 per cent) who responded that no services had been put out to tender since January 1982, with the remainder lacking the resources to respond or being unwilling to provide data. For the NHS, questionnaires were sent to each of the District Health Authorities in England. Out of 192 questionnaires distributed, 119 replies were received (62 per cent of total). However, only 10 questionnaires (5 per cent of total) provided data on actual contract experience, while a further 80 (42 per cent) indicated their plans and offered views on the likely savings from competitive tendering; others declined on grounds that the issue was currently under discussion in the Health Authority. On this basis, the results should be regarded as tentative since there were insufficient replies to provide reliable generalisations based on *actual* experience and the responses based on expectations are subject to all the standard problems of bias, beliefs, and personal opinions. Questionnaires were also sent to 81 firms, comprising 41 members of the Health Care

Table 2. The Arguments

THE CASE FOR CONTRACTING-OUT	THE CASE AGAINST CONTRACTING-OUT
• Public sector 'in-house' monopolies are inefficient bureaucracies satisfying the wishes of producer groups rather than consumers	• Private contractors offer a poor quality and unreliable service
• Public sector inefficiency is reflected in restrictive labour practices and low productivity with its effects on rates, taxes, subsidies, and government expenditure	• Private contractors are liable to default and bankruptcy, and are less able to respond to emergencies
• There is an 'open-ended' financial commitment to public sector 'in-house' units	• In the NHS, private contractors put profits before people so placing patients at risk
• 'In-house' units seek to provide 'Rolls-Royce' standards of service regardless of cost	• Awarding contracts to private firms leads to industrial relations problems and strikes
• Competition allows regular re-contracting by public procurement agents	• Contractors use low bids to 'buy into' attractive contracts and eliminate the 'in-house' capacity so that the public authority becomes dependent on a private monopoly
• Competition leads to new ideas, modern equipment, and changes in traditional methods of working	• Competitive tendering is not costless: there are costs to the public authority in specifying, monitoring, and enforcing contracts
• Successful firms in a competition are subject to the incentives and penalties of a fixed price contract	• Private contractors achieve cost savings by cutting jobs, reducing wages, and worsening working conditions
• Contractors can be penalised for poor quality, delays, and unreliability	
• *Result: cost savings and 'better value for money'*	• *Result: Cost savings, if any, are short-lived and offset by reductions in the quality of services supplied*

Services Section of the Contract Cleaning and Maintenance Association, 11 members of the British Hotels, Restaurants and Caterers Association, and 29 other firms selected from the journal *Contract Services*. Out of 81 questionnaires distributed, we received 26 replies (32 per cent of total) which provided 19 completed questionnaires (23 per cent) with the remainder having no experience of such contracts. Nearly all the replies were from members of trade associations mostly involved in hospital and school cleaning.

IV. What has been happening?

At the outset, it has to be stressed that the results of our survey are subject to all the standard limitations of a postal questionnaire, particularly the difficulties of obtaining a representative sample. Nevertheless, the replies from local authorities provide the basis for more reliable generalisations than some of the previous excursions into this field. For ease of presentation, the results will be reported as answers to some of the major questions concerning current contracting-out policy.

(i) *Which services are being put out to tender?*

For the 75 local authorities which reported actual examples, 32 were for building maintenance and repair, 22 were cleaning contracts, 9 were for refuse collection and waste disposal, 7 for pest control, and the remainder for security services, management services, and horticultural supply. Within the NHS, and as a result of DHSS policy, many District Health Authorities expected to put cleaning, catering, and laundry services out to tender within the next two years. Some Health Authorities also planned to use competitive tendering for transport, portering, gardening, vehicle maintenance, painting, medical engineering, and management services.

(ii) *Is competition possible?*

The case for contracting-out depends upon industry providing a *competitive* response. The local authorities and health authorities with actual experience of contracting-out invited an average of *eight* firms to bid and typically *six* bids

were received. Interestingly only 25 per cent of the respond-
ing local authorities had an open competition policy. As for
the beliefs of the District Health Authorities about future
policy, the majority felt that an effective competition involving five or six firms was possible and many thought that outside contractors would respond quickly to an increase in
demand. Questions arise about the role of in-house units in
any competition. For the 75 local authority contracts, the
in-house unit competed in 57 and won in 35 cases. In other
words, where competition is introduced, in-house units are
being awarded contracts. In addition, competitions are usually
restricted to a given specification. Out of 75 local authority
contracts, only 4 invited firms to offer alternative specifications for the work. This is an important finding since the
magnitude of any cost savings might be further affected if competition was extended to embrace different levels and qualities
of services.

(iii) *Are contracts always awarded to the lowest bidder?*

The survey showed that contracts are *not* always awarded to
the lowest bidder. Out of the 75 local authority contracts, 18
were not awarded to the lowest bidder. Of the 40 contracts won
by firms, 29 were lowest bids; similarly 28 of the 35 contracts
awarded to councils were lowest bids. In the 57 cases where
both firms and in-house units competed, 43 contracts went to
the lowest bidder, of which 28 were in-house organisations and
15 were firms. Predictably, supporters and opponents of
contracting-out will claim bias, favouritism, patronage, and
preferential treatment where contracts are not given to the
lowest bidder (unfair competition). Where both private and
public sector enterprises competed (57 cases), 14 contracts
were not awarded to the lowest bidder and these were shared
equally between in-house units and firms. However, the survey
provided no explanation of why in-house units did not compete for all 75 local authority contracts.

(iv) *What is a typical contract?*

The questionnaire responses embraced a wide variety of contracts, with lengths ranging from two months to sixty-five
months and values of £1,656 to £12.6 million. For the 75 local

authorities, the average duration of contract was twenty-seven months and the average value of contract was £1.3 million. For the small number of NHS contracts, the typical duration was thirty-six months at an average value of some £600,000. Firms reported a typical contract length of thirty-six months and an average value of £846,000. Contracts were generally on some form of fixed price basis, either a firm fixed price or with an allowance for inflation. Labour costs usually accounted for 68 per cent of the winning tender price, with equipment costs representing a further 14 per cent.

(v) *What are the costs of tendering?*

Local authorities provided some data on the costs they incurred in the organisation and administration of competitive tendering. These costs included the man-hours spent in organising the competition, preparing specifications, visiting sites and analysing the tenders. Such costs averaged £10,000 for local authorities and usually the time taken to complete the tendering process (i.e. between drawing up a specification and awarding a contract) was about five months. Firms also incur tendering costs and estimates were given of outlays of £1,000 to £3,000 when bidding for NHS contracts and £4,000 to £5,000 in competing for local authority contracts.

(vi) *Are contractors more efficient?*

Our results are based on those cases where a firm was contracted to provide the *same* level of service as previously supplied by the in-house unit. In these cases, the evidence from local authorities and the NHS based on a comparison of the contract value per annum with the cost of providing the same service in the previous year suggested that the percentage savings from competitive tendering would average 26 per cent per annum. The figures ranged from potential savings of 68 per cent to extra costs of 28 per cent. Such evidence can be usefully compared with beliefs and expectations. Health authorities without recent experience of contracting-out were asked whether they expected the policy to result in cost savings. Out of 59 replies from such Health Authorities, 23 expected cost savings of 11 to 20 per cent and 27 expected savings of 10 per cent or less. Our replies indicate some pessimism and under-estimation of likely cost savings amongst Health Authorities. When firms were asked about the percentage savings on actual contracts, they estimated an average of 30 per cent, a figure which is somewhat higher than the average actually experienced or estimated by local authorities and the NHS.

(vii) *What is the source of cost savings?*

Questions arise as to whether actual cost savings result from reduced employment, the increased use of part-time staff, lower rates of pay, fewer fringe benefits, the use of modern equipment, or better management and organisation. There was evidence that all these factors contributed to cost savings, although it was not possible to quantify their separate contributions. Firms in the sample claimed that 'more efficient organisational methods' were the main source of savings. One firm was more specific, explaining that the savings were made by 'using less people and fewer hours'. For the firms in our sample, part-time staff usually represented 50 per cent of the workforce. Certainly there was evidence of contractors substituting part-time for full-time labour with part-timers being more 'flexible' and firms using only a minimum of full-time staff. Out of 40 local authority contracts won by firms, not one contractor *actually* re-employed all the Council's staff on a full-time basis; for 33 contracts less than 10 per cent of the Council's staff were re-employed as full-timers and on 26 contracts less than 10 per cent of the in-house staff were re-employed on a part-time basis. Of course, contractors might *offer* to re-employ substantial proportions of a council's staff but workers might be unwilling to accept the wage rates, hours, and conditions of service in the private sector. There were also examples of contractors paying lower wage rates. From our survey of firms, in 14 cases out of the total sample of 26 local authority and NHS contracts won by firms, the contractors paid lower wage rates than the in-house unit. Similarly, contractors often 'economise' on conditions of service, especially superannuation, holiday pay, and sickness benefits (e.g. superannuation is unlikely to be inflation-proof). Nonetheless, one industry representative claimed that even if contractors were required to use identical labour inputs, rates of pay, and conditions of service, private firms could still save 10 to 15 per cent compared with in-house units.

(viii) *Can outside contractors provide the same level of service?*

Usually, contractors and in-house units competed for a given level of service as specified by the public procurement agents. In some cases, firms were required to provide performance bonds and such bonds increased contract prices by up to 5 per cent. All firms reported that contracts always contained penalty clauses. In the 40 cases where firms had won local authority contracts, there were 9 instances where penalty clauses had been invoked for poor quality of work and 7 cases where penalties had been applied for delays in carrying out the work. However, a proper evaluation requires data on the extent to which in-house units satisfactorily fulfil their contractual requirements. It is not unknown to encounter poor quality and delays in work performed by council and NHS staff. In this context, out of 35 cases where the in-house unit won the contract, there were 26 instances where the local authority stated that sanctions would be imposed if the terms of the contract were not met, with the remaining 9 stating that no sanctions would be imposed.

V. Conclusion: Problems and prospects

Contracting-out policy offers extensive opportunities for experimentation and a proper evaluation of actual experience. There is no shortage of questions to be asked and hypotheses to be tested. However, acceptance or rejection of the policy will ultimately depend on society's views about its desirability: who gains what, who loses and by how much? For example, the extent of cost inefficiency in the public sector will be reflected in the magnitude of job losses. Within the NHS, will such efficiency gains result in improved patient care and will any improvements be located within the hospital which increases the efficiency of its ancillary services, or will patients in some other District or Region benefit; or, will doctors gain through more funds to purchase expensive high technology equipment which benefits the users rather than patients? Equity and distribution of income issues cannot be ignored. If contracting-out is restricted to manual groups, savings might be achieved at the expense of the poorly paid members of society, whilst inefficiencies amongst professional groups (e.g. administrators, doctors) remain untouched.

A comparison of actual experience with our criteria for a competitive tendering policy shows that rivalry and the threat of rivalry can produce substantial cost savings. Nevertheless, there are deficiencies in current policy and, to meet the criteria for a competitive tendering policy, action is required on the following points.

- *The need to provide opportunities for new entrants.* Safeguards are required against the potential danger of private cartels and collusive arrangements replacing public monopolies. New entry might be encouraged by greater use of open competitions and by ensuring that some bids are obtained from firms which are not members of an established trade association. Furthermore, regular re-contracting avoids monopoly problems by allowing competitions at regular intervals—say, every three years.

- *Competitions are needed for both a given and alternative levels of service.* By stressing competitive tendering for a given specification only, current policy is failing to exploit all the opportunities for efficiency improvements. Both contractors and public procurement agents should be encouraged to provide and to seek information on the costs of a little more or a little less in the level of service.

- *In-house units winning a competition need to be subject to the same incentives and penalties offered to private contractors.* One possibility would be to allow in-house units to operate as worker co-operatives. Admittedly, such a proposal is fraught with difficulties! However, failure to recognise the problem could lead to the 'in-house' units bidding low to eliminate rivals and then seeking a larger budget later.

- *Contracting-out policy should be subject to the current legislation on monopolies, mergers, and restrictive practices.* The behaviour of public sector authorities, the performance of in-house units, the extent of competition for contracts, and the award of contracts should be subject to investigation by the Office of Fair Trading and its regulatory agencies. In other words, it is not at all obvious that special discretionary powers need to be given to an individual Secretary of State allowing actions to be taken against authorities which 'unreasonably set aside or frustrate the objective or results of fair competition' (Department of the Environment Consultation Paper, February 1985). Issues of anti-competitive actions by public authorities, including cases where contracts are not awarded to the lowest bidder, need to be treated as a general problem and not one confined to the Department of the Environment; hence such problems should be subject to the established machinery of UK competition policy. If this policy is inadequate, then it needs to be revised to remove its deficiencies.

Part VI

LABOUR AND FINANCIAL ISSUES

16

THE UNION RESPONSE TO DENATIONALISATION*

David Thomas

It is also hard to see how a policy of outright sale of the entire Corporation could be compatible with the over-riding need of any government to achieve some kind of *modus vivendi* with the trade unions.
(Internal memorandum, written in March 1979, by Gerry Flanagan, planning director of the National Freight Corporation (NFC), quoted in McLachlan, 1983, p. 15)

I. Union interest in denationalisation

Mr Flanagan, like many people at the time, misjudged the new Conservative Party. The Government has not only rejected consensus on the nationalised industries and the unions, but it has linked the two issues together. For Ministers, the power given to unions by public ownership is part of the problem of nationalisation. 'Public sector trade unions have been extraordinarily successful in gaining advantages for themselves in the pay hierarchy by exploiting their monopoly collective bargaining position', as the Financial Secretary to the Treasury has put it (Moore, 1983, in Part I).

Unions have both practical and ideological reasons for resisting denationalisation. They were central to the debate which preceded the Attlee nationalisations (Weiner, 1960). They were key participants in the few recent cases of nationalisation (see, for example, the report which prefigured the nationalisation of shipbuilding: Labour Party–TUC–Confederation of Shipbuilding and Engineering Unions, 1972). And the nationalisation statutes often required management to

* This article was first published in D. R. Steel and D. A. Heald (eds), *Privatizing Public Enterprises*, 1984, Royal Institute of Public Administration.
At the time of writing this article, David Thomas was Industrial Correspondent on *New Society* magazine; he is now on the Labour Staff of the *Financial Times*.

recognise and consult unions, and to promote collective bargaining. So it is not surprising that unions have won clear benefits from public ownership.

In 1980, more than 90 per cent of white collar and manual workers in nationalised industries were in unions; in private manufacturing, 75 per cent of manual workers and a mere 39 per cent of white collar workers were unionised. In the nationalised sector, management recognised manual unions in 98 per cent of establishments and white collar unions in 94 per cent; the corresponding figures for private manufacturing were 68 per cent and 32 per cent. Among manual workers in the nationalised industries, 72 per cent were in a closed shop, compared with less than half in the private sector (Daniel and Millward, 1983).

There is evidence too—though more controversial and uncertain—that nationalised industry workers are pace-setters in wage rises (Foster, Henry, and Trinder, 1984; Heald, 1983, 221–6; though see Zabalza, 1984, for a contrary view). This was most noticeable in the 1970s, when the turbulent pay bargaining in the nationalised industries contributed to the general crisis of the public sector (Heald, 1983, Chap. 9; Winchester, 1983). Their pay bargaining is highly centralised, with few important negotiations at plant level (Daniel and Millward, 1983, 188), a factor which moulds the style of their industrial relations and channels power in nationalised industry unions towards the most senior national officials.

Given their historical, ideological, and practical attachment to nationalisation, unions have been singularly unsuccessful in countering denationalisation. They came nowhere near deflecting any of the asset sales completed by the first Thatcher Government, even though some—like the British Transport Docks Board (BTDB)—were traditional centres of union power. Only in one case—gas showrooms—could a strong case be made for union action having helped to thwart a proposed sale,[a] though the steel unions also claimed credit for the collapse of the proposed US–Ravenscraig link (*Morning Star*, 28 December 1983).

This is not to say that denationalisation has been trouble-free. The 1979 manifesto pledge to sell British Shipbuilders

(BS) is still unhonoured. Other sales have been protracted affairs; but the delays have been due to the recession, not to union opposition. If a medal were struck for defence of the public sector, it would belong, not to militant unions, but to the Board of the British Gas Corporation (BGC) for their epic manoeuvres over Wytch Farm.

This article concentrates on 'denationalisation'—the sale of assets in traditional nationalised industries and Company Act companies. Denationalisation is a central part of the Government's privatisation programme which also encompasses 'liberalisation'—the introduction of more competition into the nationalised sector. So far, liberalisation has had a major impact in the coaching and civil aviation industries, a moderate impact in telecommunications, and a minor impact in some other industries like post, gas, and electricity. Liberalisation has forced enterprises like the National Bus Company to cut back their least used, less profitable services and concentrate on their more profitable operations. As such, liberalisation poses similar problems for nationalised industry unions as the recession has posed for unions throughout the economy. The main difference is that liberalisation usually requires legislation, which allows unions to oppose it during the legislative process.

Denationalisation will remain at the top of the political agenda. The candidates for partial or total sale mentioned either in the last Parliament (Howe, 1981), the 1983 manifesto, or in this Parliament (Moore, 1983) now cover almost every nationalised industry.[b] The unions believe that the influence of the Government's wish to sell the public sector is even more pervasive. On this view, it has been the over-riding objective which has determined the industries' path since 1979. Thus, the financial turnaround which the Government has demanded of the industries is a prologue to denationalisation. It has entailed major redundancies in the loss-making enterprises. Liberalisation is another spur to privatisation: it forces public corporations to become more efficient, thus making them more attractive to buyers; and it helps meet the charge that denationalisation means the transfer of monopoly from the public to the private sector. Fashionable management tactics like decentralisation aid denationalisation by hindering cross-subsidies and facilitating the piecemeal sale of a corporation (see the 1983 comment of the National Union of Mineworkers (NUM) on Monopolies and Mergers Commission (MMC), 1983).

This view—widely held in the union movement—is, however, too broad. Some of these policies, like the financial squeeze, might have been followed by a government uninterested in selling assets. This article takes a narrower focus. What have unions done *before* denationalisation in the corporations that have been sold in whole or in part? What have unions done *after* denationalisation in those enterprises which have been sold? The broad answers are nicely double-edged. The unions have failed to stop sales, but they have achieved many of their subsidiary bargaining objectives. After denationalisation, the first results are opposite to what would be implied by the thesis that public ownership boosts union power.

II. Union response before denationalisation

(i) *Spreading the word*

Faced with the threat of denationalisation the least a union can do is to lobby influential groups, and to try to win public opinion against the sale. Lobbies of Parliament, delegations to Ministers, press briefings, special conferences of members and of other sympathetic groups, and reams of publicity material—these are routine union responses.

Whilst of itself this activity is uninteresting, it means that denationalisation has had two, presumably unintended, consequences. First, unions have drawn even closer to the Labour Party. They have been in close touch with Opposition spokesmen, particularly at committee stage, on specific issues like pensions rights. Second, unions have developed more professional press and publicity capabilities, having in the past been a by-word for amateurishness.

The most professional campaign has been run by the telecommunications unions against the privatisation of British Telecommunications (BT) (POEU, 1984). The Post Office Engineering Union (POEU, now the National Communications Union) and the British Telecommunications Union

Committee (BTUC) have taken on extra staff, hired media consultants and spent some £1½ million in about eighteen months. The campaign material has varied in sophistication and targeting. Much of it, including a special video, has been aimed at the unions' own members. Target campaigns were launched in marginal constituencies during the 1983 election. The unions have issued pamphlets directed at special groups: rural communities; the poor; the blind and disabled; consumers; trade unionists; and British business. They commissioned an American consultant's report on telecommunications liberalisation in the United States (BTUC, 1983). They have advertised in the local and national press, and were prepared to spend £¼ million on television advertisements, but the Independent Broadcasting Authority (IBA) rejected their request as 'political' (*Labour Weekly*, 10 February 1984). Opinion polls conducted by Gallup in December 1982 and November 1983 showed a movement in public opinion against the BT sale, but it is impossible to know whether this was due to the unions' campaign. At the very least, however, it must have raised public awareness about the complex issues involved in selling BT. It may also have contributed to assurances given by the Government about the position of special groups, like rural inhabitants and the blind.

(ii) *Looking for friends*

Unions have been careful to build alliances against denationalisation. The POEU's campaign, as already noted, has been aimed at distinct sections of the population. The gas unions cultivated consumer groups when opposing the sale of gas showrooms in 1981 (Lord, 1983). The unions' attempts to win over consumer opinion, however, have been hindered by the fact that consumer groups are often weak and suspicious of public sector unions.

A useful group for unions to win over is the corporations' top management. It is excellent publicity if a board states openly that denationalisation would damage its enterprise. In the early days, such utterances were not uncommon. The British Aerospace (BAe) Board issued a statement in August 1979 stressing 'the uncertainty and distraction of changes effected by parliament'. Lord Kearton, British National Oil

Corporation (BNOC) Chairman, described the sale of its oil and gas interests as a 'bad business decision' (*Financial Times*, 1 September 1979). Robert Atkinson, BS Chairman, said there would be board resignations if the warship yards were sold separately (*Financial Times*, 6 August 1980). Atkinson for one mentioned union pressure as a factor in talking of resignations. But the Government closed this potentially fruitful channel for union lobbying by appointing supporters of denationalisation when board vacancies arose.

At the TUC level, the unions tried to enlist the support of the Nationalised Industries' Chairmen's Group (NICG) (TUC, 1980, p. 271). The NICG expressed concern at any fragmentation of the industries which might result from sales, but would not be drawn on the basic issue. After that, the TUC stressed the more oblique theme that the public and private sectors were interdependent. The TUC conceived such ideas as part of a long-term struggle against new orthodoxies, like privatisation (TUC 1981a, pp. 276 and 294). At the depth of the recession, stressing 'interdependence' was a thinly disguised call for a public-investment-led reflation. This struck a receptive chord in the NICG. Both the TUC and the NICG pushed the issue at the National Economic Development Council (NICG, 1981; National Economic Development Office (NEDO), 1981), though without any apparent impact on the Government.

As the failure of such conventional alliances became clear, the TUC was forced back to basics. This took the form of arguing for the necessity of public provision across the whole of the public sector—nationalised industries and public services (TUC, 1983, p. 267). More recently, the TUC has published more aggressive material designed to undermine privatisation by highlighting factors like the under-pricing of public assets (see the anti-privatisation material published by the TUC on 12 March 1984). It was pushed this way partly by certain unions, like the POEU which moved a resolution at the 1983 Congress demanding a TUC-led campaign in defence of the public sector, and partly by a growing awareness in the unions of the low esteem in which the nationalised industries are held.

(iii) *Changing the line*

Unions have adopted new policies which they hoped would help avert denationalisation. Two examples will be given, a 'hard' and a 'soft' one. Firstly, if the Labour Party were committed to renationalising corporations without compensation, then investors would not buy shares in those corporations. That was the view of many unions. Traditionally moderate unions like the Iron and Steel Trades Confederation (ISTC), Transport Salaried Staffs' Association (TSSA), and the Boilermakers spoke in favour of no compensation resolutions which were carried at TUC Congresses and Labour Party Conferences after 1979.

The policy had no effect even on the early sales (like BAe) which were completed when the Government was doing badly in the polls and even though it was noted in several denationalisation prospectuses, it was ineffective because it was incredible; and it immediately brought reservations from the TUC General Council about its implications for shareholdings held by employees, pension funds, and foreigners (TUC, 1979, p. 610). All denationalisation share issues, bar one, were heavily over-subscribed. The exception, Britoil, was launched *after* the TUC and Labour Party had abandoned the policy at their 1982 Conferences. So incredible was the idea that one union which was party to it—the National Union of Railwaymen (NUR)—itself bought shares in a denationalised asset, the Gleneagles Hotels Group.

The sole impact of the no compensation policy was to embarrass the Labour Party. By 1982, with an election in sight, this albatross could no longer be ignored. The TUC–Labour Party Liaison Committee drew up a statement changing the policy to one of 'no speculative gain' (TUC–Labour Party, 1982). This too had no impact on the sales. But it can be judged successful to the extent that Labour's opponents failed to make capital out of it during the 1983 election campaign, which was its purpose.

Secondly, the TUC adopted a policy of a quite different kind, one of whose aims was to head off denationalisation. In 1981, there was widespread debate about the industries having access to the private capital markets to finance profitable investment. The TUC published a paper (TUC, 1981b) which concluded that 'the nationalised industries, like their EEC counterparts, should be free to issue bonds to the general public and raise loans in all appropriate ways on the capital markets'. This was a departure in Labour movement thinking, which had previously accepted uncritically National Loans Fund arrangements. The TUC felt sufficiently nervous about it to underline that it remained 'totally opposed to privatisation' (TUC, 1981a, p. 295).

The TUC was party to the Treasury–NICG–CBI–TUC report on nationalised industries' investment (National Economic Development Council (NEDC), 1981), which discussed 'hybrid' projects owned by the public sector and financed by the private sector. As with 'interdependence', the unions formed an easy alliance with the NICG on 'hybridity'. Both wanted to increase the investment funds available to the industries through this route.

Additionally, the TUC backed the idea because 'in the current circumstances of some nationalised industries, bonds were an alternative to privatisation' (TUC, 1982, p. 275). The NEDC report had said that direct access to risk capital should be allowed only if it improved efficiency by introducing private sector disciplines; hence the notion of a 'performance bond'. The unions thought this half-way house to denationalisation might be acceptable to the Government; the telecommunications unions were particularly keen on the 'Buzby bond'. In the end, though, the idea came to nothing. An opportunity was missed to supply public corporations with limited amounts of extra capital in return for commitments from management and unions to improve efficiency.

(iv) *Pulling out the troops*

Few unions have used their strongest sanction—industrial action—against denationalisation. Yet the most substantial analysis to date of a particular sale (McLachlan, 1983) underlines the vulnerability of a public corporation in metamorphosis. City and management opinion was very nervous about the novelty of the National Freight Corporation (NFC) buy-out and the impact of the recession. Well-timed industrial disruption might have sunk the flotation.

There have been few strikes of any size against privatisation. Unions in the gas industry, the Royal Ordnance Factories (ROFs), and Sealink have carried out token stoppages. The gas unions' action was probably the most successful (Lord, 1983). In 1981, they held a one-day strike against the proposed sale of the gas showrooms. It was only a token stoppage, though the unions were threatening further action. Yet in the autumn of 1981 the Government rescinded its decision.[c] The strong doubts voiced by the BGC, consumer groups, and appliance manufacturers must have weighed with the Government; but so too, one supposes, must the readiness to strike of the traditionally moderate gas unions. For their part, the unions motivated their members because of fears that the sale would have a quick impact on jobs.

The POEU has waged by far the most extensive campaign of industrial action against privatisation (both denationalisation—the sale of BT—and liberalisation, in the guise of Mercury). Between August and November 1983, the union took action against BT's rival, Mercury; Mercury's parent companies; City and government targets; and the international exchanges. The action included strikes, working to rule, the blacking of maintenance, and the refusal to interconnect Mercury. The union spent over £3 million on the action, partly financed by a £1 a week levy on members working normally (POEU, 1984).

BT responded by 'bussing in' engineers to exchanges in dispute, and by suspending or sacking POEU members who were working to rule, striking, or refusing to cross picket lines. In November, Mercury secured an injunction under the 1982 Employment Act against the POEU's refusal to interconnect it. BT warned that this made legal action by its Board a stronger possibility (*Financial Times*, 18 November 1983). By early December, the POEU acknowledged defeat by returning its members to work.

The POEU's conduct of the dispute will remain controversial. It was tactically correct to focus the action. It aimed at business traffic and companies involved in privatisation, knowing that it would be counterproductive to inconvenience the public. Its shock troops were therefore in the inner London branches most likely to take action. The small number of

members involved (two to three thousand) allowed the union
to pay those on strike or suspended average take-home pay.

However, the union displayed fatally poor tactics in other
respects. First, the POEU overestimated the speed with which
its action would bite. Mercury told the High Court that the
action had cost it £1½ million (*Financial Times*, 18 October
1983), but its impact in other areas was not great. Second, paying average take-home pay to those on strike or suspended was
over-generous: it drained the union's finances, especially since
management began to court suspensions at the international
exchanges and since the levy was under-subscribed (*Financial
Times*, 22 December 1983). Third, Mercury's successful court
action, coupled with BT's threat of litigation, damaged the
union's morale: like the rest of the union movement, the
POEU had no credible strategy to counteract the Government's industrial relations legislation. The Mercury decision
appears to jeopardise any industrial action against privatisation, though the law is evolving almost from case to case
and it was not invoked against later strikes at the ROFs and
Sealink.

Fourth, and most important, the basic objectives were badly
thought out. The union voiced only one aim: to force the
Government to withdraw the Telecommunications Bill and
abandon the sale of BT. It appeared to have no fall-back position at the time, even though it pursued the kind of subsidiary
objectives described in the next section once the industrial action had collapsed. Given this Government's political psy-
chology, there was never any chance of it securing its basic
aim. To compound matters, the action was badly timed: a
union just might disrupt a sale by sustained industrial action in
the weeks before flotation, but not during the early stages of
the parliamentary procedure.

(v) *Making the best of a bad job*

Normally, however, unions are nothing if not flexible. They
have demonstrated their ultimate pragmatism by at times accepting denationalisation as the lesser of two evils, when the
alternative was complete closure of an enterprise or plant. The
ISTC was ready to see Shotton hived off, rather than closed
as an integrated works (*Financial Times*, 9 February 1980).

Unions accepted the merger of the private Hoverlloyd and British Rail (BR)'s Hovercraft, because they doubted Hovercraft's independent viability (MMC, 1981b). Unions backed the buy-out of Tyne Shiprepair rather than see it close (*Financial Times*, 25 January 1984). And similarly with Scott Lithgow private ownership was an offer the unions could hardly refuse when the only alternative was closure.

In more typical examples, unions have adopted two subsidiary bargaining objectives. First, they have wanted public corporations to pass into the private sector intact. The unions sought assurances on this in three companies to be denationalised which had distinct subsidiaries or production units with variable profit levels: the NFC, the BTDB, and BAe where the Amalgamated Union of Engineering Workers (Technical, Administrative and Supervisory Section) (AUEW–TASS) was worried that the Dynamics Group would be sold separately. None of these was fragmented on privatisation. On the other hand, BNOC, where union influence was weak, was split in two. Equally the sale of British Steel Corporation (BSC), British Leyland (BL) and BR subsidiaries can be interpreted as fragmentation before the sale of the main business.

Second, unions have wanted guarantees that their members' jobs and terms and conditions would be unaffected. It is central to the concept of denationalisation—a return to market disciplines—that such guarantees are impossible. The Transfer of Undertakings Regulations are the main legal provisions governing terms and conditions on transfer of ownership, though the Courts have not ruled definitively on whether they apply to denationalisations. They imply only that the new owner takes over the terms and conditions existing on denationalisation; thereafter, however, the new owner can open renegotiations (Hepple, 1982).

Nevertheless, pensions have to be considered before denationalisation. Many public sector schemes are index linked and substantially in deficit. Few private buyers would take that on. The Government, eager to sell, has an interest in ending index linking and in seeing to proper funding. The unions also want proper funding, but in addition to retain the best possible benefits.

Pensions negotiations before denationalisation have been varied and horrendously complex. In one case, BAe, there was no real problem since there was no index linking. In others, the Government paid heavily to ensure that the pensions issue was not a blockage: four-fifths of the money from selling the NFC found its way back to the pension fund and the resulting pension settlement was generous (McLachlan, 1983, Chap. 8). In yet others, management moved decisively to end index linking even before the sale of a corporation (British Airways (BA) statement, 25 January 1984). But given that it was unrealistic to try to keep index linking, unions have in general negotiated good pension settlements, especially for existing employees. If there are exceptions to that generalisation, they are in peripheral areas, like the BR hotels and former BSC subsidiaries like Redpath Dorman Long (on the latter, see TUC, 1982, p. 318; TUC, 1983, p. 310). The steel unions complained to the Industry and Trade Committee about the pensions implications of previous denationalisations; as a result, this all-party committee recommended that future spin-offs from BSC should involve adequate provision for pensions (Industry and Trade Committee, 1984, para. 34 and Qs 114 and 122).

A striking example of a union receiving assurances before a sale is a letter dated 4 November 1983 from BT's board member for personnel to the general secretary of the POEU. With varying degrees of firmness, the letter assures the POEU about foreign take-over, excessive price rises for domestic customers, the run-down of rural services and non-domestic services like kiosks, the abandonment of emergency services, the splitting and piecemeal sale of the corporation, and the implications for POEU members' jobs, pay, conditions of employment, and pensions (see also BTUC, 1984 for the unions' assessment of what their campaign achieved).

Some items on which unions have sought assurances—like the foreign take-overs of BAe and BT—the Government had no intention of allowing in the first place. Others—like keeping the corporations intact—are goals shared by management. It is also arguable that assurances given to unions, like those in the BT letter just mentioned, have been couched in such general and qualified terms as to be worthless: management will always be able to say that they have been nullified by circumstances. Yet it is unlikely that the unions' efforts have accounted for nothing: at the very least, they have helped furnish unions with a platform of expectations from which to defend their members' interests after denational-isation.

(vi) *Unions change too*

The run-up to denationalisation has brought contradictory pressures to bear on unions. Their final significance is unclear. Two examples have already been noted: some unions have improved their lobbying and publicity and have drawn even closer to the Labour Party.

Preparing for denationalisation has strained some already fragile inter-union relations. The NFC unions held different views on the buy-out, ranging from the Transport and General Workers' Union (TGWU) which campaigned for its members not to buy shares to the United Road Transport Union which explained the scheme and its objectives in its journal. The TSSA and the Merchant Navy and Airline Officers' Association had to withdraw their support from some of the publicity material issued by the Sealink unions against Sealink's sale because it went too far for their tastes in condemning the NFC buy-out.

Conversely, the Union of Communication Workers (UCW)'s support (including a £½ million donation) for the POEU in the autumn 1983 dispute has improved traditionally prickly POEU–UCW relations. Similarly, the Civil and Public Services Association (CPSA)'s backing helped smooth the way for the merger of the CPSA's post and telecom members with the POEU. The TGWU's national secretary for the docks has told the author that denationalisation has drawn the unions closer together in Associated British Ports (ABP), where union relations have often been difficult.

Denationalisation has also fostered militancy in normally quiet unions. The POEU, traditionally moderate and unused to industrial action, is an example. Though the union has been slowly moving left for almost a decade, anger about the sale of BT contributed in 1983 to the left's capture of the executive for the first time since 1948 (Batstone, Ferner, and Terry, 1984, pp. 237 ff.).

Privatisation, coupled with the Government's views of public sector managers, has had an effect on the small management unions in the nationalised industries like the Society of Telecom Executives (STE), the Engineers' and Managers' Association (EMA), the British Association of Colliery Management, and the Steel Industry Management Association. High union densities in managerial and professional grades are a special case of the high union densities among white collar staff in general in the nationalised industries, which has already been noted (Heald, 1983, 217–18). Squeezed between senior management and the clerical and manual unions, the relations of the specialist unions with other sections of the workforce are under strain, as when STE members were pressed to do POEU work in the international exchanges in autumn 1983. The general secretary of the ultra-moderate EMA has warned that a sale of the electricity supply industry might be met with industrial action (*Financial Times*, 19 April 1984). These unions' traditionally non-political outlook is also under threat. The STE's membership even voted to set up a political fund in 1983. This trend could catch on if the Trade Union Act means that unions' publicity against privatisation will have to come from their political funds, as Ministers have suggested (*Financial Times*, 2 March 1984).

Some unions have adjusted their structures as the corporations have reorganised before denationalisation. The POEU used to negotiate for members on the same grade across BT, the Post Office, and National Girobank. Now it has three separate negotiations. Faced with quicker management decision-taking and decentralisation in BT, the POEU's national executive has reorganised its committee structure to speed up its decisions and give a bit more power to its regions.

The run-up to denationalisation is bringing another change in unions which could turn out to be the most important of all. Many public sector unions are industrial unions of sorts: they have restricted their attentions to public sector workers within their industrial sphere of influence. That self-denying ordinance cannot continue if public monopolies are sold and liberalised. The National and Local Government Officers'

Association (NALGO, which organises white collar staff in gas, electricity, water, and buses) has agreed a rule change so that it can recruit workers in the private sector. The POEU changed its rules to allow recruitment outside its traditional areas in 1981. The bracing wind of competition could sweep through the unions, as well as the corporations. The Association of Scientific, Technical and Managerial Staffs (ASTMS) is seeking recognition in Mercury; if BT is sold, if Mercury is a success, and if ASTMS is recognised in Mercury, how long will it be before ASTMS and POEU start fighting about the recruitment of telecommunications engineers? Whether the Government will extend a welcome to this form of competition is doubtful.

III. Union response after denationalisation

(i) *The logic of denationalising*

If union power is a characteristic of public ownership, denationalisation should roll back that power. What might this actually mean? The nationalised industries, as has been noted, have high union densities often sustained by the closed shop; a preponderance of formal national agreements regulating pay and conditions; and a 'good employer' tradition which stresses 'fairness' in wage setting and the rights of unions to be consulted on corporate plans. There is also evidence that workers in public corporations have led the pack in wage settlements. Logically, therefore, a free marketeer should expect denationalisation to bring a more abrasive management attitude to unions, moves against high densities and the closed shop and increased reluctance to consult unions. Also, managements might try to depress wage settlements and fragment national bargaining into plant level bargaining.

(ii) *Early days*

The honest answer is that it is too early to assess the impact of the first round of sales. And before attempting even a preliminary analysis, several caveats should be entered. It is wrong to see a particular industrial relations tactic (like the decentralisation of bargaining) as the preserve of either unions or management, or as necessarily leading to one outcome (like lower wage settlements). Not long ago, devolving bargaining to plant level, with the consequence of 'wage drift', was the pace-setting tactic in the unions (Undy, 1978). Even more recently, bargaining decentralisation in road haulage, where the NFC is the largest company, was a union tactic. The unions have pushed for a return to plant bargaining in BL which would overturn the centralised bargaining painfully erected by management under Sir Michael Edwardes (*Guardian*, 17 February 1984). Some shop stewards in BS's naval yards have pressed for a return to yard bargaining, which management killed off after nationalisation to general acclaim (*Financial Times*, 18 February 1984).

Moreover, nationalised corporations can display all the characteristics which a free marketeer would expect of the private sector. BSC has decentralised its wage bargaining. BSC, BA, and BS have led the economy in shedding jobs and have made zero national pay awards. Since nationalisation, manual workers' pay in BS has fallen from fourth to lower than twentieth in the earnings league. BA has introduced a profit sharing scheme linked to performance. The nationalised airline has also withdrawn facilities from some union representatives, following the management strategy pioneered at the publicly owned BL (*Morning Star*, 15 September 1983).

These examples of managerial toughness might be attributed to the recession and the new political climate. Yet one study says that 'commercialism' (the attempt to find a set of objectives and criteria which act as market proxies in the nationalised industries) has increasingly formed the context of management's industrial relations strategy in the key area of telecommunications during the past two decades (Batstone, Ferner, and Terry, 1984). Management's wish to commercialise the telecom business has meant greater flexibility in the use of labour; pay being more closely related to effort; more power for local managers; and more stress on management's right to initiate change, as opposed to the traditional consensual style of industrial relations.

(iii) *A preliminary assessment*

In order to make a preliminary assessment of how unions have perceived denationalisation, the views of key union officials in the main enterprises so far affected were canvassed. The limitations of this exercise should be stressed. Only one official was interviewed for each enterprise, though in every case that official had substantial bargaining responsibilities. The interviews were conducted by telephone, though a standard set of questions was asked. The officials' responses might be coloured by an awareness of the political implications: they might feel pressure to describe their experiences after denationalisation optimistically to demonstrate their competence in defending their members' interests; conversely, they might feel pressure to describe their experiences pessimistically to reinforce their unions' stance against privatisation. Also the relatively optimistic responses reported below might change. Denationalisation brings with it the uncertainties of the private sector; a striking example is the possible merger of BAe with a company like GEC or Thorn–EMI which was mooted after the interview with the AUEW–TASS official and which must alter radically union perceptions of the BAe denationalisation.

Nevertheless, some interesting patterns emerge from the responses received. They are summarised in Table 1 and amplified in the text below. Broadly speaking, the results fit neither what a free marketeer might expect nor the dire forecasts made by unions. According to the respondents, only in Amersham International (AI) and Cable & Wireless (C&W) have managements attempted to change the bargaining system. This was inevitable in AI, since before denationalisation bargaining was done centrally through the United Kingdom Atomic Energy Authority, of which it was a subsidiary. In C&W, there has been a move to bargain around new profit centres, but Jim Mercer (the divisional officer responsible for C&W in ASTMS, interviewed on 5 March 1984) saw this as an 'opportunity for bargainers' since many C&W staff possess scarce 'high tech' skills. However, management in C&W has had success in amending certain fringe benefits such as expenses.

Views on pay settlements after denationalisation followed the same pattern. Chris Darke (national officer for aerospace, AUEW–TASS, interviewed on 14 February 1984) said that the question was academic because settlements in BAe followed the going rate. Freed from public sector constraints,

Table 1. How Union Officials Perceive Denationalisation

	Associated British Ports	Amersham International	British Aerospace	Britoil	Cable & Wireless	National Freight Corporation
Changes in bargaining system?	No	Yes, better	No	No	Yes	No
Tougher attitude on pay?	No	No, easier	No	No	Mixed	In some respects
Acceleration in job losses?	Yes	No, more jobs	Yes	No, more jobs	Yes	No
Change in consultation?	No	Worse	Better	Better	Yes	No
Change in attitude to unions?	No	Worse	Better	Better	Yes	No
Change in closed shops?	No	Irrelevant	Irrelevant	Irrelevant	Irrelevant	No
Impact of worker shareholders on unions?	None	None	None	None	None	None

Note: This is a very broad summary of the responses received. Refer to the text for amplification.

pay has improved considerably in the profitable AI, according to Veronica Bayne, assistant secretary in the CPSA, who was interviewed on 5 March 1984: AI settlements were 7½ per cent in November 1983 and 9½ per cent in November 1982 (Incomes Data Report, 1983a and b). The other respondents reported no change, except that Jack Ashwell, the TGWU's national secretary for commercial vehicles (interviewed on 7 March 1984), complained that the NFC had unilaterally made pay increases before negotiations had been concluded.

Unions in BAe, ABP, and C&W are concerned about job losses after denationalisation. John Connolly, the TGWU's national docks secretary interviewed on 5 March 1984), said that recent job losses in ABP—for example, the contracting-out of cleaning staff—stemmed from denationalisation. ASTMS added, however, that job losses at C&W were as much due to technological change as to denationalisation. Unions in AI and Britoil said that the companies were expanding.

In half the enterprises—BAe, Britoil, and C&W—respondents noted changes and in some cases improvements in the way companies consulted unions and in their general attitude to unions. AUEW–TASS said that BAe's need as a private company to lobby for the Government's financial backing for aerospace projects had drawn management and unions together; while nationalised, the employer had seemed 'more remote'. In Britoil, according to Tom Robertson (Glasgow divisional officer, Association of Professional, Executive, Clerical and Computer Staff (APEX), interviewed on 7 March 1984), unions and management were discussing ways to improve information flows between the two sides. Unions in Britoil were building up membership, unlike 'in the bad old days of BNOC'. In C&W, decisions are taken 'more rapidly', with a 'harder, less personal approach'. This has disadvantages for ASTMS, but also means that decisions are 'less tortuous'. Union facilities at C&W are 'just as good, if not better than before privatisation' but there is less attempt at genuine consultation. In AI there were other complaints. The company, according to the CPSA, has brought in outside staff at director level, consultants, and job evaluators who 'have a different attitude. They try to cut corners'.

The closed shop is irrelevant to most enterprises so far denationalised. However, there has been no attempt to dismantle the closed shop in ABP. ASTMS said that there was no closed shop in C&W, but the high union membership had stayed firm after flotation.

Finally, all the respondents said that worker shareholders made no difference to industrial relations. This is unsurprising. Unions will clearly ignore workers *qua* shareholders: to do otherwise would undermine their relations to workers *qua* union members. Also, many managements (including the NFC's) have taken a policy decision not to discriminate between worker shareholders and other employees. Unions and management typically do not know if a particular worker is a shareholder. In most denationalised enterprises, the majority of workers became shareholders, not least because shares were given away free. Yet workers typically hold less than 5 per cent of the total shares and worker shareholders lack an independent input into the industrial relations system. The exception is the NFC, where there was a worker buy-out and no free share issue. Only about a half of the NFC workforce are shareholders, but they own more than four-fifths of the shares; even here the industrial relations framework has been largely unaffected, though it will be interesting to see whether the decision of the NFC's 1984 AGM to appoint a director who represents the worker shareholders will make any difference.

BR hotels are an exception to the denationalisation experiences reported above. Former BR hotels are now held by a number of groups and individuals. Unions are particularly critical of two groups: the Virani brothers who originally bought eight hotels, and the Barclay brothers who own three former BR hotels in London. According to the TSSA, in the Virani hotels workers have been sacked and replaced by others with worse conditions, for example, without travelling concessions or pensions, and have received no pay rises for two years. The TSSA took the Virani brothers to court to get sick pay for one of its members. One new owner has said to the TSSA that BR hotel staff were overpaid by 20 per cent. Both Virani and Barclay are ignoring closed shop agreements and refuse to meet union officials or answer their letters, despite assurances given to the unions before denationalisation, according to the TSSA general secretary (interviewed on 8 March 1984; see also Bagwell, 1984, pp. 47–51).

(iv) *Unions changing after denationalisation*

There is usually a time-lag before unions change their structures to meet changes in the organisations with which they deal. So it is even more premature to assess how denationalisation has affected unions. But AI provides some pointers, even though it is unusual in other respects. AI used to be part of the highly centralised civil service bargaining machinery. Negotiations were carried out by the civil service unions' senior officials. With the detachment of AI from this system, bargaining skills—and private sector ones at that—have had to be learned by the next layer down of officials. The sale of the ROFs could give fresh impetus to this diffusion of responsibility within the civil service unions.

The most interesting analysis to date of these sorts of changes is in an NUR paper (NUR, 1984). Describing the former BR hotels, it says 'the demands on the union's organization have been transformed'. Before, pay and conditions were dealt with centrally and grievances were referred upwards through the machinery. Now, NUR divisional officers deal with these issues with the separate hotel owners. In consequence, the union is 'conscious of the need to invest more resources' in its weak local organisation. With the closed shops in the hotels gone, the NUR has 'to start almost from square one with some of our members re-establishing the benefits of belonging to a trade union. This has had fundamental implications for our recruitment and educational policies'. Much needs to be done, the NUR says, before the union is fully equipped to deal with the new position in the hotels. But, it concludes, 'we recognise that much of this groundwork is a necessary part of progressive trade unionism anyway'.

IV. Conclusion

This concluding comment by the NUR points to what may be one of the most unforeseen consequences of denationalisation.

If it ends the cosy, centralised management/union understandings which often characterise the public corporations, unions will have to establish a new form of legitimacy among their members. This might entail unions paying greater attention to what their members want and pursuing those wants even more aggressively. Their recruitment activities too might become more competitive, if liberalisation dents the monopolies. These developments would not necessarily entail a weakening of the union movement; possibly the reverse.

This is uncertain, as much that is written about denationalisation has to be at present. The major utilities, the core of public enterprise, are mainly untouched. Yet three tentative conclusions can be reached. First, unions have in almost all cases failed to stop the sale of public enterprises. A qualification is needed even here, however. Unions may have been exercising negative power in that most early sales have skirted clear of the strongest union bastions. Two economists who have influenced the Government's thinking on privatisation have described the National Coal Board (NCB) as one of the 'prime candidates for privatisation' (Beesley and Littlechild, 1983). Yet the Government has taken no steps to sell the NCB or its main subsidiaries, even though, for instance, open-cast mining could be sold easily. Second, unions have generally achieved their bargaining objectives before denationalisation. Third, unions have in the main protected or even improved their own position and that of their members after denationalisation.

The exception to the third conclusion, BR hotels, suggests a fourth, more speculative conclusion. There is no reason to suppose that denationalisation will affect workers in different enterprises, and the unions which represent them, in the same way. Some may gain, others will lose. The highly skilled workers in AI improve their wages and numbers; the unskilled workers in the hotels suffer. Highly profitable enterprises have dominated the early sales, so it is unsurprising that their workers and unions have reaped rewards. The fate of the BR hotel workers is so far untypical of the sale of public enterprises, though it is a more familiar outcome in the contracting-out of public services like street cleaning.

Moreover, it is logical to expect the impact of denationalisation to vary within enterprises, as well as between enterprises. No large, monopoly-supplier, long-established corporation has yet been sold to test this thesis.[d] But there is evidence for realistic speculation. For example, the MMC found that NCB clerks, tied by internal relativities to miners' pay, were paid 23 per cent above the national average for clerks (MMC, 1983), p. 304). It is unlikely that NCB clerks would retain these external relativities if the NCB were sold and liberalised. The highly skilled operational managers at the pits, on the other hand, might see improvements in their pay and conditions.

Public ownership may have bid up the terms and conditions of less skilled staff (like clerks and some manual workers) with poor bargaining power, and depressed the rewards which highly skilled workers (like managers and engineers) would expect in the private sector. In this precise sense, public ownership has been an egalitarian force. How denationalisation will affect the staff of an enterprise will vary, depending not least on what, if any, productivity improvements result and on whether (as is likely) staff experience these productivity increases as fewer jobs, but higher pay. On this issue, as on many others, what happens in BT will be the most interesting case yet.

These speculations suggest a final conclusion. Perhaps the unions' greatest success has been to hold a united, anti-privatisation line. Denationalisation has a variable impact on workers organised by different unions. It could also have a differential impact on workers organised by the same union: the senior grades covered by unions like the EMA might benefit, while the more junior staff lose out. The privatisation programme could have split the unions asunder.

EDITORS' NOTES

a. Subsequently the Government has introduced proposals to privatise the whole of the British Gas Corporation.
b. See also the 1985 Moore speech reproduced in Part I.
c. Subsequently the Government has introduced proposals to privatise the whole of the British Gas Corporation.
d. This article was written before the privatisation of British Telecom.

17

SELLING PUBLIC ASSETS: TECHNIQUES AND FINANCIAL IMPLICATIONS*

Colin Mayer and Shirley Meadowcroft

I. Introduction

By any account, the British Government's privatisation programme has been a large-scale exercise in new capital issues.
The sale of British Telecom alone raised around £1.6 billion
in November 1984 (with £2.3 billion in two subsequent instalments) which compares with a total of £1.4 billion subscribed
by the whole of the private sector in 1984 to new ordinary
shares. In the financial years 1982/3 and 1983/4, £0.38 billion
and £1.10 billion[1] were raised by sales of public assets which
represent 32 and 55 per cent of total private ordinary share
issues respectively. In the next two years it can be expected
that substantial sums will be sought from the capital market
as the Government brings such companies as British Airways,
the British Airports Authority and British Gas into the
private sector. Privatisation therefore has fundamental financial implications for both the private and the public sectors
and in this article we consider some of the most important of
these.

Leaving aside such questions as efficiency and managerial
control, the Government has had a number of financial
objectives in transferring assets to the private sector. These

* This article was first published in *Fiscal Studies*, 1985, 6, 4.

Colin Mayer is a Fellow of St Anne's College, Oxford and a Research Associate of
the Institute for Fiscal Studies.

Shirley Meadowcroft is a Research Officer at the Institute for Fiscal Studies.

The authors are grateful to John Kay and David Thompson for helpful comments,
and to Evan Davis for research assistance. The research on which this article is based
was financially supported by the Economic and Social Research Council.

[1] Net receipts from special sales of shares.

objectives have had a significant influence on the way in which the privatisation programme has been arranged. First and foremost, the Government has wished to transfer public corporation assets to the private sector at the earliest possible opportunity. This has involved the sale of a sufficiently large proportion of their equity capital to extinguish their accounts from the public sector. Secondly, the Government has repeatedly stated that it wishes to encourage a wide ownership of formerly public assets. It views privatisation as an opportunity to broaden the participation of small investors in UK equity markets. As Table 1 records, the proportion of UK equity held by private individuals is indeed unusually low in comparison with Germany, Sweden, and the US. While only just over 40 per cent of equity is held by private individuals in the UK, over 70 per cent is held by households in Germany and the US. While in the former case it must be recalled that the equity market is substantially smaller than its UK equivalent, the US demonstrates that private shareholdings are not incompatible with large equity markets.

Thirdly, an obvious objective has been the maximisation of the return from the privatisation programme. The costs to the Government of making an issue are twofold: first there are the direct costs of the promotion and underwriting of an issue and secondly there is a cost associated with setting a subscription price below the per share value of the assets being sold. We shall begin, in Section II, by estimating the costs that the Government has borne in privatisation to date.

Table 1. Domestic Ownership of Corporate Equity in 1979/80

				(*Per cent*)
	Germany	Sweden	UK	US
Household	73	60	43	74
Tax-exempt institutions	21	30	41	22
Insurance companies	6	9	16	4

Source: King and Fullerton, 1984.
Note: Figures may not add because of rounding.

Finally, in the light of the scale of the activity, the Government will wish to minimise disruption to the capital market. The disruption essentially arises from a flow of funds effect created by the cash requirements of the issues. These cash flows have to come from existing balances, bank borrowing, or sale of or reduced subscriptions to other assets. Despite the staggering of the payment from the BT issue mentioned above, there is some evidence that the timing of other private sector new issues was strongly influenced by consideration of availability of funds.

In this article we shall consider how successful the Government has been at meeting these objectives and we consider ways in which performance might have been improved and should be improved in the future. We shall also discuss, in Section III, the effects of the privatisation programme on the financial position of the Government and the private sector at large. We shall argue that a clear presentation of the financial implications is required to address such issues as the effect of privatisation on the private sector's cost of capital and the pure financial benefits of privatisation.

In Section IV we summarise the results.

II. Meeting the objectives

The Government has used two methods to denationalise public assets: offers for sale and tender offers, with the former being the more widely applied. In an offer for sale, shares are offered to the public at a fixed price which is determined in advance of the sale. In a tender offer, the offer price is not fixed in advance of the sale; instead, bids are invited at or above a stated minimum price. The striking price is then determined once all the bids have been received. It can be set above the market clearing price if preferential investors are allowed to purchase at the minimum price, or below the clearing price if the Government preferred allocation can be achieved by rationing certain subscribers. In addition to permitting applicants to tender above the minimum price, applicants have been allowed to offer to buy at the striking price—it was felt that the latter alternative would be attractive to small investors with little experience of the bidding mechanism.

The obvious advantage of the tender offer is that it does not require that a precise estimate of the value of a firm be made. Since most assets sold to the private sector have not had a previously quoted value there has been very little information on which to base value estimates. A procedure that permits the market to establish the valuation therefore has substantial appeal. Its drawback, however, is its supposed complexity, with the view prevailing that the bidding process discourages the participation of small investors. While such techniques as permitting purchases at striking or minimum prices may increase its attractiveness, it was still felt that simplicity was of the essence; the offer for sale has therefore been the preferred method.

(i) *Discounts*

As Table 2 records, a large proportion of the biggest asset sales have been by offers for sale. The crucial issue here is the price at which the offer is made. One way of judging the success of the Government and its advisers in pricing the issues is to compare the offer price with the price at which shares sell once trading opens. Table 2 records discounts in relation to trading prices one day and one week after trading commences. The penultimate column records movements in share price since issue adjusted for market-wide share price movements. Discounts on public offers for sale range between 3 and 91 per cent at or shortly after the issue and average 26 per cent. Subsequent movements in share prices relative to the market have usually been in an upward direction (British Petroleum being the notable exception) thereby accentuating the size of the discounts. The last column of the table records the extent to which the issues were over-subscribed. The application multiples range between 1½ and 34. Buckland, Herbert, and Yeomans (1981) estimate that in times of bullish equity markets, as prevailed over much of the period of these issues, discounts on private offers for sale averaged 12 per cent and application multiples averaged 26. Discounts on offers for sale of public assets thus seem well in excess of the average for private issues.

Table 2. Asset Sales: Discounts and Application Multiples

| Company | Offer/ minimum tender price (*pence*) | First trading day | Discount at end of first day (%) | Discount after 1 week[1] (%) | INCREASE FROM ISSUE TO CURRENT SHARE PRICE[2] | | Application multiples[3] |
					relative to market move-ments	relative to industry move-ments	
OFFERS FOR SALE							
Amersham International	142	25.02.82	32	35	10	−78	25
Associated British Ports (1983)	112	16.02.83	23	28	169	113	34
British Aerospace (1981)	150	20.02.81	14	15	66	111	3.5
British Aerospace (1985)	375	14.05.85	22	19	13	15	n/a
British Petroleum (1979)	363	12.11.79	3	6	−130	−11	1.5
British Telecom	130	03.12.84	86	91	111	131	5

Britoil (1985)	185	12.08.85	22	22	24	24	4
Cable and Wireless (1981)	168	06.11.81	17	15	295	375	5
Jaguar	165	10.08.84	8	8	45	24	8
TENDER OFFERS							
Associated British Ports (1984)	250	19.04.84	2	-2	14	-4	n/a
British Petroleum (1983)	435	26.09.83	3	3	-14	15	1.3
Britoil (1982)	215	23.11.82	-19	-21	-67	-64	u.s. = 0.3
Cable and Wireless (1983)	275	05.12.83	-2	-3	69	119	u.s. = 0.7
Enterprise Oil	185	02.07.84	0	2	-35	-17	u.s. = 0.7

Notes:
1. Discounts after 1 week are calculated relative to market movements.
2. Share price movements from the issue date to the current date (30 September 1985) are measured relative to the full subscription price (or, in the case of British Telecom and Britoil (1985), the current subscription price), and are calculated relative to market movements and to industry movements.
3. n/a = not available.
  u.s. = under-subscribed.

While it was suggested above that the tender offer is an attractive alternative to an offer for sale, Table 2 records some substantial failures in practice: sales of Britoil, Cable and Wireless, and Enterprise Oil were all substantially undersubscribed. In each case the minimum tender price was too high to clear the market. The Britoil and Enterprise Oil failures can be attributed to adverse movements in world oil prices. It has, however, been suggested that there is a more inherent weakness in the tender offer system (see Buckland and Davis, 1984). Each of the tender offers was underwritten by a City institution. These same institutions are in many instances prime bidders for shares. Since a failure of a bid to be fully subscribed involves the underwriter in purchasing remaining shares at the minimum underwritten price, there is an incentive for these institutions to abstain from the bidding process and acquire unsold shares at this low price. The tender price that an institution will favour will, at least in part, balance the risks of being landed with too large a holding of unsold shares and the gain to be had from this cheap method of subscription. This conflict of interest was thought to be particularly troublesome in the case of Cable and Wireless (see *Financial Times*, 12 February 1984).

(ii) *Costs of issues*

A new issue involves three types of cash expenses. Firstly, there are fixed expenses associated with the printing of a prospectus and the advertising of the new issue. Secondly, there are payments to accountants, bankers, solicitors, and other advisers who are party to the issue. These payments are related to the scale of activity involved. Finally, there are payments to institutions (sub-underwriters, issuing houses, stockbrokers, allotment commission, and listing fees) that are determined by the size of the issue and are usually fixed as a certain percentage of the issue.

There are a number of alternative sources of information on the costs of the privatisation exercise. In the case of offers for sale, government estimates suggest costs between 2 and 4 per cent of the size of issue. Public Accounts Committee estimates are more in the region of 4 to 6 per cent. Tender offer costs are consistently around the 2 per cent level according to government estimates.

While there is substantial variability in the estimates from different sources the overall picture that is conveyed is that, with the exception of British Telecom, the direct costs of the privatisation exercise have not been substantially out of line with those in the private sector. Dimson (1983), for example, quotes 4½ per cent as being the costs associated with large private issues.

One might then be led to conclude that since the losses that can be associated with the incorrect pricing of an issue are so large in relation to the direct costs, the Government was quite justified in devoting substantial resources to obtaining the best advice. A casual glance at Tables 2 and 3 would not suggest a very close relationship between expenditures on issue and accuracy of pricing. But even if there were substantial returns to this type of expenditure it is not clear that it would be warranted. For what has been ignored to date is the unique position of the Government as a guardian of public assets. The relevant question therefore is not whether direct and indirect costs have been large in relation to those incurred by equivalent private corporations but whether the Government could in fact have met its objectives more successfully.

(iii) *Alternative procedure for asset sale*

There are several respects in which the Government is in a unique position when it comes to make a disposal of assets. First, unlike a private corporation the Government is not subject to a flow of funds constraint. It does not need the cash to float a project and while there may (or may not) be substantial benefits to privatisation these benefits do not have to be instantaneously realised. As we will see below, while an asset sale does reduce the Government's borrowing requirement, the beneficial effects that are normally associated with this do not apply here. The sale imposes a corresponding financing burden on the private sector thereby offsetting any tendency for the private sector cost of finance to fall.

Secondly, the major uncertainty that a private corporation faces in marketing a new issue is the price at which a share can be sold. As in the case of an auction of a good, the

Table 3. Asset Sales: Costs of Share Issues

Company	Gross proceeds of sale £m	COSTS OF SALE (£m)		COSTS AS A PERCENTAGE OF SALE (%)	
		Government estimate[1]	Other estimate[1,2]	Government estimate	Other estimate[1]
OFFERS FOR SALE					
Amersham International	63[3]	1.3[4]	2.4[5] (PAC)	2.1	3.8
Associated British Ports (1983)	45[6]	1.8	2.6 (PAC)	4.0	5.8
British Aerospace (1981)	149[7]	4.3	5.6 (PAC)	2.9	3.8
British Aerospace (1985)	550	n/a	10[8] (FT)	n/a	1.8
British Petroleum (1979)	290	5.2	14 (PAC)	1.8	4.8
British Telecom	3,863[9]	189.5	263[10] (NAO)	4.9	6.8
Britoil (1985)[11]	450	n/a	15[12] (FT)	n/a	3.3
Cable and Wireless (1981)	224	5.4	7 (NAO)	2.4	3.1
Jaguar	294	n/a	5.5 (Prospectus)	n/a	1.9
TENDER OFFERS					
Associated British Ports (1984)	52	1.1	n/a	2.1	n/a
British Petroleum (1983)	565	9.4	n/a	1.7	n/a
Britoil (1982)	549	11.3	12.5 (PAC) / 17 (NAO)	2.1	2.3 / 3.1
Cable and Wireless (1983)	275	5.0	12.5 (HC)	1.8	4.5
Enterprise Oil	392	9.0	11 (NAO)	2.3	2.8

Notes:
1. n/a = not available.
2. PAC = Public Accounts Committee.
   FT = *Financial Times*.
   NAO = National Audit Office.
   HC = House of Commons Library.
3. The gross proceeds of £70.6 million from the sale of Amersham International were divided £63.3 million and £7.3 million between the Department of Energy and Amersham International.
4. The government estimate of total costs (= £1.5 million) is the same as that quoted in the offer documents. The cost borne by the Government comprises fees of £1.15 million and £0.13 million plus VAT payable.
5. The PAC estimate of £3.12 million is divided £2.45 million and £0.67 million between the Department of Energy and Amersham International. Note that costs are gross of interest on application returned.
6. The loan equivalent of Associated British Ports (book value of £81.3 million but estimated current value of £44 million) was extinguished and converted into an equity interest with an initial market value of £26.8 million.
7. Includes a payment of £100 million by the Government for new shares subscribed.
8. The £18 million cost of issue includes capital duty but excludes VAT and selling commissions. £10 million was borne by the Government and £8 million by the company.
9. Net of shares given to employees under free and matching offers.
10. Includes incentives for small shareholders amounting to £23 million for bill vouchers and £88 million for bonus shares.
11. Around 20 per cent of the 243 million shares were placed with investors abroad.
12. The FT estimate of £15 million covers City fees and advertising costs.

vendor will wish to attach a reservation price below which a sale will not be acceptable. To avoid the risk of an asset being underpriced in this sense private issues are underwritten, the underwriter agreeing to purchase if the price falls below a certain level. The role of the underwriter then is to absorb the risks that would be borne by the vendor and to spread these amongst its investors.

The Government is, however, in a very different position. The price at which a public asset is sold will determine the revenue that will accrue to the Government and thus the future tax and debt burden that the Government will have to impose on the public. The cost associated with a low-price issue is thus borne by the economy as a whole. There is no more effective way in which risks can be spread. The notion that there should be further risk-spreading is clearly nonsensical and the procedure by which asset sales have been underwritten at substantial costs is hard to justify. The costs of £0.7 million, £0.4 million, £4.6 million, £22.4 million, £9.8 million, and £4.5 million associated with the underwriting of Amersham, Associated British Ports, British Petroleum, British Telecom, Britoil, and Cable and Wireless respectively should therefore have been avoided.[2]

The absence of a cash constraint on the Government makes it difficult to understand why issues have, for the most part, been made in one go. Since the primary cost of issues to date has been that associated with incorrectly forecasting trading prices, any information that assists in determining these prices is of immense value. One of the easiest ways of generating such information is to make an initial issue of a very small percentage of the total stock to be sold. This sale could be made either by offer or by tender. The costs associated with the mispricing of these initial sales would be minute in relation to the costs incurred in current procedures.

Having established an active market in the stock of the company under public ownership, the pricing of subsequent sales is very much more straightforward. Furthermore, there is no reason why the Government should not minimise dis-

[2] Source: Public Accounts Committee, 1982 and 1984; National Audit Office, 1985. The underwriting costs represent 29 per cent, 17 per cent, 33 per cent, 9 per cent, 78 per cent and 64 per cent respectively of the recorded costs of the issues.

ruption to the market by bringing out subsequent issues in instalments rather than as one large sale. At the very least, the issues could be timed carefully to coincide with favourable movements in the market. It is no accident that the more successful issues recorded in Table 2 are those of British Petroleum in 1979 and 1983; in each case a comparatively small tranche of shares (5 per cent and 7 per cent respectively) was issued in an enterprise with a well-established share price.

(iv) *Concentration of ownership*

One of the primary objectives of the Government in the privatisation campaign has been the encouragement of wider share ownership. Many of the issues have offered small investors favourable terms or preference in the allocation of an over-subscribed issue.

However, evidence to date does not suggest that diversity of ownership has been sustained for long after the issues. In the case of Amersham International there were approximately 65,000 shareholders at the first date of trading (25 February 1982). By 14 June 1982 this had fallen to 8,600 and at 1 June 1984 there were 8,129 shareholders. Most of the decrease in the number of shareholdings occurred in the first month of trading as smaller buyers sold out to institutions who had not been allocated their total subscriptions.

At the date of quotation (20 February 1981) there were 158,000 shareholders in the British Aerospace issue. By the end of 1981 this had dropped to 27,000 with around 70 per cent of the shares not owned by the Government or employees being held by 179 shareholders. In the case of Cable and Wireless, shareholdings dropped from 157,000 to 26,000 within one year of the first issue. Within six months of the Jaguar issue the number of shareholders dropped from 120,000 to 50,000. The greatest effort of the Government in maintaining wide share ownership went into the British Telecom issue. At issue there were 2.3 million shareholders with shares distributed 4.6 per cent to employees, 34.4 per cent to the public, 47.4 per cent to institutions, and 13.7 per cent overseas. According to recently published accounts there are currently 1.7 million shareholders with individual holdings accounting for 27.7 per cent of non-government shares. The maintenance of individual shareholders in British Telecom has, therefore, been much more successful than its predecessors.

Encouraging private investors to participate in windfall gains has been relatively straightforward. Inducing them to retain their shareholdings thereafter has clearly been very much more troublesome. Further inducements could no doubt be tried but at some expense to the rest of the community. The most effective way is to require people to hold equity stakes in firms, which is precisely what public ownership so successfully achieves via the tax system!

Should the Government anyway be concerned about the distribution of ownership? The answer is probably yes and no. It is no to the extent that there are potential real benefits to be derived from the concentration of ownership. A well-known difficulty with dispersed shareholdings is that there is little incentive to monitor the performance of firms. Institutions can diminish the free-rider problem by concentrating shareholdings and diversifying their portfolios across companies (see Diamond, 1984). By holding a significant proportion of the outstanding equity, institutions internalise the benefits to be derived from monitoring management. Thus through deliberately diversifying shareholdings the Government may be undermining one of the ways in which the privatising of a corporation encourages productive efficiency. Since many of the companies that the Government is contemplating privatising will be large enough to avoid any serious risk of being taken over and are unlikely to be allowed to go into liquidation, a discouragement to shareholder involvement effectively ensures that there is no way in which the capital market will exert control over these firms.

On the other hand, to the extent that there are external interferences that distort the desired concentration of ownership, concern about a large institutional involvement may be justified. The distortion that is most obviously built into the British system comes from taxation. There are substantial tax inducements to channel savings into institutions in preference to direct investment in equity and debt (see Hills, 1984). In particular the tax deductibility of contributions to pension schemes and the tax-free nature of lump-sum payments make savings through pension funds very tax-efficient. To the extent that the Government wishes to rectify the dominance of institutions in equity markets then attention would more appropriately be directed towards the long-term incentives that the tax system gives to institutional savings, as against some artificial inducements to temporary equity holding that privatisation offers. Furthermore, if the Government believes that there is an inherent prejudice against direct equity investments by personal investors then a case for a subsidy of shareholdings by the personal sector in preference to the institutional sector may be justified. There is, however, no case for an implicit subsidy to hold a very limited number of formerly publicly owned assets. Such subsidies can only act as a further distortion to the savings decisions of individuals.

III. Financial implications

It is well known that the sale of public assets reduces, at least in the short term, the public sector's borrowing requirement. According to accounting conventions the proceeds of a sale are treated as a revenue receipt. Set against this are the net earnings that would have accrued to the Government had the corporation remained under public ownership. However, since market values reflect future as well as current earnings there is a net revenue gain.

Table 4 records the effect of privatising British Telecom on the 1985/6 PSBR. During this fiscal year the Government received proceeds of £1.2 billion from the second instalment of last year's sale. The removal of BT from public sector accounts reduces public corporations' gross trading surplus by an estimated £3 billion but of this some £1.9 billion would probably have been allocated to capital investment. The net increase of £1.1 billion in the PSBR is further reduced by taxes (Advance Corporation Tax—ACT) collected on dividends paid to British Telecom shareholders, interest paid to the Government, and interest that would have been paid by BT to the rest of the private sector had it remained under public control. Finally, since the Government is retaining a 49.8 per cent share of BT, it receives dividends on its investment. The net effect is to reduce the £1.2 billion sale receipts

Table 4. The Effect on the 1985/6 PSBR of Privatising British Telecom

(£ million)

Proceeds from the sale second tranche, collected June 1985	−1,200
Removal of BT's gross trading surplus from public revenue	+3,000
Removal of BT's capital requirements from public spending accounts	−1,900
ACT receipt on all BT dividend pay-outs	−170
Interest paid by BT to Government	−350
Interest paid by BT to rest of private sector	−150
Receipt by Government of its dividend on 3 billion shares (net)	−200

Source: HM Treasury (1984b) and the British Telecom Prospectus.
Note: Gross trading surplus in 1985/6 assumed to be 10% higher than in 1984/5.

by just £230 million. A very favourable impression is then created of the effect of the privatisation on the public sector's accounts. In fact, to the extent that there has been any effect on the public deficit it is probably in exactly the opposite direction.

To understand why current accounting conventions are so misleading let us go back to the 1984/5 account and pose the question: how was the public sector affected by the BT privatisation decision? On the day of the issue the assets (net of future payments) that the Government sold were valued at £2.80 billion (3.012 billion shares at 93 pence). The Government received £1.24 billion (3.012 billion at 50 pence less an issue cost of £263 million). Public sector cash holdings increased by £1.24 billion and public sector financial investments declined by £2.8 billion. The net *worth* of the public sector then fell by £1.56 billion—this is the 1984/5 loss associated with the privatisation decision at the date of privatisation.

Since the date of the issue the market has revised its estimate of the value of BT. Some of these revisions were genuinely unpredictable at the time of issue, e.g. movements associated with aggregate market changes; others reflected more realistic assessments of the Government's regulatory stance, the ineffectiveness of the Office of Telecommunications (OFTEL), and the dominant position of British Telecom. Table 2 records a 111 per cent rise in BT's share price from the issue date relative to the market. If all of this is associated with a more accurate valuation of BT then the net loss of the privatisation rises to £3.34 billion—over 80 per cent of the sale value and just under £65 for each British citizen.

The 'net loss' is, of course, in large part merely a redistribution within the population. This is not entirely true since 13.7 per cent of BT shares were issued to overseas investors;[3] thus in making the sale the UK subsidised the rest of the world to the tune of at least £200 million. Within the UK it might be argued that the wide ownership of shares at the time of sale renders the redistributional consequences relatively insignificant. In fact there were 2.3 million shareholders at issue including institutions and overseas investors. At most then approximately 4 per cent of the population directly shared in the windfall gain of the underpricing, though many more clearly indirectly benefited through their investments in financial institutions. Furthermore, within the 4 per cent there were variations in shareholdings thereby creating inequalities within this group as well as between those who did and did not participate. One would be hard pushed therefore to defend the assertion that the redistribution associated with the BT issue was comparatively insignificant.

We turn now to a consideration of how the private sector's financial position is affected by the sale of a public asset. We will abstract from redistributional considerations and assume that the sale price accurately reflects the expected present

---

[3] Nominee shareholdings complicate the interpretation of this figure. However, a consideration of nominees would suggest that 13 per cent is, if anything, an underestimate of the overseas proportion.

value of the asset's earning stream. The effect of the sale is dependent on the assumption that is made about the Government's response to the cash proceeds. A reasonable assumption to make is that the Government's monetary policy is set independently of revenues raised from sales, though in the short term there may well be monetary repercussions as investors borrow from banks to finance purchases (see *Bank of England Quarterly Bulletin*, December 1984). Since the PSBR is reduced by the proceeds, the Government can either reduce borrowing or re-establish the previous borrowing requirement by cutting taxes or raising expenditure.

If there is a reduction in government borrowing, which in the short term is the most likely response, then the private sector's holding of debt will fall by the equity value of the sale.[4] There will then be a reduction in aggregate debt/equity ratios. Assuming that an optimal aggregate debt/equity ratio exists (see Miller, 1977, and Auerbach and King, 1983) then this will reduce the ratio of the cost of debt to equity finance.

If the Government redistributes the proceeds through increases in expenditure or reduction in taxes then the aggregate debt/equity ratio will be unchanged. The most straightforward example is if the Government makes an equal cash payment to each member of the population—the sale is then equivalent to the Government giving all UK citizens an equal shareholding in the public assets and then allowing trading to develop in those shares. In this case an implicit equity holding in a public asset is being made explicit by establishing a market for shares.

In either case there is no effect on total financial requirements and therefore no effect on the aggregate cost of capital. There has merely been a transfer of ownership from the public at large to a limited number of shareholders. The crowding-out literature is thus particularly misleading in that regard. According to simple IS–LM analysis a reduction in the Government's borrowing requirement as reflected in a fall in the PSBR shifts the LM curve to the right and reduces interest rates. Thus, since the Government is borrowing less,

---

[4] Note that if restructuring of the corporate balance-sheet occurs prior to privatisation then the reduction in the private sector holding of debt only corresponds to the equity, not the debt, component of the balance-sheet.

the cost of finance will fall thereby reducing the extent to which the public sector is crowding out private sector investment. In this case it is indeed possible that the Government will borrow less but only at the expense of the private sector having to raise more equity. Thus while relative costs of capital may be affected (the cost of capital of debt being reduced and that of equity being raised), aggregate costs will not be. This is merely another illustration of the extent to which the PSBR as against changes in the public sector *net worth* can present a very misleading impression of how government actions affect the private economy.

IV. Conclusion

Whatever one's views about the desirability of a programme of privatisation, considerable concern must be felt about the techniques that have been employed in implementing the programme to date. As set out at the beginning of this article there are three primary considerations that may have influenced the form of the asset sales: extent of ownership, costs of sale, and disruption to markets. Certainly on the first two there is little evidence that objectives have been met: costs have been high, primarily as a consequence of underpricing of assets, and large personal shareholdings have only been maintained for very short periods. Furthermore, there would appear to be a simple way of avoiding high costs by staggering sales, which would also diminish financing disruptions to equity markets. As yet there has been no clear statement as to why huge corporations have to be brought to the market in one single sale and one can only presume that timing considerations are heavily influenced by political and PSBR considerations.

On the question of the PSBR we have shown that accounting conventions give very misleading impressions of the effects of asset sales on the private and public sectors. As a consequence of underpricing, what look like net cash receipts are in fact balance-sheet deficits when proper public sector accounts that measure net worth are constructed. The confusion created by illusionary PSBR figures has permeated to discussion about the effect of sales on the private sector's cost of capital. A mere transfer of capital cannot, *ceteris paribus*, affect aggregate costs of capital, though, as was shown, it can influence relative costs of different types of finance.

BIBLIOGRAPHY

Ashworth, M. H., and Forsyth, P. J. (1984), *Civil Aviation and the Privatisation of British Airways*, IFS Report Series 12, London: Institute for Fiscal Studies, summarised in Part III of this volume.

Auerbach, A. J. and King, M. A. (1983), 'Taxation portfolio choice and debt-equity ratios: a general equilibrium model', *Quarterly Journal of Economics*, 97, 587–609.

Averch, H. and Johnson, L. (1962), 'Behaviour of the firm under regulatory constraint', *American Economic Review*, 52, 1052–69.

Aylen, J. (1973), 'Memorandum to the Monopolies Commission on the supply of cross-Channel car ferry services', unpublished.

Bagwell, P. S. (1984), *End of the Line? The Fate of British Railways under Thatcher*, London: Verso.

Bailey, E. E. (1973), *Economic Theory of Regulatory Constraint,* Lexington, Mass: D. C. Heath & Co.

—— (1985), 'Price and productivity change following deregulation: the US experience', paper given to Royal Economic Society conference.

Batstone, E., Ferner, A., and Terry, M. (1984), *Consent and Efficiency: Labour Relations and Management Strategy in the State Enterprise*, Oxford: Blackwell.

Baumol, W. J., Panzar, J. C., and Willig, R. D. (1982), *Contestable Markets and the Theory of Industry Structure*, New York: Harcourt Brace Jovanovich.

—— and Willig, R. D. (1981), 'Fixed cost, sunk cost, entry barriers and sustainability of monopoly', *Quarterly Journal of Economics*, 95, 405–31.

Beesley, M. E. (1981), *Liberalization of the Use of the British Telecommunications Network*, London: HMSO.

—— and Gist, P. (1984), 'The role of market forces', in J. Grieve-Smith (ed.), *Strategic Planning in the Nationalised Industries*, London: Macmillan.

—— and Littlechild, S. C. (1983), 'Privatization: principles, problems and priorities', *Lloyds Bank Review*, no. 149, 1–20, reprinted in Part I of this volume.

Bennett, J. T. and Johnson, M. H. (1979), 'Public versus private provision of collective goods and services: garbage collection revisited', *Public Choice*.

Bosanquet, N. (1981), 'Sir Keith's reading list', *The Political Quarterly*, 52, 3, 324–41.

Boyfield, K. (1985), *Put Pits into Profit*, Policy Study 73, London: Centre for Policy Studies.

British Airports Authority (1983a), 'Heathrow traffic—cost related charges', BAA Position Paper TCG/BAA 1.

—— (1983b), 'Gatwick traffic—cost related charges', BAA Position Paper TCG/BAA 5.

British Airways (1977), *Civil Air Transport in Europe*.

British Telecommunications Union Committee (1983), *The American Experience*, London: BTUC.

—— (1984), *The Battle for British Telecom*, London: BTUC.

Brock, G. (1981), *The Telecommunications Industry*, Cambridge, Mass: Harvard University Press.

Buckland, B. and Davis, E. W. (1984), 'Privatisation techniques and the PSBR', *Fiscal Studies*, 5, 3, 44–53.

Buckland, R., Herbert, P. J., and Yeomans, K. A. (1981), 'Price discount on new equity issues in the UK', *Journal of Business Finance and Accountancy*, 8, 1, 79–95.

Butler, A. (1979), speech given at a luncheon for Aldridge and Brownhills businessmen on 14 December.

Caves, D. W. and Christensen, L. R. (1978), 'The relative efficiency of public and private firms in a competitive environment: the case of Canadian railroads', Social Systems Research Institute, Workshop Series, October.

Chadwick, E. (1859), 'Research of different principles of legislation and administration in Europe of competition for the field as compared with competition within the field of service', *Journal of the Royal Statistical Society*, Series A, 22, 381–420.

Coopers and Lybrand Associates Ltd (1982), *Report on the Review of the Bulk Supply Tariff*, London: Department of Energy.

Courville, L. (1974), 'Regulation and efficiency in the electric utility industry', *Bell Journal of Economics and Management Science*, 5, Spring.

Crain, W. M. and Zardkoohi, A. (1978), 'A test of the property rights theory of the firm: water utilities in the United States', *Journal of Law and Economics*, XXI, 2.

—— and Zardkoohi, A. (1980), 'Public sector expansion: stagnant technology or property rights', *Southern Economic Journal*, 46, 4.

Daniel, W. W. and Millward, N. (1983), *Workplace Industrial Relations in Britain: The DE/PSI/SSRC Survey*, London: Heinemann.

Davis, E. H. (1984), 'Express coaching since 1980: liberalisation in practice', *Fiscal Studies*, 5, 1, 76–86, reprinted in Part III of this volume.

De Alessi, L. (1974a), 'Management tenure under private and government ownership in the electric power industry', *Journal of Political Economy*, 82, May/June.

—— (1974b), 'An economic analysis of government ownership and regulation: theory and evidence from the electric power industry', *Public Choice*, 19, Autumn.

—— (1975), 'Some effects of ownership on the wholesale prices of electric power', *Economic Inquiry*, 13, December.

—— (1977), 'Ownership and peak load pricing in the electric power industry', *Quarterly Review of Economics and Business*, 17, Winter.

—— (1980), 'The economics of property rights: a review of the evidence', *Research in Law and Economics*, 2.

Dean, A. J. H. (1975), 'Earnings in the public and private sectors 1950–1975', *National Institute Economic Review*, no. 74, November, 60–70.

—— (1977), 'Public and private sector manual workers' pay 1970–77', *National Institute Economic Review*, no. 82, November.

Deloitte, Haskins and Sells (1983), *British Gas Efficiency Study*.

Demsetz, H. (1968), 'Why regulate utilities?', *Journal of Law and Economics*, 11, April, 55–66.

Department of Energy (1983), paper on energy projections methodology, Sizewell B Inquiry.

Department of the Environment (1985), 'Competition in the provision of local authority services', Consultation Paper, February.

Department of Trade (1982), *The Future of Telecommunications in Britain*, Cmnd 8610, London: HMSO.

Department of Transport (1984), *Airline Competition Policy*, Cmnd 9366, London: HMSO.

Diamond, D. W. (1984), 'Financial intermediation and delegated monitoring', *Review of Economic Studies*, 51, 393–414.

Dimson, E. (1983), 'The UK new issue market', in J. Broyles, I. Cooper, and S. Archer, *The Financial Management Handbook*, London: Gower.

Domberger, S. (1985), 'Economic regulation through franchise contracts', paper given to IFS conference on Competition and Regulation, May, reprinted in Part V of this volume.

—— and Middleton, J. (1985), 'Franchising in practice: the case of independent television in the UK', *Fiscal Studies*, 6, 1, 17–32.

Douglas, G. W. and Miller, J. C. (1974), *Economic Regulation of Domestic Air Transport*, Washington DC: The Brookings Institution.

Drucker, P. (1974), *Management: Tasks, Responsibilities, Practices*, London: Heinemann.

Dyos, H. J. and Aldcroft, D. H. (1974), *British Transport*, Harmondsworth: Penguin Books.

Edwards, F. R. and Stevens, B. J. (1978), 'The provision of municipal sanitation services by private firms: an empirical analysis of the efficiency of alternative market structures and institutional arrangements', *Journal of Industrial Economics*, 27, December.

Findlay, C. C. and Forsyth, P. J. (1984), 'Competitiveness in internationally traded services: the case of air transport', ASEAN—Australia Joint Research Project Working Paper.

Finsinger, J., Hammond, E. M., and Tapp, J. (1985), *Insurance: Competition or Regulation? A Comparative Study of the Insurance Markets in the United Kingdom and the Federal Republic of Germany*, IFS Report Series, London: Institute for Fiscal Studies.

Forsyth, P. J. (1983a), 'The cost of convenience in transport: the case of airlines', mimeo, University of New South Wales.

—— (1983b), 'Airline deregulation in the United States: the lessons for Europe', *Fiscal Studies*, 4, 3, 7–22.

—— (1984), 'Airlines and airports: privatisation, competition and regulation', *Fiscal Studies*, 5, 1, 61–75.

—— and Hocking, R. D. (1980), *Economic Record*.

Foster, N. A., Henry, S. G. B. and Trinder, C. (1984), 'Public and private sector pay: a partly disaggregated study', *National Institute Economic Review*, no. 107, February, 63–73.

Furubotn, E. G. and Pejovich, S. (1972), 'Property rights and economic theory: a survey of recent literature', *Journal of Economic Literature*, December.

Graham, D. R., Kaplan, D. P., and Silbey, D. S. (1983), 'Efficiency and competition in the airline industry', *Bell Journal of Economics*, 14, 118–38.

Griffiths, R. P. (1947), *The Cheshire Lines Railway*, Surrey: Oakwood Press.

Gunderson, M. (1979), 'Earnings differentials between public and private sectors', Canadian Journal of Economics, May.

Hammermesh, D. S. (1975), 'The effect of government ownership on union wages', in D. S. Hammermesh (ed.), *Labour in the Profit and Non-Profit Sectors*, Princeton.

Hammond, E. M., Helm, D. R., and Thompson, D. J. (1985), 'British Gas: options for privatisation', *Fiscal Studies*, 6, 4, reprinted in Part IV of this volume.

Hartley, K. and Huby, M. (1985), 'Contracting-out in health and local authorities: prospects, progress and pitfalls', *Public Money*, September, reprinted in Part V of this volume as 'Contracting-out policy: theory and evidence'.

Heald, D. A. (1980), 'The economic and financial control of UK nationalised industries', *Economic Journal*, 90, 243–65.

—— (1983), *Public Expenditure: Its Defence and Reform*, Oxford: Martin Robertson.

—— and Steel, D. R. (1982), 'Privatising public enterprise: an analysis of the Government's case', *Political Quarterly*, 53, 333–49, reprinted in Part I of this volume.

Hepple, B. A. (1982), 'The transfer of undertakings (protection of employment) regulations', *Industrial Law Journal*, 12, 29–40.

Hicks, J. (1956), 'Process of imperfect competition', *Oxford Economic Papers*.

Hills, J. (1984), 'Public assets and liabilities and the presentation of budgetary policy', in M. H. Ashworth, J. Hills, and C. N. Morris, *Public Finances in Perspective*, IFS Report Series 8, London: Institute for Fiscal Studies.

Hirsch, W. Z. (1965), 'Cost functions of an urban government service: refuse collection', *Review of Economics and Statistics*, 47, February.

HM Treasury (1961), *Financial and Economic Obligations of the Nationalised Industries*, Cmnd 1337, London: HMSO.

—— (1967), *Nationalised Industries: A Review of Economic and Financial Objectives*, Cmnd 3437, London: HMSO.

—— (1978), *The Nationalised Industries*, Cmnd 7131, London: HMSO.

—— (1983), *The Government's Expenditure Plans 1983–84 to 1985–86*, Cmnd 8789, London: HMSO.

—— (1984a), *Nationalised Industries Legislation: Consultation Proposals*.

—— (1984b), *The Government's Expenditure Plans 1984–85 to 1986–87*, Cmnd 9143, London: HMSO.

—— (1985), *The Government's Expenditure Plans 1985–86 to 1987–88*, Cmnd 9428–II, London: HMSO.

—— (1986), *The Government's Expenditure Plans 1986–87 to 1988–89*, Cmnd 9702, London: HMSO.

Home Office (1983), *The Development of Cable Systems and Services*, Cmnd 8866, London: HMSO.

Hotelling, H. (1938), 'The general welfare in relation to problems of taxation and of railway and utility rates', *Econometrica*.

Howe, Sir Geoffrey (1981), speech given to the Selsdon Group on 1 July, Conservative Central Office Press Release 533/81.

Incomes Data Report (1983a), no. 393, 18.
—— (1983b), no. 414, 13.
Industry and Trade Committee (1984), *The British Steel Corporation's Prospects*, London: HMSO.
Joskow, P. and Schmalensee, R. (1983), *Markets for Power: An Analysis of Electricity Utility Deregulation*, Cambridge: MIT Press.
Joy, S. (1964), 'British Railways' track costs', *Journal of Industrial Economics*, 13, 74–89.
Kay, J. A. (1984), 'The privatization of British Telecommunications', in D. R. Steel and D. A. Heald (eds), *Privatizing Public Enterprises*, London: Royal Institute of Public Administration.
—— and Silberston, Z. A. (1984), 'The new industrial policy—privatisation and competition', *Midland Bank Review*, Spring, 8–16.
—— and Thompson, D. J. (1985), 'Privatisation: a policy in search of a rationale', Institute for Fiscal Studies Working Paper 69.
King, M. A. and Fullerton, D. (eds) (1984), *The Taxation of Income from Capital: A Comparative Study of the United States, the United Kingdom, Sweden and West Germany*, London: The University of Chicago Press Ltd.
Kitchen, H. M. (1976), 'A statistical estimation of an operating cost function for municipal refuse collection', *Public Finance Quarterly*, 4, 1.
Labour Party–TUC–Confederation of Shipbuilding and Engineering Unions (1972), *Nationalisation of Shipbuilding, Ship-Repair and Marine Engineering*, London: Labour Party.
Lawson, N. (1982), speech to a conference on energy, Cambridge.
Little, I. M. D. (1950), *A Critique of Welfare Economics*, Oxford: Clarendon Press.
Littlechild, S. C. (1979), '*Elements of Telecommunications Economics*, London: Institute of Electrical Engineers.
—— (1981), 'Ten steps to denationalization', *Journal of Economic Affairs*, 2, 1, 11–19.
—— (1983), *Regulation of British Telecommunications' Profitability*, London: Department of Industry.
Lord, S. (1983), 'Gas and electricity shops', in S. Hastings and H. Levie (eds), *Privatisation?*, Nottingham: Spokesman.
Mackay, K. R. (1979), 'A comparison of the relative efficiency of Australian domestic airlines and foreign airlines', *Domestic Air Transport Policy Review*, Volume II, Appendix A6.1, Australia: Department of Transport.
Mann, P. C. and Siefried, E. J. (1972), 'Pricing in the case of publicly owned electric utilities', *Quarterly Review of Economics and Business*, 12, Summer.

Mayer, C. P. and Meadowcroft, S. A. (1985), 'Selling public assets: techniques and financial implications', *Fiscal Studies*, 6, 4, reprinted in Part VI of this volume.

McLachlan, S. (1983), *The National Freight Buy-Out*, London: Macmillan.

Memorandum of Understanding between the Government of the United States of America and the Government of the United Kingdom of Great Britain and Northern Ireland on Airport User Charges (1983), 6 April.

Meyer, R. A. (1975), 'Publicly owned versus privately owned utilities: a policy choice', *Review of Economics and Statistics*, November.

Miller, M. H. (1977), 'Debt and taxes', *Journal of Finance*, 32, 261–75.

Millward, R. (1978), 'Public ownership, the theory of property rights and the public corporation in the UK', Salford Papers in Economics, 78, I.

—— (1982), 'The comparative performance of public and private enterprise', in Lord Roll (ed.), *The Mixed Economy*, London: Macmillan, reprinted in Part II of this volume.

Monopolies and Mergers Commission (1979), *British Gas Corporation*.

—— (1980), *Domestic Gas Appliances: A Report on the Supply of Certain Domestic Gas Appliances in the United Kingdom*, HC 703, London: HMSO.

—— (1981a), *Central Electricity Generating Board: A Report on the Operation by the Board of its System for the Generation and Supply of Electricity in Bulk*, HC 315, London: HMSO.

—— (1981b), *British Rail Hovercraft Limited and Hoverlloyd Limited: A Report on the Proposed Merger*, HC 374, London: HMSO.

—— (1981c), *European Ferries Limited, Sealink Limited: A Report on the Proposed Merger*, HC 65, London: HMSO.

—— (1982), *Contraceptive Sheaths: A Report on the Supply in the United Kingdom of Contraceptive Sheaths*, Cmnd 8689, London: HMSO.

—— (1983), *National Coal Board: A Report on the Efficiency and Costs in the Development, Production and Supply of Coal by the NCB*, Cmnd 8920, I and II, London: HMSO.

Monopolies Commission (1974), *Cross-Channel Car Ferry Services: A Report on the Supply of Certain Cross-Channel Car Ferry Services*, HC 14, London: HMSO.

Moore, J. (1983), 'Why privatise?', speech given to the annual conference of City of London stockbrokers Fielding, Newson Smith at Plaisterer's Hall, London Wall on 1 November, HM Treasury Press Release 190/83, reprinted in Part I of this volume.

—— (1985), 'The success of privatisation', speech made when opening Hoare Govett Ltd's new City dealing rooms on 17 July, HM Treasury Press Release 107/85, some of which is reprinted in Part I of this volume.

Moore, T. G. (1970), 'The effectiveness of regulation of electric utility prices', *Southern Economic Journal*, 36, April.

Morrell, P. S. and Taneja, N. K. (1979), 'Airline productivity redefined: a study of US and European carriers', *Transportation*, 37–49.

Morrison, H. (1933), *Socialisation of Transport*.

National Audit Office (1985), *Department of Trade and Industry: Sale of Government Shareholding in British Telecommunications plc*, Report by the Comptroller and Auditor General, HC 495, London: HMSO.

National Consumer Council (1981), 'The nationalised industries', Consumer Concerns Paper.

National Economic Development Council (1981), 'Report of working party on nationalised industries' investment', mimeo, NEDC (81) 53.

National Economic Development Office (1981), 'Interdependence of the public and private sectors in the UK', mimeo, National Economic Development Council (81) 25.

Nationalised Industries' Chairmen's Group (1981), 'Interdependence of the public and private sector businesses', mimeo, National Economic Development Council (81) 31.

National Union of Mineworkers (1983), *Hands Off the Pits—No Privatisation of Coal*, Sheffield: NUM.

National Union of Railwaymen (1984), *Privatisation*, mimeo presented to the Post Office Engineering Union's London Regional Council conference, January.

Neuberg, L. G. (1977), 'Two issues in the municipal ownership of electric power distribution systems', *Bell Journal of Economics*, 8, 1.

Office of Fair Trading (1982), *London Electricity Board*, 29 April.

Panzar, J. C. (1979), 'Equilibrium and welfare in unregulated airline markets', *American Economic Review*, 69, 92–5.

Pashigian, B. P. (1976), 'Consequences and causes of public ownership of urban transit', *Journal of Political Economy*, 84.

Peacock, A. T. and Shaw, G. K. (1981), 'The public sector borrowing requirement', University College at Buckingham Occasional Papers in Economics 1.

Pearson, R. J. (1976), 'Airline managerial efficiency', *Aeronautical Journal*, November.

Peltzman, S. (1971), 'Pricing in public and private enterprises and electric utilities in the United States', *Journal of Law and Economics*, 14, April.

Pepper, M. P. G. (1985), 'Multivariate Box-Jenkins analysis: case study in UK energy demand forecasting', *Energy Economics*, July.

Pescatrice, D. R. and Trapani, J. M., III (1980), 'The performance and objectives of public and private utilities operating in the United States', *Journal of Public Economics*, 13, 2, 259–76.

Pier, W. J., Vernon, R. B., and Wicks, J. H. (1974), 'An empirical comparison of government and private production efficiency', *National Tax Journal*, 27, December.

Plowden Committee (1976), *The Structure of the Electricity Supply Industry in England and Wales*, Cmnd 6388, London: HMSO.

Pommerehne, W. W. and Frey, B. S. (1977), 'Public versus private production efficiency in Switzerland: a theoretical and empirical comparison', *Urban Affairs Annual Review*.

Posner, R. A. (1972), 'The appropriate scope of regulation in the cable television industry', *Bell Journal of Economics*, 3, 98–129.

Post Office Engineering Union (1984), 'The privatisation of British Telecom', mimeo presented to POEU London Regional Council conference, January.

Price, C. M. (1984), 'Distribution costs in the UK gas industry', University of Leicester Department of Economics Discussion Paper 31.

—— (1985), 'Competition in UK gas distribution: the effect of recent legislation', *Energy Policy*, 13, 1.

Price Commission (1979), *Area Electricity Boards*.

Primeaux, W. J. (1977), 'An assessment of x-efficiency gained through competition', *Review of Economics and Statistics*, February.

—— (1978), 'The effect of competition on capacity utilisation in the electric utility industry', *Economic Inquiry*, April.

Private Wagon Federation (1983), *The Future of Rail Freight: An End to Uncertainty*, a submission to Government.

Pryke, R., (1971), *Public Enterprise in Practice*, MacGibbon and Kee.

—— (1981), *The Nationalised Industries: Policies and Performance Since 1968*, Oxford: Martin Robertson.

—— (1982), 'The comparative performance of public and private enterprise', *Fiscal Studies*, 3, 2, 68–81, reprinted in Part II of this volume.

Public Accounts Committee (1982), *Tenth Report from the Commit-*

tee of Public Accounts, Session 1981–82 HC 189, London: HMSO.

—— (1984), *Report from the House of Commons Public Accounts Committee: Sales of Government Shareholdings in Publicly-Owned Companies*, HC 243(i), London: HMSO.

Savas, E. S. (1974), 'Municipal monopolies versus competition in the delivery of urban services', *Urban Affairs Annual Review.*

—— (1976), 'Policy analysis for local government: the private delivery of a public service', *Policy Analysis.*

—— (1977a), 'An empirical study of competition in municipal service delivery', *Public Administration Review*, November/December.

—— (1977b), 'Policy analysis for local government: public versus private refuse collection', *Policy Analysis*, no. 3.

Scherer, F. M. (1985), *On the Current State of Knowledge in Industrial Organisation*, Seminar Proceedings of Ottobeuren Seminar, September.

Schmalansee, R. (1979), *The Control of Natural Monopolies*, Lexington: D.C. Heath & Co.

Select Committee on Energy (1984), *Electricity and Gas Prices*, First Report, Session 1983–84, HC 276, London: HMSO.

—— (1985), *The Development and Depletion of the United Kingdom's Gas Resources*, Seventh Report, Session 1984–85, London: HMSO.

Select Committee on Nationalised Industries (1974), *The Ownership, Management and Use of Shipping by Nationalised Industries.*

—— (1977), *The Role of British Rail in Public Transport*, First Report, Session 1976–77, HC 305, London: HMSO.

—— (1978), *Minutes of Evidence*, 24 January.

Select Committee on the Treasury and Civil Service (1980/1), *Report on the Financing of the Nationalised Industries*, Session 1980–81, HC 348, London: HMSO.

Serpell Committee (1983), *Railway Finances*, Report, London: HMSO.

Sharkey, W. W. (1982), *The Theory of Natural Monopoly*, Cambridge: Cambridge University Press.

Sherman, R. and Visscher, M. (1982), 'Rate of return regulation and two-part tariffs', *The Quarterly Journal of Economics*, 97, 27–42.

Slater, M. and Yarrow, G. (1983), 'Distributions in electricity pricing in the UK', *Oxford Bulletin of Economics and Statistics*, 45, 317–38.

Spady, R. H. (1979), *Econometric Estimation for the Regulated Transportation Industries*, New York: Garland.

Spann, R. M. (1974), 'Rate of return regulation and efficiency in production: an empirical test of the Averch–Johnson thesis', *Bell Journal of Economics and Management Sciences*, 5, Spring.

—— (1977), 'Public versus private provision of government services', in T. Borcheding (ed.), *Budgets and Bureaucrats: The Sources of Government Growth*, Duke University Press.

Starkie, D. N. M. (1984), 'BR: privatisation without tears', *Economic Affairs*, October-December, 16–19, reprinted in Part IV of this volume.

—— and Starrs, M. (1984), 'Contestability and sustainability in regional airline markets', *Economic Record*, September.

—— and Thompson, D. J. (1985), *Privatising London's Airports: Options for Competition*, IFS Report Series 16, London: Institute for Fiscal Studies, summarised in Part IV of this volume.

Steel, D. R. and Heald, D. A. (eds) (1984), *Privatizing Public Enterprises*, London: Royal Institute of Public Administration.

Stigler, G. J. (1971), 'The theory of economic regulation', *Bell Journal of Economics*, 2, 1, 3-21, reprinted in G. J. Stigler, *The Citizen and the State* (1985), University of Chicago Press.

Stiglitz, J. E. (1984), 'Information and economic analysis: a perspective', *Economic Journal*, Supplement, 21–41.

Taussig, W. M. (1977), *British Airways: An Analysis of Efficiency and Cost Levels*, US Department of Transportation.

Thatcher, M. (1981), economic address at Georgetown University on 27 February, quoted in a press release, reported in the *Financial Times*, 28 February.

Thomas, D. (1984), 'The union response to denationalisation', in D. R. Steel and D. A. Heald (eds), *Privatizing Public Enterprises*, Royal Institute of Public Administration, reprinted in Part IV of this volume.

Trades Union Congress (1979), *Report of the 111th Trades Union Congress*, London: TUC.

—— (1980), *Report of the 112th Trades Union Congress*, London: TUC.

—— (1981a), *Report of the 113th Trades Union Congress*, London: TUC.

—— (1981b), *Financing the Nationalised Industries*, London: TUC.

—— (1982), *Report of the 114th Trades Union Congress*, London: TUC.

—— (1983), *Report of the 115th Trades Union Congress*, London: TUC.

—— and Labour Party (1982), 'Re-acquiring public assets', in TUC (1982), 274.

Undy, R. (1978), 'The devolution of bargaining levels and responsibilities in the TGWU 1965–75', *Industrial Relations Journal*, 9, 3, 44–56.

Vickers, J. and Yarrow, G. (1985a), *Privatization and the Natural Monopolies*, London: Public Policy Centre.

—— and Yarrow, G. (1985b), 'Telecommunications', in J. Vickers and G. Yarrow (1985a), reprinted in Part IV of this volume as 'Telecommunications: liberalisation and the privatisation of British Telecom'.

Wallace, R. L. and Junk, P. E. (1970), 'Economic efficiency of small municipal electricity generating systems', *Land Economics*, November.

Walters, A. (1982), 'Externalities in urban buses', *Journal of Urban Economics*, 11.

Webb, M. G. (1984), 'Privatisation of the electricity and gas industries', in D. R. Steel and D. A. Heald (eds), *Privatizing Public Enterprises*, London: Royal Institute of Public Administration.

Weiner, H. E. (1960), *British Labour and Public Ownership*, London: Stevens.

White, P. R. (1983), 'Express coach services in Britain since deregulation', in *Transport Policy*, proceedings of Seminar M, PTRC summer annual meeting.

Williamson, O. E. (1976), 'Franchise bidding for natural monopolies—in general and with respect to CATV', *Bell Journal of Economics*, 7, 1, 73–104.

Winchester, D. (1983), 'Industrial relations in the public sector', in G. S. Bain (ed.), *Industrial Relations in Britain*, Oxford: Blackwell.

Yarrow, G. (1985a), 'Regulation and competition in the electricity supply industry', paper prepared for Institute for Fiscal Studies conference on Competition and Regulation, May, reprinted in Part IV of this volume.

—— (1985b), 'Strategic issues in industrial policy', *Oxford Review of Economic Policy*, 1, 3.

Young, D. R. (1974), 'The economic organisation of refuse collection', *Public Finance Quarterly*, January.

Yunker, J. A. (1975), 'The economic performance of public and private enterprise: the case of US electric utilities', *Journal of Economics and Business*, 28, I.

Zabalza, A. (1984), 'Comment on Foster, Henry and Trinder, 1984', Centre for Labour Economics, LSE, Working Paper 611.